HISTORY IN MY BONES

Episodes in the 500-Year Story of My Father's Fathers

WILLIAM HOWARD

To order additional copies of this book, contact:
Xlibris
844-714-8691
www.Xlibris.com
Orders@Xlibris.com

ISBN: Softcover   979-8-3694-3173-3
        Hardcover   979-8-3694-3175-7
        EBook   979-8-3694-3174-0

Library of Congress Control Number: 2024921851

Print information available on the last page

Rev. date: 12/14/2024

Author on Luanda Bay, Angola

Homo sapiens Idaltu found in Ethiopia's Great Rift Valley in 1997. Idaltu is about 160,000 years old and thought to be among humankind's earliest ancestors.

Contents

Acknowledgments

My sincere thanks go out to my friends and two sisters, Julia and Linda, who provided support to me to complete this project. Many thanks also to the numerous unnamed others who contributed their time and resources even though I hardly knew them.

Special thanks to Bill Micks and the volunteers at Friends of the Rappahannock and Steve Walker of the Rappahannock River Campground for making a way when there seemed to be no way for me to visit the historical grounds of the Shackaconia; to Jessie Neal and Cindy Kay for organizing two different and challenging itineraries to get me into and out of the Banda and the Philippine Islands; to Pak Abba for sharing your understanding of Banda islands' cultural history and making the necessary connections for me to complete my research while I visited Banda Neira in 2017; to Peter V. Lape for sharing with me your eye-popping PhD dissertation of the Banda islands (I read it like most would enjoy a 350-page novel); to Edgar Hisoler of the Filipino Travel Center for quickly understanding what I needed to do and helping me meet those challenges while in Manila Bay; to Monica Moody, wherever you are, for laying before me files on the Howards of Halifax County, North Carolina, especially the precious information about Miles Howard; and to Art Lyons for being patient when editing the manuscript.

My travels through northern Angola and my meetings with the *sobas* of Malanje would not have been possible had it not been for TravelGest and its staff.

While the foregoing, along with others, deserve much credit for helping me to bring my research to the conclusions I have reached, I am the one responsible for any shortcomings that might remain.

William Daniel Howard's American Family Tree

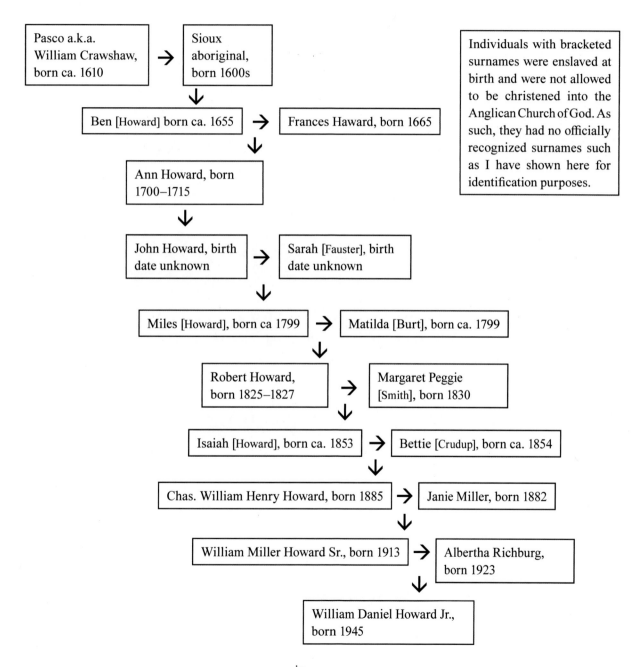

Pasco a.k.a. William Crawshaw, born ca. 1610 → Sioux aboriginal, born 1600s

Individuals with bracketed surnames were enslaved at birth and were not allowed to be christened into the Anglican Church of God. As such, they had no officially recognized surnames such as I have shown here for identification purposes.

Ben [Howard] born ca. 1655 → Frances Haward, born 1665

Ann Howard, born 1700–1715

John Howard, birth date unknown → Sarah [Fauster], birth date unknown

Miles [Howard], born ca 1799 → Matilda [Burt], born ca. 1799

Robert Howard, born 1825–1827 → Margaret Peggie [Smith], born 1830

Isaiah [Howard], born ca. 1853 → Bettie [Crudup], born ca. 1854

Chas. William Henry Howard, born 1885 → Janie Miller, born 1882

William Miller Howard Sr., born 1913 → Albertha Richburg, born 1923

William Daniel Howard Jr., born 1945

Chronology

ca. AD 1400 Southwest Central Africa's Mbundu people end their long trek from the Cameroon-Nigeria area to the Congo River. The migration began hundreds of centuries earlier in or near Ethiopia.

1482/83+ Portuguese explorers accompanying Diogo Cão visit the Kongo Kingdom, later stepping up their Mbundu slave raids, which handsomely profited *converso* Portuguese merchants, the Portuguese Crown, Kongo kings, and even some Mbundu chiefs too.

Early 1500s My proto-Howard Mbundu male ancestor is taken by the Portuguese from Africa to Lisbon.

Mid-1500s Proto-Howard Mbundu converso and Portuguese male arrives in Southeast Asia's Malacca, then on to Ternate in the Moluccas. After the start of the 1536 Portuguese inquisition (ca. 1546), this proto-Howard marries a mixed-race Catholic Melanesian living in Ternate.

1565 After Magellan's unsuccessful first attempt at Spanish settlement in the Philippines, a Legazpi permanent settlement begins on April 27, followed by October 8's galleon trade.

1572–1626 Reverend William Crashaw was born and died in England.

1606–1624 Virginia Company of London is chartered and finally dissolved.

1607 Virginia Colony is founded when English settlers arrive in Jamestown on May 13.

ca. 1610 Pasco is born to Mbundu/Bakongo/Portuguese/Melanesian/Converso and a Filipina in Manila.

1625 "William Crawshaw an Indian Baptised," says a 1624/25 muster in Elizabeth Cittie, Virginia.

ca. 1655 Ben is born to a Manahoac (possibly mixed with Nahyssan) Siouan woman and William Crawshaw, formerly known as Pasco.

1656	Battle of Bloody Run happens outside Richmond, Virginia.
	Colonel Mainwaring Hammond sells the Indian boy Ben to white Joseph Crowshaw.
1665	Frances Haward is christened in St. Peter Priory, Dunstable, England, on April 9.
	On July 1, Major Joseph Crowshaw sells Indian boy Ben to William Calvert for £24.
1666	July 20: "One Indyan boy called by ye name of Ben willed by William Calvert to son Robert."
1666/67	"Indyan" Ben is inherited by Henry Heywood (Howard) because of the death of his half brother Robert Calvert.
1682	New Virginia law relabels its off-reservation "Indians:" *Negroes and other slaves.*
1691	New Virginia law forbids "intermarrying" of white women with any nonwhite male.
1692	Frances Haward is fined in the Virginia court for "committing the sin of fornication with a Negro."
1705	In Virginia, descendants of female Indians who were slaves before 1705 are "slaves for life."
ca. 1711	Ann Howard is born free to an English mother, Frances Haward, and enslaved Indian Ben.
ca. 1799	Miles (unbaptized and enslaved) is born to an enslaved woman and free mulatto John Howard.
1818	Miles is emancipated and marries mulatto Matilda, whom he purchases as his slave.
ca. 1828	Robert Howard is born free to the now-free woman Matilda and Miles Howard.
1836	Miles and Matilda's children Henry, Fanny, and John are emancipated on December 10 by North Carolina.
1838	Miles Howard (barber, landowner, and musician) baptizes himself and his family as Catholics on June 19.
1842/44	Matilda dies.
1846	Miles marries free mulatto Caroline Valentine on May 6.
ca 1853	Isaiah is born to black enslaved Margaret Peggie and free mulatto Robert Howard in March. Robert Howard marries free mulatto Antonette Meacham on October 6, 1852. Betsy Crudup (mulatto), the future wife of Isaiah Howard, is born about 1854.
1857	Miles Howard dies on July 1 without leaving a will, thus leading to . . .
1858	*Howard v. Howard*, North Carolina Supreme Court Case decision.

1875	Isaiah Howard (a blacksmith) marries mulatto Betsy Crudup on February 2.
1885	Charles William Henry Howard is born on August 12 to married couple Isaiah Howard and Betsy Crudup-Howard.
ca. 1909	Charles William Henry Howard moves to New York City.
1911	Isaiah Howard dies on December 16.
1913	William Miller Howard is born on April 16 to Charles and Janie Howard in New York City.
1945	William Daniel Howard is born on July 8 to William M. Howard and Albertha Richburg-Howard in New York City.
1947	Julia Howard is born on January 29 to William M. Howard and Albertha Richburg-Howard in NYC.
1951	Linda Howard-Ryan is born on April 14 to W. M. Howard and Albertha Richburg-Howard in NYC.
1976	Charles William Henry Howard dies on June 11.
2003	William Miller Howard dies on August 28.

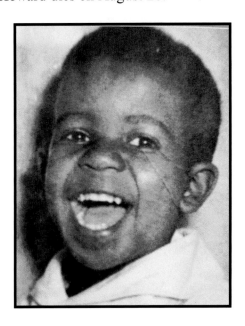

Author William Howard photographed when about 4 years old.

Introduction

Sometimes, I wonder whether I should thank you or just forget the whole thing. The tangled stories that used to excite the imagination of an inquisitive, young grandson still refuse to leave me alone. But you knew that would happen. You said they were two young boys who, like you, were anxious to run away from home. But unlike your own, the home their father made was rich. Still, they chose to leave it.

Fell into the hands of some white pirates, you say, survived on uncooked rice kernels the pirates threw into the ship's hold. Bet you thought I wouldn't remember any of it! I remember, but it just did not add up. I mean, an Indian ancestor who sailed here from London? And if the father and the home he provided were so rich, then why did the boys want to leave it, even at the risk of enslavement by strangers or even death?

I have been trying to confirm for you and me what most said was, by now, unverifiable. But you knew I was that kind of grandson—the one who would chase down what seemed to others impossible to find. I guess that is why it was me you told more times than I can remember. You told the one who you figured would track down the impossible-to-find origins of our family's memory, the history in our bones, making sense of our place since the olden times.

Today, Grandpa's casual mention remains a vivid memory. During one of my visits to his house in the 1950s–1960s, my father's father started talking to me again about our ancestors—the ones he called Indian. The occasion stands out because he told me our last name could have been Crawshaw. Other than his claim that Crawshaw was an Indian and that none of our Indian ancestors was ever enslaved, I recall two other things he brought up that afternoon. First, Crawshaw lived a long time ago in a place far away from New York City. England and Virginia both come to mind. Although there was mention of Chesapeake Bay, he did not mention Africa. Second, Crawshaw's first name was William. I remember wondering how it was that we jumped from being African to Indian and how a stranger named William Crawshaw managed to play such an outsized role in changing the last name of generations of our family from Crawshaw to Howard.

I am sure Grandpa told me more back then. Maybe he even gave me answers to some of the very questions I still think about today. But we are, after all, talking about more than sixty years ago.

It would not be until some forty years later that I gave more serious thought to finding out what I could about my African ancestors, William Crawshaw, and the Howard family.

Strange as it may at first seem, my search began with a career change. Resigning from investment and industry research at a Fortune 500 company in 1979, I returned to graduate school, where I studied political economy and social welfare policy. Shortly after graduation, I was a consultant to the newly formed John D. and Catherine T. MacArthur Foundation, at the same time I was appointed Associate Director of the University of Illinois at Chicago's Center for Urban Economic Development. At both places, a major part of my job portfolio required me to use the social science research and policy skills I developed recently at the University of Chicago—skills I found useful in my Africa/Crawshaw/Howard research.

At work, my research and policy projects focused on quality-of-life measures concerning low-income people of color. These projects motivated me to look closely at the historical circumstances of my own family and the generations who preceded them. Access to a major university library and interlibrary loan privileges enabled me to find virtually any kind of data and publication I wanted from any part of the world.

One day, while reading a publication about Virginia's colonial history, I ran across the name William Crawshaw. In *Virginia Immigrants and Adventurers, 1607–1635* by Martha W. McCartney, the author writes:

> In early 1625, when a muster was compiled, William Crawshawe (Croshaw, Croshair, Crowshaw) was living in Elisabeth City in Captain William Tucker's household and was identified as an Indian who had been baptized. William, three baptized Africans, and several white people appear to have been servants. William Crawshawe may have been one of the Christianized Indians living in Elizabeth City who in March 1622 warned the settlers about an impending attack. Presumably he was named after the well-known English clergyman whose name he shared.

In another publication, William Crawshaw was listed in the 1624–25 muster of Captain William Tucker as "an Indian Baptised." He was the only nonwhite member of the household other than three "negroes." The source here was John Frederick Dorman, CG, FAS G, editor and compiler of *Adventurers of Purse and Person: Virginia 1607–1624/5*. But the publisher was the same: Genealogical Publishing Company. The Crawshaw mention was on page 51.

Although both publications agreed with Grandpa that William Crawshaw was an Indian, there was no mention of Crawshaw's African origins, which I learned about after Grandpa's death, and no mention of his being a Howard family ancestor.

By then, my research told me that William Crawshaw was not in Virginia in 1622. He could not have been there at the time the article alleged because, just barely hanging on to his life, he had fled the Spanish Empire's Philippine Islands to escape being worked to death as a serf. He also wanted to escape the food blockade orchestrated by the Dutch and the English against Spain and its Portuguese-allied traders. My ancestor was on the brink of starvation in Manila in 1622. Had he stayed, he would have died.

Attempts to reach the author and publisher were fruitless. I found distortions, omissions, and outright mistakes in other publications that briefly mentioned William Crawshaw. Not only did the authors not understand the hard circumstances under which my ancestor lived, but they also failed to describe the dire political economy of the times.

It was time for me to publish the truth as I knew it and could document and otherwise defend it.

Among my first sources for *History in My Bones* was a book written by Walter L. Howard, PhD. His 1949 publication, *Ten Generations of Virginia Howards*, self-published in 1949, was just what I needed. *Ten Generations of Virginia Howards* contains wills, probate records, related white Howard family documents, bits of Howard family history, genealogies, as well as estate records going back to 1661. The wills and other material provided names, commentaries, and birthdates of some of my enslaved ancestors who were part of the estate of these white Howards. Among them was

> one Indyan boy called by ye name of Ben . . . listed among John Heyward's (Howard) 1665–1672 York County, Virginia estate papers. (p. 76)

Ben was the son of William Crawshaw, formerly named Pasco, who was from Manila.

History in My Bones turned to other reliable, sometimes-hard-to-find published sources related to my seventeenth-century ancestors—information found in such rarely mentioned archives and journals as *Hotten's List*, Paul Heinegg's *Native Heritage Project*, colonial Virginia records, the 1665–1672 records of York County, Virginia, and much more. As I continued to research, write, and travel—learning more about my ancestors as I continued while forming more and more questions—I was able to construct a complete list of William Crawshaw's descendants, beginning in Africa.

I spent more than seven years conducting research and undertaking travels to Angola, Southeast Asia, and the southern United States to complete *History in My Bones*.

Along the way, as I followed a zigzag path of questions and answers, I discovered several facts about the history of these peoples and the places where they lived, especially about southwest Central Africa, in general, and Angola, in particular, and the history of my paternal ancestors who lived there. Some of these discoveries, no doubt, will upset the expectations and values of some readers. I have reported them as I found them, however, and I ask the reader to appreciate the findings in their historical contexts. At a minimum, these discoveries will certainly fascinate the reader as much as they enlightened me. I invite everyone to join me in reflecting on the discoveries shared in *History in My Bones*, and I welcome comments and inquiries.

Pasco: El Mestizo de Portugués (ca. 1610–1623)

BILL HOWARD is what they call me now. To my family, though, I will always be William. After leaving New York City in 1969 to attend school and launch my first career, I wanted to be recognized by my father's nickname, so I started introducing myself as Bill. But if some of my father's paternal ancestors could rewrite history, my name today might indicate descent from Pasco.[1] One of the names chosen by *his* mother over four hundred years ago, the name Pasco suggests her child carries the moniker of the first Catholic male born into her indigenous family,[2] an event that occurred following the arrival of Augustine missionaries in the early 1580s.[3] The last of these Pasco-named ancestors was born about 1610 in the Manila *arrabal*[4] of Malate, perhaps in the part soon called the village of Ermita. Pasco's foreign-born father, whom I call in this story Pascoal (his earliest ancestors were Mbundu), lived in the Portuguese and Spanish East Indies. A *homen de negócio* (businessman), he profited handsomely from the trade and international distribution of cloves. His well-heeled kinsmen and associates had surnames like da Silva, Viera, Bravo, Lima, Veloso, Ribeiro, Ribaldo,[5] de Carvalho, Mendes, Garcia, Silveira, and Brandao.[6] In Spain and Portugal, they were mostly Jews or ex-Jews converted to Catholicism, known as conversos. By circa 1610, Pasco's father[7] tied to such surnames thanks to a vibrant, international spice trade linked to prosperous conversos, included in his compound live-in female servants.[8] Into this setting, Pasco was born. Though he was raised Catholic, it was in 1624

Daddy was born April 16, 1913, and the two of us grew up in San Juan Hill's West Sixty-Third Street. His parents, Charles and Janie, were married in a civil ceremony on February 20, 1909, then moved to the Hill in 1910. The family worshipped at St. Cyprian's Episcopal-Anglican Chapel on Sixty-Third Street,, where Daddy and sisters, Harriet May and Rebecca Louise, were all baptized on February 9, 1919. Why didn't they attend a Baptist Church like us? I wondered. More than just sharing names, Dad and I traveled similar paths: attended Public School 141, loved exotic animals, liked travel, and relished Latino food and friends. It wasn't until a couple of years before he died that I learned we both liked classical music too. He liked Stokowski's symphonic orchestrations. Dad never attended high school but took it for granted that my sisters and I would. He died on August 28, 2003.

London that Pasco was baptized into the Church of England. Buried among the sepia-toned pages of history went any mention of a Jewish past. The boy now carried the name of his godfather, a Puritan reverend. It is after this William Crawshaw whom the future sons called William in my Howard family have since been named. Today, knowledge of such things has disappeared from my family's memory.

While working on this project, I also learned that archeological digs in Ethiopia's Omo and Rift Valleys uncovered approximately two-hundred-thousand-year-old remains of early *Homo sapiens*. It is likely that prehistoric proto-Howards were among a particular group of these early people, according to an analysis of my Y-chromosome markers.[9] As both habitat *and* its people can share the same history, these hunter-gatherers might have been surrounded by the same kinds of acacia trees and big lakes filled with hippos, giant Nile crocodiles, and catfish as big as human infants such as the ones I witnessed when I visited Ethiopia in 2016. It was out of the Omo-Rift Valley where these early humans undertook their thousands-of-year-long trek westward through Africa.

The journey from East to West Africa began in the Great Rift Valley–Omo River area of eastern Africa. From there, families probably entered today's Sudan, then the vicinity of Lake Chad, and later to what is now the Cross River Region of Nigeria and Cameroon in West Africa. By the 1400s, these Bantu-based Kimbundu speakers had moved down through the Congo River Basin, then into the Hungu territory of the Kongo Province known as Mbata, and later south to the Lukala River and just north of the Kwanza—all located in today's Angola.[10]

But not all proto-Howard ancestors went to Angola. Some left East Africa for Northwest Europe. Other proto-Howards chose Southeast Asia, including Taiwan, Polynesian Brunei on today's Borneo Island, the Philippines, and such Spice Islands as Ternate. Others left East Asia for North America, becoming the continent's first *Homo sapiens*.[11] Some proto-Howards left Ethiopia to settle in the Middle East's Levant and in Europe's Iberia, the latter including Portugal and Spain. Among the Howards' Portuguese and Spanish ancestors were Levantine Muslims and Jews, and, later, so-called New Christians (*cristaos-novos*), Jews who converted to the Catholic faith (conversos). After the destruction of Israel's second Temple in AD 70, surviving Jews were forced from Israel to the Roman Empire's Iberian lands. Some claim that Jews have lived in Spain and Portugal at least since the era of King Solomon and in Portugal since 1200 BC when the Phoenicians traded there. Whichever the case, at least one distant proto-Howard ancestor was a Sephardic Jew.[12]

In 1607, Virginia was England's first permanent colony that was established on today's North American mainland. The second colony in the hemisphere was Bermuda, established in 1609. Seventeenth-century England presented its citizens with many reasons to undertake the dangerous and expensive journey to the frontier colony of Virginia.[13] English overpopulation was one reason. Between 1520 and the last decades of the 1600s, the number of people who called England home doubled from 2.5 million to 5 million. The situation in its cities was even more striking. In places like London, the population increased eightfold, from 50,000 during the 1520s to 400,000 in the mid-1600s. Living conditions in these cities were unsanitary, noisy, and crime-ridden. Unemployment was high everywhere in the island kingdom.

Conditions in England's countryside were especially ripe for significant emigration. After the 1500s, the effects of England's enclosure policies caused large numbers of peasants and yeomen living in rural areas to search for off-the-farm work.[14] Before the enclosures, fields and pastures were open to families who wanted to grow provisions to feed themselves and the small number of farm animals reared by local yeomen and other commoner households. By the 1800s, however, most of these lands were fenced off by private owners who raised for themselves a growing number of farm products for private commerce. The consequences were not good for ordinary citizens and yeomen farmers like my "Haward" ancestors. With increasing enclosures, the yeoman lost the land rights granted under old English customary law. The yeoman no longer had land on which to plant and raise crops for his family. Enclosure policies also meant that for the yeoman and his family to survive, they had to search for hard-to-find labor employment to earn the wages that could pay for the provisions they once could plant and grow for themselves. Consequently, crime and poverty rose throughout the English countryside.

Religious upheaval all over England was another reason to emigrate. Starting in the 1530s, King Henry VIII outlawed the Catholic Church, replacing it with an egocentric Anglicanism. The consequences for those clinging to the old religion were dire. Not only did they include religious prohibitions, but they also had implications that were economic, political, and even deadly. For the recalcitrant, the results included unemployment and impoverishment, torture, imprisonment, state confiscation of valuable real estate and property, and even beheading.

Those seventeenth-century English siblings who did not have the good fortune to be first-born males had one more incentive to emigrate. Under the English system of primogeniture, unless one was the firstborn male, younger sons would never inherit their father's assets while the firstborn remained alive. Second-born sons and their younger brothers stood to gain more by leaving England for Virginia, hoping to strike it rich in prospective but dangerous frontier conditions. Material success for daughters depended on being a wealthy heiress or marrying well. Some of these daughters struck out for Virginia, hoping to find their (white) Prince Charming.

The prospect of venturing to far-off Virginia was not without its private, profit-seeking promoters who often played folly with the truth. The Virginia Company of London, authorized to promote development in Virginia by King James I in 1606, was the organization used by these promoters to sell the colonial settlement to the English public. The joint venture was a privately owned, profit-making stock company designed to accomplish several ends, including[15] to make money for its investors; turn Virginia's "savages" into compliant, friendly Christians and thereby save their condemned souls as well as increase wealth-making opportunities—like land ownership, farm exports, and trade—for the Crown; promote English emigration to the colony and so relieve England of its increasingly high rates of beggars, orphans, criminals, and unemployed; and, finally, create work and land ownership opportunities for an English public that had grown much too large for an island kingdom whose continued political endurance was threatened by the rising unemployment. To promote such ends, claims made by the company to English citizens were often exaggerated, frequently sugarcoating the fact that the voyage was dangerous. Passengers often endured the cold, hunger, and storms. More than half the émigrés died before the fifth year of their arrival. Starvation and war with the natives were not mentioned in the promotions, but those were the real facts of life in early Virginia. Yet English men, women, and their children continued to voyage there.

With all that said, as you read this narrative, remember the opinion held by more than one observer of the period: "It would have been inconceivable to a seventeenth-century Englishman to picture Virginia as anything but a disreputable penal colony since it was largely peopled by the scouring from English prisons, vagrants, waifs and strays, and these lured into migration by promises of land and wealth."[16]

While 105 English settlers arrived in Virginia in 1607,[17] the earliest Jamestown muster showed that of these 105 original English settlers, there were only 2 still living in 1623/24. Accounts of the *entire* Virginia population during its first seventeen years indicate that some 7,000 people had arrived in the colony. Of these, only 1,200 were alive at the time of the 1623/24 muster. Appearing later in Virginia's

Elizabeth Cittie muster of 1624/25 was the name of a young nonwhite male. This boy was listed as William Crawshaw, and as far as I could tell, this immigrant from the Spanish Indies was the sole Christian "Indian" resident counted among the colony's original settlers.[18] Crawshaw was also listed in the February 1625 Elizabeth Cittie household of wealthy Englishman Captain William Tucker, a member of Virginia's first House of Burgesses in 1619.[19] Besides William Crawshaw and the Tucker family, the captain's 1625 household included 14 white servants plus a Negro couple and their child.[20]

The 1624/25 muster listing of Crawshaw reads: " Indean, baptised."[21] The description referred to the fact that he had only recently been baptized into the Church of England. Unbeknownst to most Virginia colonists of the day—but brought to my attention thanks to DNA history including my own Y-chromosome link—was another important fact about him: Indian William Crawshaw had African roots too, and they were planted in the same land as the Angolans Antoney and Isabell's, the two Negroes who were part of Tucker's 1624/25 household. Crawshaw's sixteenth-century paternal ancestors came from a south-central African people collectively called by their Kongo lords the Mbundu:

> The Ndongo Kingdom [an Mbundu location] lay in a plateau 4,000 feet in elevation, some 30 miles wide and 50 miles long between the Lukala and Lutete Rivers. The Ndongo Kingdom consisted of large towns enclosed within woven grass stockades. Kabasa [the royal capital situated in the interior about 200 miles southeast of Luanda] contained 5,000 to 6,000 dwellings and 20,000 to 30,000 people. The rural people raised millet and sorghum . . . Ndongans tended large herds of cattle and also raised domestic animals such as goats, chickens, and guinea fowl. They wore bark and cotton clothing they both made themselves and imported from the kingdom of Kongo to the north. Ndongans traded in local and regional markets where they bought iron, steel, and salt from the region south of the Kwanza River.[22]

The Mbundu people consisted of seven subcultural groups, including a group who lived in early Hungu.[23] The Hungu lived north of what later became the Ndongo Kingdom. They were the northernmost Mbundu, original inhabitants of a territory increasingly occupied by their more powerful immigrant lords, i.e., the Kongo Kingdom. By the early 1400s, Kongo immigrants had begun settling among the Hungu. Many married their women and absorbed Hungu villages into their increasingly Catholic Kingdom.[24] Many of these Hungu became assimilated into the world of the Kongo Kingdom, including some becoming members of the royally sanctioned Catholic Church. As the assimilated Hungu population accepted the new faith, they held on to their traditional beliefs too, gaining political and economic advantages along the way. By 1526, villagers living within and outside the Kongo Kingdom proper—including

Mbundu living near the Lukala, Kwije, and Kwanza Rivers farther south—increasingly were kidnapped, becoming inventory of freelance Portuguese merchants and errant soldiers illicitly seeking slaves for sale abroad. Some captives became tributes to the court of King Afonso I.[25] Others wound up at the Portuguese Court,[26] courtesy of unofficial, freelance Portuguese merchant-adventurers.[27] All but the humble villager were complicit, leading to the sixteenth-century capture of the son of one Hungu villager. He was Pasco's Mbundu ancestor.[28]

It was only a few decades before—in the early 1480s after launching an Age of Discovery—when Portuguese explorer and navigator Diogo Cão became the first European to visit Angola and Kongo.[29] During these years, explorers like Cão aimed to strike it rich for kings and queens of the age. As part of his quest, Cão joined fellow explorers in their search for gold, along with silver and spices. Europe at the time was determined to find profitable, Western- and Christian-controlled maritime routes to Asia—routes leading to the source of the world's most valued flavorings. From Asia, therefore, European explorers raced to monopolize trade in the world's most highly valued spices in those days: nutmeg, mace, and cloves. The only place in the world where the clove spice grew wild and plentiful was on the tiny Moluccan volcanic island of Ternate and on the nearby volcanic atolls of Tidore, Moti, Makian, and Bacan. Since biblical times, cloves had been transported from there and used throughout the world as food; breath anesthetic; and exchange for Asian cloths, Chinese silk, and its porcelain, as well as for gold, Japanese silver, and knives, glass, and more. Until just before the Age of Discovery, the only way spices, silk, porcelain, and precious cloths could reach their European markets was through Venice on the overland Silk Road. But compared to as-yet-undiscovered sea routes, overland avenues were outrageously costly and largely controlled by those whom Christians vehemently disliked: the Moors or Muslims and the Arabs. The AD 1453 conquest of Constantinople by Muslims sparked fear in the Christian West that the secret Eastern sources of these precious commodities would be cut off to them or at least be rendered unaffordable. Enforced by the church-backed AD 1494 Treaty of Tordesillas[30] and its sequel, the 1529 Treaty of Zaragoza, maritime explorer Afonso de Albuquerque won from the pope Portugal's exclusive right to the precious Eastern trade, disappointing rival Spain.

Albuquerque reached India's Goa in 1510, and by 1511, he and his crew went on to conquer Malacca on the Malaysian Peninsula, which linked the all-Muslim trade route called the South China Sea to the Indian Ocean commercial corridor. There, Albuquerque learned the source of nutmeg and mace was the Banda Islands located over 1,900 miles to the southeast of Malacca and that cloves were grown on islands to Banda's north.[31] With a crew of 120 mixed-race and white Portuguese sailors and soldiers,[32] plus 60 mostly Asian slaves, Captain António de Abreu (a friend of Albuquerque) sailed to the Bandas guided by Javanese and Lusong pilots. Portuguese explorers reached the Bandas and then Ternate in 1512 and 1513, respectively.

In AD 1511-cosmopolitan Malacca and its suburbs,[33] Portuguese explorers found a bustling metropolis of some 100,000 to 200,000 Malaysians, Indians, Javanese, and Tagalog-speaking Lusongs (Hispanicized term for today's Filipinos).[34] Since sixteenth-century Malacca, Luzon (viz. Lusong) merchants living in the city's suburbs included traders from Luzon's Manila Bay, where the people who spoke Tagalog[35] lived. Luzon sailors had been transporting valuable spices plus Chinese silk and porcelain between China and the rest of Southeast Asia since before the Ming Dynasty, which began in 1368.

Because the spices were worth more than gold, Malacca and her traders' boats were frequently under threat of attack by pirates.[36] Besides piracy, the port city was situated amid powerful Muslim neighbors, and the Catholic Portuguese there had to be always on guard for possible attack from religious enemies. Sailors who went to Asia in the early- to midsixteenth century to help secure Portugal's budding investment there included a mixed-race Portuguese and African ancestor of my Howard family. He was descended from the early-sixteenth-century captive carried from Africa's Kongo-Mbundu area to Lisbon, after which he became part of the progeny of a converso Portuguese family and African Catholics.[37] Having established important conjugal links to Filipino-area families and their trading activity, he was further able to tap into his mercantilist converso connections likely supported by European Jewish capital.[38] Such credentials led to the respectable mestizo trader who was able to earn profits for himself and the Crown. No matter to what social class Lisbon might have earlier relegated the descendants of converted Jews and Africans, the mixed-race Catholic was now an upright middle-class Portuguese citizen. He became a *casado morador*.[39]

But upon first reaching the Asian city, life for any nonindigenous trader-soldier[40] in sixteenth-century Malacca entailed a competitive struggle for survival.[41] His first years in Portuguese-controlled Asian port cities such as Goa and Malacca saw my ancestor learning how to outmaneuver the city's everyday challenges to support himself and common-law dependents: wives and concubines (the latter constituted the majority of the cities' domestic arrangements) were famously independent of their male paramours.[42] It was the normal state of affairs that the hustling soldier in those days would only be "employed" in the event that he was called to duty by the city's captain.[43] This would only occur when Malacca—where, before moving elsewhere, my ancestor spent his initial period in Asia—was under attack or was itself the aggressor. Normally, however, soldiers received no support unless lucky enough to join maritime foreign trade expeditions organized by the city's captain or by another official or perhaps hire himself out to a foreign king for warfare or partake in similar opportunities that would allow him to trade and plunder. He started by capitalizing on his early converso connections; eventually, the trade deals, strategic domestic arrangements, and profitable Northern Moluccas trade links became his métier. Such was the surest way for a rise to wealth and to middle-class respectability in Portugal's Estado da Índia[44] and advancement from *soldado* to *casado*. By the mid- to late sixteenth century, the Afro-European bachelor had risen in Asia from the lowliest rungs of Portugal's urban and town society.[45] His male descendants went on to develop commercial arrangements associated with clove-rich Ternate, including marriage to a mixed-race Melanesian woman. From there, the trade activity of descendant sons widened to include markets in Macao, Nagasaki, Makassar, and a territory today called the Philippines. With converso ties to friars and profitable markets facilitated by his mixed-race wife's local family, Pascoal was a true casado morador and no stranger to the ports lining Manila Bay and Makassar.[46]

On the morning of October 31, 2017, I boarded the first of three flights and then a six-hour "fast boat" to Southeast Indonesia's Banda Sea Islands. Getting there from Chicago would test every fiber in my body, but I undertook the four-day journey to be able to speak with the islands' current occupants about the aftermath of the Dutch massacre that occurred there on May 8, 1621. Current residents who live on nine of the archipelago's eleven Indonesian islands are descendants of enslaved Asians and the *perkeniers* whom Dutch sailors brought there after murdering and forcing into exile the islands' natives so that Holland could begin its monopoly of the islanders' nutmeg and mace. One highlight of the trip was Banda Neira Island's little Rumah Budaya Museum, which housed a collection of artistic, cultural, and historical items from Banda's past.

Before leaving Chicago, I thought that my ancestor Pasco (whose name I did not know at the time) was born and spent his early years in tiny Banda Neira's Labbetácca village and that he was among the natives exiled from the Banda archipelago by Dutch soldiers in 1621. The name and a brief description of one of my paternal ancestors appeared in the 1624/25 muster of Elizabeth Cittie, Virginia.

To get to Banda, I spent a couple of nights on the Indonesian island of Ambon. Enjoying my short stay there, I nevertheless did not realize then how important Ambon itself was to the ancestors I was on my way to Banda to investigate. Before Pasco was born in around 1610, his "black Portuguese" father counted Manila Bay and Makassar among his homes: domiciles where he undertook trade, conducted other business, and housed his Christian family, including servant-concubines.[47]

After visiting the Bandas, I questioned whether Pasco was born in today's Indonesia or in the Philippines instead. In pursuit of an answer, writing *William to William* (an earlier book) necessitated a reformulation of some earlier assumptions I held before my 2017 trip to the Bandas.

One constant that stayed with me, however, was a conundrum my granddad laid before me when I was a boy: our ancestor came from a "rich 'Indian' family" from whom he wanted to run away.

While that last piece of memory stayed with me, it seemed unimportant at the time. The research concluded some years later enabled me to uncover the complicated historical circumstances that support my granddad's claim.

When Granddad said these so-called Indians were rich, I thought it unlikely given my limited understanding back then of so-called Native American history. Besides, it never occurred to me or to my grandfather that by Indians (the term my grandfather used), the indigenes could have been Asian—ones who, in fact, were subjects of empires known as Portuguese East India (Estado da India) and the Spanish East Indies. Recent DNA evidence has shed more light on these possibilities, as I will explain below.

Believing Southeast Asia's island of Makassar to have played a prominent role in his life,[48] I concluded Pascoal was familiar with the nearby Moluccas as well.[49] Before Makassar, I came to believe Pasco's father lived on or near Ternate Island in the Northern Moluccas. It was on these islands where cloves grew wild and where private Portuguese traders had been cultivating the plant ever since they first came there in 1513.[50] Pasco's elders arrived sometime later, but it was on Ambon Island in Southern Moluccas where Pasco's father or even his grandfather[51] logically would have chosen to live after fleeing Ternate in 1575, for it was then that Ternate's irascible sultan ordered all Portuguese civilians and soldiers who lived there to leave in response to the earlier murder of the sultan's father. The sultan promised, however, to grant the Portuguese safe passage to Ambon if they left quietly within twenty-four hours. It was while in the Northern Moluccas that Pascoal established links with the Spanish Indies based in nearby Manila Bay. It was also during this period's late sixteenth to early seventeenth centuries when he enhanced ties not only with the Spaniards of Manila, who *militarily* dominated the North Moluccas from 1606 to 1663, but also with Los Indiós de Luzon, along with the Portuguese community also living there on Manila Bay. Since these Luzones had maintained trade links to the Chinese Court for centuries at Manila Bay's large port of Tondo, Portuguese traders later took advantage of the already-established links and created commercial ties of their own not only to China but also to India and, separately, Japan.[52] It was these Portuguese traders who constituted the link between China and the Spanish Empire's galleons, which carried to America Chinese silk and precious spices arriving at Tondo from Molucca.[53] About the Portuguese civilians accompanying the soldiers to Ambon in 1575, a modern-day author tells us:

> The missionary zeal of the Portuguese was . . . good politics; Christian Natives almost automatically became enemies of the Muslims, the most feared opponents of the Portuguese, and thus automatic allies. . . . In order to have a ready made Christian Colony on hand when they established themselves on Ambon, a colony which would act as a bulwark against the Muslims and perhaps as a catalyst for the Ambonese to adopt Christianity themselves, the Portuguese had brought with them seven Ternatese Catholic families.[54] These were granted many privileges: they did not have to render compulsory labour services [for instance],[55] they were allowed to ply a trade, own businesses and slaves and they were granted a plot of land [on which to grow cloves] near the Portuguese fort on which to build houses and establish gardens. Their settlement became *Kampong Mardika* (from Sanskrit *Mardaheka* = free from servitude) [which still] exists in Ambon.[56]

The Portuguese now had a virtual monopoly in the spice trade,[57] while rival Spain looked on with jealous envy. That is, until their forced 1580 union under the Habsburg dynasty's Spanish king Philip II (son of the Holy Roman Emperor Charles V), described in the pages that follow.

Portuguese Escape from Ternate to Ambon

The sultan of Ternate proposed to deliver the besieged Portuguese, if they chose, to the island of Ambon in southern Moluccas, where Portuguese soldiers were already building a new fort named Victoria. These Portuguese in Ternate accepted the sultan's terms. They put the Ternate fort in order after having been under siege there for five years, piled up their arms in the courtyard, and marched in orderly files through the great gateway, the priests in the lead, the rest of the fort company following, the black Portuguese (half-castes), and others, including numerous wives and children, in the rear, everyone carrying what he could in the way of personal possessions, including a small clove tree and seeds. Intent on continuing their worldwide clove monopoly, the Portuguese were a presence in the area since 1512, and they chose to transfer their monopoly to Ambon.

Genealogical History of Pasco a.k.a. William Crawshaw: Before 1500s to 1625 and Beyond

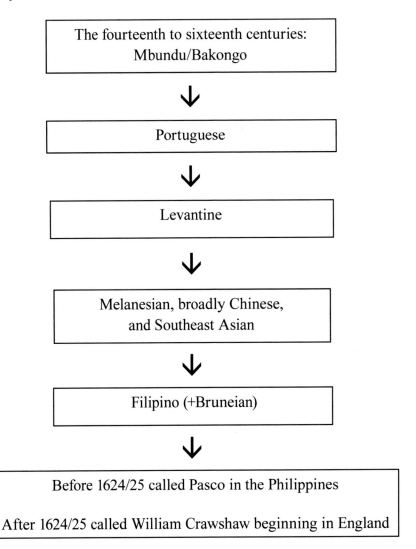

Source: Africanancestry; 23andme; Ancestry.com. Note that the genealogy testing services established definite links to the Mbundu, Kongo, Iberians, Levant (Jews), Melanesians (Ternate or Ambon area), and the Philippines. Additionally, proto-Howard family DNA was found by these sources to be tied to "broadly Chinese and other Southeast Asian" such as the Javanese, Makassarese, and Malaccans.

1640-1650 Manila existed solely within protective walls. Ermita
was outside these walls on the lower left.

Pasco's Manila Bay mother was likely mixed with one of these, especially the Chinese and Muslim Javanese who had been engaged in trade with Manila Bay for centuries.

Instead of joining the 1575 exodus to Ambon, a few Portuguese other than Pascoal stayed behind on the Ternate and Tidore Islands. Some had married into the sultan's family,[58] remaining there until 1605 when the Dutch expelled them.[59] About 400 of these expelled Portuguese then withdrew from Ternate and Tidore and moved to Manila Bay, especially to Ermita,[60] which was about to emerge from Malate Village in 1606.[61] In the following year, some of the expelled returned to Ternate as part of a force of Spanish (mostly Mexican) troops plus 1,672[62] Manila Bay auxiliaries,[63] whereupon the Dutch were routed and the Spanish refurbished the previously Portuguese fortress into their military post to prevent a Dutch return. But the Dutch returned. After they did, control of Ternate's trade and defenses against rivals changed back and forth among the Dutch, the Portuguese, and Manila Bay's Spanish until 1619. It was then that Ternate's military fortifications and—on paper anyway—its clove trade were divided between the Dutch and Spanish, each of whom did everything possible to win to their side the favors of Ternate area leaders in control of the islands' clove trees. In the end, the Dutch were unable to control who native growers in the Ternate area chose to sell their cloves to. Most of these North Moluccans chose to sell their cloves to the Portuguese traders who had moved to Makassar after their 1605 exodus from Ambon.

Reaching Manilla Bay in 1606, four years later, one of these mixed-race Portuguese traders, Pascoal, fathered a son, Pasco. He partnered with a Manila Bay woman whose family included fishermen and natives engaged in coastal trade with mainland Chinese and Southeast Asian visiting merchants.[64] The Chavacano-speaking[65] mother facilitated Pascoal's commercial trade while fulfilling his domestic needs as a member of the casado's large household.[66] Monsoons and trade responsibilities required Pascoal to live in Manila Bay's Ermita[67] in the spring, spending the remainder of the year in Makassar.

Meanwhile, like Ternate about three hundred miles to the south, the Dutch attacked the South Moluccas Island of Ambon. The Island's Fort Victoria, a Portuguese fortress, was captured by the Dutch East India Company (VOC) on February 22, 1605. If Pascoal was trading in Ambon at the time, he would have joined the Portuguese exodus—the so-called "'big Portuguese' . . . private merchants" there, who fled Ambon and "took a large volume of the spice trade with them to Makassar."[68] From Makassar, these Portuguese traders carried on "a very rich trade with the Philippines," living there part-time while carrying on a trade whose major inventory, in addition to Chinese silk and American silver, included the clove spice.[69]

From Ambon or Ternate, Makassar and Manila offered Pascoal a tremendous opportunity to prosper from the area's entrenched intra-Asia market barters. The free-market metropolis of Makassar became heir to the once-Muslim-dominated, pre-Portuguese Malacca emporium, among the places where my proto-Howard ancestors first launched a life in Southeast Asia. Beginning in 1607, when it adopted Islam, the Gowa-Tallo Kingdom and Sultanate of Makassar let it be known throughout Southeast Asia that it welcomed people of all religions to settle in its major trade port, especially the Catholic Portuguese and Anglican English, who traded in the area through their English East India Company that was permitted to establish a factory in Makassar in 1613.[70] By extending a hearty welcome to all merchants and traders regardless of religion—except the hated Dutch—Makassar was banking on the boost that such a diverse assortment of businessmen would bring to its expanding, free-market maritime economy. The strategy proved to be shrewdly successful, for according to one authority,

> as the monsoons forced the merchants to stay ashore for some time,[71] a Portuguese quarter with a trading post came into being which, after the fall of Malacca in 1641, grew into a definite town, soon reported to count more than 3,000 inhabitants. These Portuguese benefited the Makassar people in no small measure to be called "the mainstay of Makassar's prosperity" and "the key figures in the life of the Sultanate."[72]

Among Southeast Asia's most important trade links, beginning in the early 1620s, Makassar connected all the prominent Asian markets of its day, such as Malacca, Cambodia, Ache, Johor, Batavia (Jakarta), Banjarmasin, Nusa Tenggara, all of Maluku, Manila, and the Kingdom of Sulu. What traders who settled in Makassar required of any economic environment inviting them to enter and prosper were actual "security of life and property, on the one hand, and freedom of commercial and personal exchange, on the other."[73] Ruled by the highly regarded Chancellor Karaeng ("Prince") Matoaya of Tallo, Makassar provided that environment—much to the chagrin of its opposite, Holland, which wanted to begin a trade monopoly there and permanently eliminate private English and Portuguese competition as they had done when they entered Ambon and conquered the Bandas in the early 1600s. Until they got their way, the Dutch would continue to be troublesome to both the Makassarese and to the Moluccas, where the Dutch, Spanish, a few Portuguese, and natives all lived a very tense, tenuous existence until the mid-1600s.

By Pascoal's heyday, any chance of significant participation by Portugal's Royal Court in a profitable intra-Southeast Asia trade as described above had been lost to Lisbon largely because of Portuguese corruption and mismanagement at the royal court itself and among its inefficient layers of Portuguese officials active in the lucrative trade markets of Asia. In place of intra-Asia traders connected to the European court stepped small, independent, and private merchant-businessmen like Pascoal. These darker-skinned Portuguese business agents included casados and New Christians.[74] Living at different times in Makassar and on Manila Bay (near its port of Tondo in Pascoal's case), with operations in the rest of Southeast Asia[75] too, they remained the successful distributors and merchants of cloves and other spices through barter confined to markets within Southeast Asia and through silver-denominated international commercial transactions marketed through the likes of China, Japan, and Hormuz.

Spain was desperate to gain a commercial foothold in Asia. For starters, they wanted a piece of the wealth and prestige enjoyed by Makassar's Portuguese traders and sought participation in a later monopoly China granted the Lusophones in Macao.[76] After 1521, when Magellan had reached the archipelago, Spain planned to colonize the islands—called the Philippines after 1543 in honor of a young Prince Philip of Spain—along with the islands' natives whom the invaders later called Indians. By doing so, Spanish explorers hoped to bring a part of Asia's spice trade under the control of its own empire while adhering to the 1493 papal bull and the consequential 1494 Treaty of Tordesillas, both of which, in deference to Portugal, prohibited Spain from trading in Asia.[77] Despite trying, the Spanish were unable to establish any durable trade in the islands or in Asia's spices or even in its gold.[78] Spain did eventually achieve economic success in Asia but not in spices and only with grudging cooperation from her erstwhile Portuguese rivals. Even after their 1580 union with Spain under King Philip II, the Portuguese continued to prohibit direct commercial trade between Spanish merchants and China,[79] thanks to their strong lobby in Madrid.

The total population of natives living in the Philippine Islands was about 1.6 million[80] when the Spanish came there in 1565. Inhabiting just a fraction of the more than seven thousand scattered islands—only about five hundred exceeded one square mile in area and eleven over one thousand square miles[81]— the indigenes,[82] for as long as anyone could remember, lived in small isolated, independent villages (barangays) consisting of parents, their children, relatives, slaves, and the village leader who was kin to the villagers. Sometimes, a barangay consisted of just one small island (although, more often, they were established along a riverbank or seacoast). Since there was no centralized, overarching political authority between these tribal villages, the scattered islands were vulnerable to European invasion. The family of Pasco's mother were natives of the land who lived on Manila Bay in the settlement of Malate, just two and a half mils southeast of Manila.

After colonization, many datus swore allegiance to the Spanish king, becoming baptized in the king's church and then rewarded by appointment to the specially created post called cabeza de barangay (village chief). Enjoying more wealth and power now, they took seats alongside their puffed-up colleagues, all of them lording over the free classes of natives who lived in their respective villages and a larger group of the less free, whose victuals depended more now on rice imported from China and less on the yields from lands on which these natives labored but could no longer claim. Where Pasco stood in this new menagerie looked as murky to any outside observer as was Pasco's curiously chocolaty complexion, for rather than from Manila Bay, his father (though favored by the Crown for the profits he garnered from the rich spice trade) was an outsider, with households not confined just to Manila Bay. This rich converso's homes bore more mestizo sons and daughters, a caste looked down upon by the pure-blooded Spaniards. Meanwhile, Pasco's indigenous mother, whose introduction to the converso was welcomed by village officials, could be seen attending to trading and fishing and performing household chores and unpaid domestic work at the all-male convent, while her son was relegated to the hard scrapple life of burdensome labor in fields assigned to him by a compromised cabeza. Under this chief, it was during the blockades when Pasco would all but starve, as he was made to pay an unfair share of the costs of Dutch war through a rising level of tribute in the form of a dwindling supply of rice yields nowadays increasingly hard to come by. Pasco's prosperous merchant father, of whom the son was immensely proud and admiring, and his pre-Hispanic Islamic-class mother, whose post-Hispanic caste was now among the lowest of the low, could offer little to a son whose own time belonged least of all to him and not very much to them but to an all-too-powerful cabeza and senior officials above him, all of them urging Augustine and secular priests to deny wards like Pasco any basic education, save for a manipulated scripture shaped by colonialist ends . And it was during the blockade too when these secular officials would permit servants like Pasco to eat only a measured share of the now hard-to-find rice, primarily arriving on the few Chinese boats able to get past the blockade, that barely grew in fields made fertile from these servants' own hard labor. But given this war, such allotted rice was the top limit of what any servant could expect to eat according to the precise calculations made by profit-maximizing superiors, faking a sincere interest in the starving servants' deserved portion.

At the beginning of the Age of Discovery, Northern Europe still craved rare spices coming from somewhere in Asia's mysterious heathen world. At first, it was only the Portuguese among these Europeans who seemed capable of meeting any meaningful proportion of the world's large demand. Chavacano-speaking Lusophones did so through their hard-won Southeast Asian trade links to the area's source of spices, cloths, and silks. Meanwhile, the financially stressed Spanish searched for a way to compete with Portugal's richly endowed Asian estate. In 1521, young Philip II's father, the Holy Roman Emperor and King of Spain Charles V, initialized attempts to colonize Las Islas Filipinas. In doing so, he hoped to find rare spices and gold[83] and maybe bring the Spanish Empire closer to *all* the valuable spices of Southeast Asia, exchanging the aromatic plants together with European trade goods for precious Chinese porcelain and silk. China, however, judged all *European* products as inferior. They were not interested in Spain's fanciful designs.

As for the spices, China already had reliable suppliers among that country's well-connected Portuguese and a reliable network of native traders. But in 1565, after Cortez and Pizarro had conquered the Aztec and Inca

Empires, Spain stumbled upon a way to overcome its dilemma. Deep silver deposits were discovered in its new American territories. An expanding Spanish Empire then shipped to the Philippines silver ingots—converted later to pesos and Spanish dollars—mined and minted in its new American colonies. Such silver became legal tender not only in China and Southeast Asia but later all over the world. Such commerce brought enormous profits to Pascoal, his fellow Portuguese traders, and the Spanish Empire. In exchange for China's silk, Spain paid American silver. For cloves, other spices, and Asian cloths, China paid Pascoal and his fellow Portuguese merchants still more silver specie and, of course, silk. American silver, in all its manifestations—be it commodity, silver-dollar coin, or other legal tender—was at the center of all East-West commercial transactions, causing Spain to mine and trade it for Chinese silk, thus fueling its galleon trade.

Young Filipino indigenes receiving Catholic religious instruction in
17th century San Agustin Church in Manila, Philippines.

Spain centered this commercial activity on the Philippines' Luzon Island, a location endowed with the excellent deep-water harbor called Look ng Maynila (Manila Bay) and its trade port of Tondo.[84] The harbor was able to accommodate large ships, which Spain operated between Tondo—gateway to the China market—and Acapulco:[85] the important portal to American silver. Manila was also located midway between China and the Spice Islands, just 435 miles between. Manila was important to Spain's commercial plans. After 1586, it was from Manila's port at Tondo that the empire exported local and American gold and raw Chinese silk carried by private Portuguese traders to Japan.[86] Given its attractive location, it was from Manila that Spaniards sucked up huge profits from its galleon Trade. Such profits would have been out of reach but for the large returns enjoyed by Pascoal and fellow converso traders.

Manila Bay's growing population of Christianized natives were made King Philip's wards. In exchange for their clear path to heaven (which Spaniards seemingly convinced the natives they needed), and along with promised protection against Muslim enemies, Dutch marauders, and local enemy tribes, Philip and his church demanded of them unwavering obedience. To the delight of these now-Christian natives, no longer would Spanish officials and soldiers refer to them by the racist terms *heathens* and *pagans*.[87] Instead, they earned the privilege of being called Los Indiós.[88] Traditional rulers (datus)—demonstrating submission to the church, in addition to being made cabezas de barangay—became *trustees* of the Spanish Empire, enjoying freedom from mandatory tribute or any field labor. They were given other privileges that were not extended to the islands' lower-caste Indians.

Since peopled by pre-Hispanic inhabitants whose descendants live on the islands today, the traditional cabeza played an essential role in local trade and family life. For instance, before colonialism, datus (as the cabezas used to be called) controlled fields and prime agricultural territory farmed by free and dependent vassals, although such land was communally owned. The rice and vegetables used to be enough to feed everyone in the village, affording each datu the prestige and renown he came to enjoy among his kinfolk and the area's commoners.[89] All this changed after the Spanish arrived.

Before the Spanish came, social norms in the islands entitled datus to rely on involuntary labor supplied by social classes below his noble status. Such labor enabled the datu to care for vast agricultural lands, which he conditionally allowed to feed the villagers. Entitled servitude to the datu meant for the vassal debt peonage, sharecropping, and warrior duties. The latter was the job description of the *maharlika*[90] social group, a class including the commercially successful family of Pasco's mother. But being the child of a prosperous Portuguese trader and maharlika-linked mother complicated the mestizo's social status, rendering him a freeborn but an illegitimately born serf-like ward of the king.[91]

The arrival of the Spaniards complicated the rights of natives, their tenure to the land, and the authority of the islands' chiefs. After colonization, title to arable land over time was transferred to friars and certain officials favored by the king. Philip II reluctantly granted these favored officials the right to receive unpaid Indian labor, requiring them to work to produce a food surplus sufficient to feed Spaniards and newly settled Chinese and, if there was enough, the wards too. Even cabezas were among the officials entitled to royal favors. Since they no longer had access to the rice they planted, ward dependents now needed to "purchase" most of their food by way of tribute labor and as imports from China. In short, under colonialism, rice from Luzon's fields was diverted from the mouths of natives to fill the stomachs of Manila's favored. Though Spaniards tried to stop the precolonial practice of involuntary labor to native chiefs, they were thwarted by these very same chiefs and, later, by the messiness of a Dutch war.

Despite the riches trade once brought to Los Indiós, Spaniards never could establish a profitable intra-Asia trade, largely because of a monopoly driven by private Portuguese traders, the Lisbon Court, and Rome. Experts report colonialism in the Philippines turned into a proselytizing enterprise[92] and was never profitable—contested by those examining activities engaged in by allied Chinese traders and workers whose 1575–1600 population compared to the Spanish came to exceed 2:1.[93] Contenders also argue that the area's private Portuguese merchants who, upon paying a mandated hefty tax, earned handsome trade profits in Manila markets.[94] Nevertheless, instead of the hoped-for riches of a bountiful trade with wider Asia, Spanish officials settled in Manila expecting to profit from the Manila-Acapulco galleon Trade. The galleon trade's profitability is traceable to the important role played by American silver, the businesses of *private* Chinese traders, and the important intermediary role played by *private* Portuguese merchants and distributors whose Southeast Asia market depended on Manila Bay's Indians, such as the family of Pasco's mother. Certain Portuguese merchants—the ones from Macao—were also primary suppliers of the Asian slaves[95] absorbed into the internationalized economy of Spain's Manila Bay.[96]

Under Spanish rule, bay-area settlements such as the one where Pasco lived among traders became as important to Portuguese merchants like Pasco's father as he was to them, given Pascoal's ties to Moluccan spice growers and

Although their royal courts were rivals ever since the early Middle Ages, Portuguese and Spanish traders found they needed to partner in Manila to make their lucrative commercial operations work well and so that the world's first global economy, one fueled by silver, could run smoothly. Spaniards relied on the Portuguese-Asia links to obtain precious Moluccan spices and prized Chinese manufactures, which Spain exported to acquire American silver. In turn, the Portuguese depended on the imported American silver to pay for the silk and porcelain purchased from China. These commodities—silk, spices, and porcelain—were among the most valuable merchandise carried on the galleons to Acapulco, and American silver enhanced the wealth of all three: Spanish, the Chinese, and, of course, the private Portuguese traders like *Pasco's* father.

Makassar's redistribution channels and given Pasco's mother's ties to domestic commercial networks and her family's resulting prosperity.[97]

At first, Manila brought wealth and prestige to Spanish merchants and the empire because it was in Manila Bay's Port of Tondo where Spain exchanged American silver and gold for Chinese silk and for the spices China imported from the Moluccas through local Indian and private Portuguese distributors and traders.[98] The silk and spices purchased with the silver were shipped to Spanish American luxury markets as part of the larger-than-Asia international galleon Trade, yielding huge profits to Spain and the small Portuguese traders directly active in this global enterprise. But according to one observer, Manila had no real purpose in the scheme of things other than to serve as a medium for the Spanish Empire and China's trade in silver and silk.[99] And in the words of yet one other observer, "until the latter half of the eighteenth century Manila [for the Spaniards] was to be commercially little more than a way-station between China and Mexico,"[100] a waystation, which the Virginia William Crawshaw (formerly Pasco) boasted to family members was where his black Portuguese father had earned a fortune in American silver and in "that brown gold they call cloves" by the early seventeenth-century.[101] The Indian family of Crawshaw's mother once prospered from their participation in Southeast Asian trading and fishing.[102]

> So long as Spaniards and Portuguese cooperated[103] in the Maluku Islands, casados[104] such as Pasco's father retained a role in the luxury spice traffic via the Philippines. These Portuguese [traders] distributed the bulk of Maluku's cloves [through Manila and Makassar] in China and in Coromandel and Bengal; a secondary market for these cloves developed in the Americas, via the Manila galleons. The Makassar-China-Manila trade axis also facilitated [an] exchange of American silver for South Asian cloth and spices from Ambon, the Bandas, and probably Ternate.[105] Importantly, it was after the 1580 Iberian Union that the Habsburg Dynasty forced the submission of both Spain and Portugal to one Catholic Crown: that of King Philip II. And it was because of this union that the two rival European powers "cooperated in the Maluku Islands" [a.k.a. the Moluccas] to bring spices and even more wealth to the Dynasty and Empire, thanks to valuable Asia trade links unique to the private Portuguese traders. After the union and their payment of high taxes, Portuguese merchants—despite the protests of Manila's Spanish merchants [who suspected many of the Portuguese traders were secret Jews and conversos anxious to steal the Spanish trade and extend it throughout the world]—enjoyed unencumbered access to the rich trade opportunities centralized in Manila Bay and its globalized galleon market. Shrewd Portuguese traders grew even wealthier by arbitraging silver.[106]

Dutch pirating in Manila Bay was not unusual during the time Pasco was abducted,[107] for the troublesome activity was part of a determined effort to take complete control of all the Portuguese and Spanish trade carried on among China's southern Fujian, Portuguese Macao, and Spain's Manila Bay.[108] Accordingly, Dutch privateers had been carrying on an annual blockade of Filipino waters ever since 1616.[109] In fact, it was from 1621 to 1622 that the Dutch East India Company implemented a most unusual blockade in partnership with its longtime enemy, anchored just outside the entrance to Manila Bay. It was a blockade conducted by using a joint Anglo-Dutch fleet to interrupt trade involving the Portuguese, the Spanish, and the Chinese.[110] It was toward the blockade's waning days that privateers seized Pasco, his brother,[111] and others.

For some one and a half years,[112] the Dutch-English blockade wreaked havoc on the lives of Manila Bay's dependents. As these circumstances shaped the events to follow, Pasco's family—given the empire's ruthless caste system and his vulnerable converso father's limited presence on Manila Bay (between March and June, when outbound galleon activity at Tondo was at its height)—[113] could be of little help to the mestizo. To the empire, he was a throwaway tributary but one with obligations to the state that he needed to fulfill in person.[114] In fact, it was the Portuguese traders and the Spanish Empire who were the real targets of these Dutch-English blockades. As far as Spaniards were concerned, El Mestizo and wards like him were obligated to struggle through "inconveniences" caused by disturbances like the blockades. During the Dutch-Spanish wars, such serf-like wards survived on disappearing Chinese food imports. The long blockade-induced scarcity caused food prices to spike. The bay-area dependents had to labor harder to satisfy per capita quotas owed to their superiors. These men, women, and children worked still harder just to make up for any in-arrears tribute owed to demanding superiors, leaving little to no time for the boys and men to hunt and fish to feed themselves and their families. The freeborn and captive indiós, mestizos, mulattoes, blacks, and Asians—all of whom were singled out for racist opprobrium by Spaniards for having been born with "impure blood"—ran the risk of violent punishment and increased peonage should any fail an obligation. Each had to decide what to do next. Many escaped Manila Bay for any number of pagan islands located well beyond the reach of he Spaniards.[115]

As recorded in the box, a few devoted Christians fled the islands altogether to join the fleet. Both free and ensnared vassals (together called slaves by European observers) complained of being "very ill used." Despite the dire consequences of the blockades, commoners remained obligated to meet all tribute quotas and other obligations. Under the empire's *vandala* and encomienda,[116] among the expanded responsibilities

"The situation in Manila had already reached crisis proportions . . . and (on) January 1622, several slaves had escaped to the Fleet from Manila, and the reason they gave for their flight was because they had been 'very ill used and the Rice exceeding deere.' These slaves reported that there were many others in Manila that were very-hard pressed as well and would also flee to the enemy if they had the chance. Consequently, the Joint Council [which oversaw the blockade] decided to send several ships to anchor near the town (out of gunshot, of course) to see if they could entice more of them away from the Spanish colony" (Blussé, 77,8).

of selected cabezas during the blockade was the collection of extra tributes and farm produce owed to opportunistic cabezas and *encomenderos* caused by the European siege. Rice, a dietary staple for all Indians, had become so "deere" that there were locals who were driven into debt slavery to acquire something to feed themselves and their families. As the blockades continued, dependents starved.

It was near their home on Manila Bay where the two brothers, seeking escape, swam southwest of Ermita to the mouth of Manila Bay. They were invited upon an enemy ship in wait there, hijacked after climbing aboard, and later launched a second escape—this one from their "white men" captors.[117] The attempt led to the drowning and death of Pasco's brother. Pasco sailed on to London.[118]

When he sailed from London to Virginia between 1622 and 1624, William Crawshaw was not the only "East Indian" so transported. Records confirm that in 1624, "Tony, an East Indian," arrived in Virginia's Jamestown from England as a servant to rich, recently arrived white English merchant George Menefie.[119] By paying for the indentured servant's passage from London, Menefie obtained a 50-acre "headright" (credit) toward his purchase of 1,200 acres of land.[120]

By the end of this narrative, I will have traced my paternal ancestors to more than five hundred years ago. To do so, statistics, history books, and the census alone were not enough.

Helping to comprehend these ancestors as historical agents, I learned, for instance, that my Angola male progenitor bequeathed me his five-hundred-to-two-thousand-year-old Y-chromosome,[121] especially important because the discovery led to a trajectory that I never would have thought possible but for DNA. My African mother gave us mitochondrial DNA.[122] Besides the Philippines, other ancestors had roots in Ireland, England, Portugal, Israel, Ternate, and elsewhere, as revealed in autosomal DNA.[123] Combined with my grandfather's wonderful stories and other oral, sometimes-complicated written histories and public records, all these gifts helped shape my Howard family portraiture.

When Charles William Henry Howard told me more than fifty years ago about William Crawshaw, I received the information with more than a little bit of incredulity. I looked at the unrecognizable couple in the daguerreotype portrait hanging in the vestibule of my grandfather's Manhattan apartment, then heard about the never-enslaved Indian who *chose* "America" after leaving England. None of this seemed relevant to any Howard family history that I could identify with at the time. That my ancestor was an Indian with agency enabling him to make choices that forever shaped his life all seemed so unreal!

Grandpa died in 1976. Before his transition, he lived for quite some time in a state of mind that was out of touch with the world we both knew. Were he alive today and in possession of the curiously keen mind he was known for many years earlier, we would both be pleased to learn that much of what he told me back then is today traceable to historical sources that I found decades later, beginning with a source that neither of us could ever imagine might one day be accessible: DNA.

Pascoal's busy chambers hugged the Manila shoreline, with its Indió mistresses, dependents, fishermen, and traders bartering with Asian and Chinese merchants visiting the bay. From nearby Tondo, Pascoal redistributed to luxury markets his Moluccan cloves shipped there from China. Famed for its Nossa Senhora da Guia[124] shrine, in 1610, the mission town[125] of Ermita separated from Malate, where Pasco and his family lived. Until 1571, the Marian statue lay buried under a Manila Bay beach when a Legazpi soldier found it, leading to the establishment of the Ermita chapel[126] and, in 1610, to the Augustine Ermita Parish.

Paseo de la Luneta [127]was a pleasant lane along the bay. Its path to Ermita was a short walk beyond the gated entrance to Manila (Intramuros). Facing west lay the glimmering bay, to its south Indió settlements,[128] some resulting from forced relocations (*reducciónes*) of families' traditional riverside and shoreline homes. They had been forced to move there and join the other newly Christianized families already there. The new settlements formed large pueblos overseen by Spanish friars and soldiers:

The main task of Spanish missionaries and soldiers in the seventeenth century was to concentrate or resettle people within hearing distance of the church bells. At the very center of a major settlement (pueblo) were a Catholic church, a convent . . . [and a town hall] surrounded by the houses of the local elite. Comprising the bulk of this elite up to the nineteenth century were the datu [or cabeza] and his personal following[129] . . . whom Spaniards had transformed into a petty ruling class that learned to profit from an alliance—sometimes uneasy—with the colonial masters.[130] These cabezas unlike the datus of old were not selected in connection with any kinship ties to village residents.

Ermita Chapel[131] was built in 1606[132] after the Dutch expelled some 400 Portuguese settlers from the Ternate and Tidore Islands, causing them to resettle in nearby Manila Bay. But Nuestra Senora de Guía (as the Spanish call her) is older than any host church built by the Spanish. The Portuguese brought her to the islands, but one would be hard-pressed to reach an agreement on this point with any Spaniard! Sailing under the Spanish flag, before Ferdinand Magellan's 1521 alleged "discovery" of the islands, his friend and putative Portuguese cousin Francisco Serrão had landed in the same area nine years before him in 1512. Serrão remained on nearby Ternate Island until he and Magellan died there in 1521. Those who argue that it was the Portuguese who brought Nossa Senhora da Guia to the islands can point to the fact that both men were Portuguese and had come to the islands as scouting soldiers long before the 1565 Spanish.[133]

The Senhora is a patron of travelers, navigators, and traders; but she certainly rejected the pirates who used to raid Manila Bay, especially Dutch-English privateers like Pasco's kidnappers. To these pirates, capturing Pasco was part of a larger plan designed to accomplish five goals: weaken the economic core of the Spanish Empire rooted in Asia and strengthen their own trade ties to Asia, divert Chinese trade away from the Spanish Empire's Manila Bay and instead to a Dutch-controlled port, disrupt the Macao-Manila trade link then currently monopolized by private Portuguese traders, and replace the Portuguese traders with Dutch and English.[134] But for the plan to succeed, an obstacle had to be overcome: secure a Dutch monopoly against the Iberian traders[135] by harassment and seizure of their cargo and then permanently remove the Portuguese merchants from the Asia trade. The fragile Dutch-English partnership hoped that the strategy would cause the Portuguese and Spanish to lose profits on their Asia trade, making the Manila economy go bust, subsequently causing Spain (together with the pesky Portuguese traders) to leave the profitable Chinese trade altogether,[136] thus yielding to the pushy Europeans a path to a monopoly controlled by the two quarrelsome partners. Nossa Senhora da Guia would never have given her blessings and guidance to such machinations.

But what made my Howard family's first American ancestor run away from what my grandfather said was a rich father to start life all over again with pirates? The simple answer? The brothers had had enough of trying to survive the miserable life of a Manila Bay mestizo during the time of a long Dutch war.[137]

It was from January 26, 1621, to May 9, 1622,[138] when an Anglo-Dutch Fleet of Defense "effectively prevented the movement of ships into and out of Manila Bay."[139] Chinese ships had become the Indiós' primary source of food. Five privateer ships belonging to the Dutch and an additional five privateer ships tied to the English harassed all Chinese and Iberian shipping between the Chinese island of Macao and Manila Bay.[140] Promising a better life for themselves, Pasco and his brother boarded the enemy's ship,[141] each cautiously calculating that his new life could not be any worse than the one left behind.

As to the fortunes faced by Pasco's father after the hijacking, I learned that following two military campaigns against Makassar, by 1663, the Dutch VOC (Verenigde Oostindische Compagnie) had monopolized Makassar's clove trade and forced yet another expulsion of what the Dutch called the kingdom's "smugglers,"[142] i.e., private Portuguese traders who had been able to skirt earlier Dutch embargoes. By the same year, the spice trade emanating from Ternate and the rest of the Moluccas had been monopolized by the VOC, and it was also in 1663 that the Spanish left Ternate and Tidore for good. By the late seventeenth century, the Dutch finally completed their monopoly designs on the trade of clove spice. All now trained their sights on Brazil.

Pasco's father and his fellow "smugglers" had temporarily managed to circumvent the Dutch monopoly when they established a distributive trading network in Makassar and Manila. Despite their short-lived success, Dutch-controlled Ambon Island remained the world's center of clove production until the 1800s, when the VOC dissolved into bankruptcy—a victim of its own two hundred years of monopolistic success.

This chapter invites the reader to consider the impact on the cultures of sixteenth- and seventeenth-century Asia and Africa of postmedieval Europe's growing demand for spices, the beginnings of its North American extension of the transatlantic slave trade, and the introduction of global capitalism. During the era of Pasco's abduction, the world's first sustained public corporation—the Dutch East India Company or VOC—began. The growth of an unregulated global economy and an international war (in which Pasco was made a victim) that lasted for eighty years and which began with a Dutch rebellion against their Spanish colonial masters all made their inaugural appearance on the world stage. Such unconstrained racist, capitalist ventures were part of an exploitation of Asian, African, and Caribbean peoples of color. In this environment, a glimpse into my family's pre-Western history is presented. But little can be gleaned from this account alone about our prospects in the tumultuous centuries that carried my family to the present. An account of my ancestors' lives in these future years is presented in the following chapters.

> The arrival of Pasco to England's first overseas colony followed by only one hundred years the 1519 generally acknowledged opening of the transatlantic slave trade. Some would argue that, technically, Pasco was not a slave. But when the used-to-be ward of the Spanish Empire—a ward descended from the West African ancestor who left the continent in the early 1500s—landed in early seventeenth-century colonial Virginia, he was among the first of his kind to be recorded and become part of the group that later called one another African Americans. The baptized Indian would become just one of millions who comprised the diaspora destined to form a complex story spanning continents, oceans, and centuries of often-misunderstood African American history.

William (ca. 1624–1656+)

Reverend Dr. William Crashaw belonged to the elite intellectual society of late-sixteenth- and early-seventeenth-century London.[143] But the circumstances from which he sprang were relatively humble.[144] Despite his modest beginnings, William Crashaw went on to become a graduate of St. Johns College, Cambridge; distinguished poet, author, and scholar; the prestigious Prebend of Rippon; esteemed rector of Burton Agnes, Yorkshire; and Puritan preacher at the upscale Inner Temple Council. At the age of just forty, the eminent reverend possessed England's third largest library after Oxford and the large collection of books and manuscripts that belonged to Richard Bancroft, Lord Archbishop of Canterbury.[145]

In 1624, when the wavy-haired, dark-skinned Pasco arrived in London, the celebrated Puritan would soon enough play an important role in the life of this slightly built mestizo.[146] The abducted youngster was not long ago destined to live the life of an enslaved pauper. But as one of the progressive investors and clerk of the Virginia Company of London and as rector of St. Mary Matfelon-Whitechapel, Reverend Crashaw turned the doomed captive into an orthodox-baptized Indian servant,[147] ensuring him a life far better than any Dutch slave could expect.

Pasco was turned into a captive by pirates—concealed in the hold of an enemy ship as he survived on uncooked rice kernels—until these enemy privateers surreptitiously transferred him to the care of Reverend William Crashaw's parish in East London. Reverend Crashaw's Virginia Company of London was an organization—actually, an institution—whose membership included individuals who were also members of the English East India Company.

It was the English East India Company, along with the Virginia Company of London, that figured importantly in the English Court's quest to become a world empire—the likes of which the years preceding and including the seventeenth century had not seen. Indeed, the English East India Company's first declared colony was the Banda Sea's nutmeg-rich island called Rhun. Reverend Crashaw endorsed the colonial plans of the English Court but with reservations. As a member of the Virginia Company, he helped to fulfill its aims as he and colleagues led by Sir Edwin Sandys maintained friendships with associates of the pro-slave-trade English East India Company[148] while they also sought to fulfill English commercial interests in Asia.

It was more than sixty years ago when Grandpa and I were alone one afternoon, and he told me about a child abduction in our family's history. My recent recollection of this story is that there were two brothers who ran away from home and decided to join the crew of a merchant ship leaving from the nearby Chesapeake Bay. They were invited aboard by two white men. Around the time of departure, the boys realized they had been hoodwinked and hijacked. Panicked, they attempted escape by jumping into the bay. A brother drowned. Sixty years later, when I sat down to write a history of my paternal family, I recalled that the two boys might have been Grandpa and his drowned brother. At the time when Grandpa told me the story, he also told me he had been raised by "some mean people," including by a relative named Paris. As I continued to write my Howard history, research revealed that the United States Federal Census of 1900 conducted in North Carolina's Lower Conetoe (pronounced cuh-NEAT-uh), Edgecombe County, records my fifteen-year-old grandfather as a member of the Paris Howard household. I also learned that this Paris Howard and a son were identified by a later census taker in the year 1910 as Pasco Howard. But I also came to realize that according to census information, Grandpa had no such brother. The story about the abduction and drowning was not about Grandpa at all. Instead, it was about a William Crawshaw, whom Grandpa said was an early American ancestor arriving from England as a free Indian. Like Grandpa, he too had left home. Unlike Grandpa's home, Crawshaw's was said to be "rich." The reality was more complicated than what I remembered.

Although the reverend endorsed the colonization of Virginia, he and Sandys did so with trepidation.[149] The two wanted more freedom for Indians and Virginia settlers, even as each sought a way to ensure profits for the company's investors. But neither entirely endorsed slavery. Most privateers familiar with the East India Company knew that among Reverend Crashaw's responsibilities as head priest of Stepney Parish, a position he occupied since 1617 when he won the position of rector at St. Mary's, he was administrator of the Elizabethan poor law in East London's Docks neighborhood.

Ah, those lowly "Docks"! It was in this area of London where my now-homeless ancestor disembarked after a very long journey from Asia in 1624. Reverend Crashaw took a delectable interest in this brave young prospect: not only was he a good candidate for religious conversion, the reverend thought, but he was a valuable Virginia laborer. He could tend tobacco and defend against enemy Spaniards too. Pasco was "heathen," though. At best, these Indians from the East—professed Christians— were said to practice a folk Catholicism, or at Pasco's young age, they might not yet have been baptized at all. And in a way, the West was right. Although Pasco declared to the reverend that he was a Christian Indian, the scholarly Puritan thought otherwise. He knew that the boy had never been *properly* baptized at all and that he even did not know, in the reverend's estimation, the true meaning of the word.[150] Before Christianity had reached his land, Pasco's people, according to the reverend, followed mixed Islamic and native beliefs, venerating spirits and practicing reverence to the ancestors while professing a belief in monotheism. The reverend thought that such behavior was not becoming of a true Christian. Pasco believed otherise.

The boy could be forgiven for his professed inclinations toward papist[151] superstitions, Reverend Crashaw concluded. But the fact that he is now *a willing* candidate for a real Christian baptism—and, to his credit, a willing candidate whom the reverend learned had fled his Catholic captors and their hellish practices and beliefs—sufficiently confirmed for him the boy's sincere *faith* in the true Christ. To the reverend, as it was for any Puritan preacher, *free will* was the minimum required of any candidate before he or she could be baptized. Staunch Puritan that he was, Reverend Crashaw believed that the heathens of the world, including all Catholics, should be converted to the church only of their own free will and only if they demonstrated a sincere faith in Christ. They should never be converted by the threat of force.[152]

Before the Spanish began their permanent settlement in the Philippines in 1565, islanders revered their women and feminized men, the latter held as spirit mediums and called catalonan and bayugin by the Tagalogs (Manila Bay natives). Women and men enjoyed the same rights and were equally privileged, children enjoyed the same, while marriages between opposite and same sexes were equal. Precolonial women possessed the sole right to name children, and they owned property and accumulated wealth. Unwed mothers and fathers back then were unashamed, as many of their gods and goddesses lived the same way. When colonists and friars arrived and witnessed all this, they were appalled. Slowly, they were successful in changing such ways, convincing converted natives (Los Indiós) that the ancient beliefs and practices were inspired by the devil.

The good reverend did not like the papists and their faith. He believed all of them were a bunch of idol-worshipping heathens who knew nothing about how to properly prepare fellow heathens to be true Christians.

"Yes," in answer to the child's imagined questions—questions aimed to measure this new way to know Him other than by way of the Moors (called Moros according to Filipino Spaniards) and the Christians back home. "Yes," he could continue to eat fish and swine after his baptism, the reverend would have answered—if you can catch the critters. "No, not rice, though. The crop is unknown in the colony."

First, though, he must quickly be made aware of the basic tenets of the catechism before baptism into the Christian Church: a spin-off of the Church of England and today's Episcopalians. But this was not what the tired and hungry young Asian wanted to hear—I can imagine Pasco thinking in response. Food was of utmost importance just now, as he craved a portion of rice and back-home sago.[153]

But Reverend Crashaw was thinking about other matters. He would have answered his young charge by preaching it was far more important that he seek spiritual sustenance in addition to mere sustenance of the flesh! He must at least *hear* the Ten Commandments and understand the importance of the baptism and Eucharist first. The Puritan decided that if the child took well to shortened lessons about the catechism, then he would be given his coveted baptism. Besides these lessons, Reverend Crashaw would see to it that the boy received parish accommodations;[154] the reverend's parish office had authority over such things as mandated by the Elizabethan poor law. These same accommodations housed parish waifs and vagrants, the city's poor, in addition to London's sizable population of prostitutes, prisoners, and beggars.

Pursuant to his plans for the boy, Reverend Crashaw thought about a prominent Virginia cousin named Raleigh Crowshaw. Raleigh was among Virginia's so-called ancient planters—"ancient" because he was among the colony's first settlers after the 1606 King James I charter. Like his cousin, Raleigh Crowshaw was a member of the Virginia Company; but he had arrived in Jamestown in September of 1608, around the same time as Captain John Smith, with whom Crowshaw was on familiar terms. As one of Virginia's ancient planters, Raleigh and his friend, the prominent William Tucker, were entitled to one of the limited number of special grants: land patents sponsored by the Virginia Company and a headright grant of at least 50 Virginia acres for each servant's transportation from England paid for by Virginia planters like Crowshaw and Tucker.

Raleigh came "from an old London merchant family and in Virginia sought the promotion of profitable trade with the Colony's Indians."[155] He could be heard voicing the same sentiments as his preacher cousin in London whenever he declared to the colony that Virginia Indians needed to be Christianized peaceably through trade, exchanging knives and mirrors and blankets for valuable beaver pelts and for corn—activities in which the East Indian could be useful as he helped facilitate such exchanges while meeting the terms of his indenture agreement.[156] But since it was well-known in Virginia and London that Crowshaw was also open to "non-peaceable" colonialization methods, the degree of sincerity he felt about establishing amicable relations with the Virginia naturals[157] caused a few in London to worry.

Ancient planter Crowshaw had received one of the coveted Virginia Company grants in 1623.[158] His connections with Sir Edwin Sandys and merchants involved in trade linked to the London and East India Companies helped lead to young Crawshaw's selection to travel to Virginia as a limited-term, baptized servant to one of Virginia's prominent tobacco planters and merchants. Company grants like Crowshaw's awarded 500 acres plus workers to a lucky-few English planters. The East Indian's Virginia arrival was associated with a valuable award to his host to be used by Crowshaw or his friend William Tucker as they planted tobacco and established trade with Virginia Indians. The award further enabled the creation of Elizabeth Cittie (present-day Hampton, Virginia). These awards were as good as money, often sold and transferred among the planters the same as legal tender. One of the conditions of grants that were tied to any Virginia-bound servant whose transportation expenses were covered was that he be given a proper Christian name before entering Virginia.[159] My first non-native American ancestor was henceforth called by the Christian name given to him by his godfather: William Crawshaw.

Given those harsh times, William Crawshaw simply *had to* be known in the colony as the Indian who was willingly baptized into the Church of England, and what better way to accomplish that than to parade him around the colony as the godson of Reverend William Crashaw! The Virginia Charter of 1609 required that all who settled in the colony be non-Catholic Christians. It forbade the immigration of Catholics because they would undermine "the conversion and reduction of the people in those parts unto the true worship of God and Christian religion . . . The governor had colonists worship 'according to the constitucions of the Church of England . . . and popery should be exemplarily punished to the horror of God.'" Elsewhere, an official pamphlet promoting English immigration to Virginia reiterated that "the colony forbade 'papists' and suggested that 'if once perceived, such a one, weede him out, and ship him home for England, for they will ever be plotting and conspiring.'"[160]

It was stipulations such as these and the circumstances that memorialized 1622 that make it clear why no more was mentioned about the boy's desire to be baptized a Catholic! He was wise enough to keep his papist sympathies to himself, with only an occasional mention to trusted members of the family.

Recall that it was in 1622 when 347 settlers, one-third of Virginia's population, were killed in a Powhatan Indian uprising stemming from many unkept promises and continued encroachments on Powhatan lands made by the colonists.[161] For most colonists and their servants, living conditions in Virginia immediately after the uprising were nightmarish and, in many quarters, led to starvation, as settlers were afraid to venture beyond their fortresses to plant, hunt, and seek water. Successful recruitment of good servants and workers from England practically stopped. Peter Arundel, one conscientious settler who lived in Elizabeth Cittie where Crawshaw arrived from England around 1624, agonized over the need to reduce food allowances to servants because they, the servants, despite their English parish grants received in London and meant to sustain them until they settled in Virginia, did not have, and could not purchase, sufficient provisions in the Virginia settlement. Complained Arundel:

> I have not at this tyme to mayntaine me & my people till Harvest but a little more than halfe a bushel of English meale.[162]

Perhaps the aftermath of the 1622 Indian revolt was worse too for Richard Frethorne, a twelve-year-old white indentured servant from London who lived in nearby Martin's Hundred, when he complained in a letter to his parents who lived in 1623 England that

> we live in fear of the enemy every hour; we are but 32 to fight against 3,000 if they should come. And the nearest help that we have is 10 miles from us. When the rogues overcame this place the last time they slew 80 persons . . . I have nothing at all—no, not a shirt to my back but two rags, nor no clothes but one poor suit, nor but one pair of shoes . . . I am not a quarter as strong as I was in England, and all is for want of victuals. I tell you that I have eaten more in one day in your home than I have here in a week . . . Your loving son, Richard Frethorne, 3rd April, 1623 [163]

Shortly after the letter was sent to his parents, Richard died.

The setting that welcomed William Crawshaw to Elizabeth Cittie in 1624 might not have been as dire as the earlier quote from Arundel and as the unfortunate circumstances of young Frethorne imply. Two weeks after worrying about how he was to find sustenance for his family and servants, for instance,

Arundel wrote home: "Any laborious honest man may in a shorte time become ritche in this Country," implying that all was now well in his household.[164] As to the general state of pending starvation after the 1622 Powhatan raid, the same source reports that "ships were expected [in the colony of Virginia] daily from Canada and Newfoundland with enough fish [caught on the shores of Virginia and sufficient to feed the colony] for the whole ensuing year [as of 1623]."[165] In addition to an abundant supply of fish, the colony had an ample supply of corn.

Raleigh Crowshaw died before 1624 ended. Following the death, records list Crawshaw as a servant and household member of William Tucker, whom Crawshaw assisted in trade with Virginia's natives. Other tasks of the Asian required duties already familiar to him through experience gained in the Philippines—duties requiring the planting, hoeing, and stringing up of what was for every Virginia colonist the valuable tobacco crop in preparation for market. Thomas Dunthorne (one of the Virginia Company's senior servants and member of Tucker's plantation) was Crawshaw's field boss.

One wonders what difference the death of Raleigh really made in the Virginia life of the young East Indian, given that both Raleigh and Tucker were rugged frontiersmen and boastful Indian fighters. Coming from a more practical variety of adventurers, neither man shared Reverend Crashaw's utopian vision of an integrated religious Virginia society, though Tucker went on to hire only Christian servants, and he honorably abided by the agreements specified in their so-called indentures—as loosely understood as some of these terms might have been. Still, many of the Virginia planters wished that the well-meaning Puritan reverend in England would simply pray more and preach less! But working under the reverend's cousin or his friend Tucker, young William's welfare, at least for his first years in the colony, rested in his indenture agreement.[166]

In theory, Crawshaw's agreement—no doubt negotiated with the aid of liberal-minded reverend Crashaw—might have guaranteed food, shelter, clothing, and even a severance consisting of a small plot of barren land located near the colony's western frontier. But at the end of his indenture, Crawshaw managed to sustain himself in part through trade with Virginia natives. Crawshaw could expect little to no assistance for any kind of an evangelical crusade such as he might have been urged in London to carry forth in Virginia—neither from official Virginia nor from the Church of England. Authorities in both places knew that the average white colonist, despite pretensions, tended more toward the faithless side, and his aim in coming to Virginia in the first place was to make as quick and as big a profit as possible, all Indians be damned.

While sympathetic to these colonists' views, the ruthlessly successful Tucker called himself a devout Christian. He was a rich merchant, recipient of numerous land grants, and member of Virginia's powerful House of Burgesses. He was the commander of Kecoughtan and its successor called Elizabeth Cittie. He had secure connections to all manner of provisions needed to satisfy the indenture requirements of his large plantation, which included seventeen servants, tenant workers, as well as his wife and child.[167]

The 1622 Powhatan uprising occurred in isolated smaller settlements lying along the James River rather than in Jamestown and Elizabeth Cittie proper. Settlements in the latter town were surrounded by fortifications from nearby forts (including Captain Tucker's own well-armed plantation fortress),[168] and they had been forewarned by the natives. But in its aftermath, survivors continued to ignore the grievances of the Powhatans, blaming the uprising on their conviction that Indians refused to be turned into Christians and that these heathens were, therefore, the treacherously ill-fated children of Satan and Ham:

> Despite [a] treaty, during the summer of 1623, carefully staged attacks were made upon the Indians and it became an accepted stratagem to go against them in March (prior to planting, when food stores were minimal), in July (while crops were growing), and in November (after harvest and when loss of shelter would be most critical).[169]

In the days following the 1622 attack, unless a professed Christian, all Indians were banned from English-claimed territory:

> It is infinitely better to have no heathen among us, who at best, were thornes in our sides.[170]

"Indean" William would have been a likewise banned Indian had it not been for his much-touted baptism into the English church while in London, vouched for by the rich Raleigh Crowshaw just before his death and by Captain William Tucker, among Virginia's most highly respected citizens and well-known Indian fighters.

In England, meanwhile, the Reverend William Crashaw had not long to live. In 1625, he chose to remain in London to care for poverty-stricken victims of that year's plague—a calamity the young Asian barely escaped. By 1626, Reverend Crashaw too succumbed.[171] Preceding his final days on Earth, however, he joined the rest of the Virginia Company Council in seeking resolution to a rather important political question that plagued the English Court in the early 1620s. There was then considerable disagreement among the members of the council of the Virginia Company of London about whether it was appropriate to continue the company's illicit practice of pirating Spanish-Portuguese ships. Such pirating was sometimes done in cooperation with Dutch adventurers. Indeed, it was this kind of pirating that explained how Pasco, a.k.a. William Crawshaw, reached Virginia.

While it is true that the Virginia Colony was in dire need of indentured labor to help grow and process tobacco and corn and that many in England still had not gotten over the Spanish armada incident, which left a serious rift between England and Spain, others on the council, including the few who remained sympathetic to Catholicism and some of whom were secret spies in league with Spain, wanted to be on friendly terms with the Catholic Spanish Empire. The English Court was especially interested in cementing ties between England and Spain, and in 1623, high-level officials had been involved in negotiations to arrange the marriage of King James I's son Charles, Prince of Wales, to Infanta Maria Anna, daughter of Philip II of Spain. These negotiations began in 1614, but they finally broke down on August 30, 1623. Relations between the two courts remained tense. Continuing to capture Spanish cargo by hijack on the high seas was not going to curry favor in the courts of England's former ally. Any inkling of these hijackings—and of how a subject of King Philip II of Spain, Pasco, a.k.a. William Crawshaw, sailed to Virginia—all needed to be sealed from public scrutiny.[172] Still, the reverend thought that young Crawshaw could be relied upon to help defend the colony against any possibility of attack from their number one enemy: the *hated* Spanish!

A final source of tension between the colonists and Spain was Pope Alexander VI's 1493 papal bull, Inter Caetera. In it, the Catholic Church decreed all rights to Virginia and its eastern shore neighbors to Spain. The English church ignored the decree, and as a result, colonists expected an imminent attack from their archenemy. Furthermore, what would the enemy do upon finding a Spanish subject baptized into the Anglican Church living and working among the hated English! No, both colonists and England did not want to give any excuse to this formidable enemy to suddenly appear on its Atlantic shore.

After the 1622 Indian-colonists clash, English settlers in Virginia were in no mood to welcome for stay among themselves yet one more heathen stranger, especially one who looked to them just like the Powhatan enemy. Everyone thought that the enemy was always plotting to kill them and that the enemy desired to interrupt their profitable tobacco industry. In fact, so angry did the colonists remain in 1623 that just before Crawshaw reached Virginia, a cool but angry Captain Tucker, representing the frightened and vengeful white settlers, went before clueless Powhatan Indians to launch a so-called peace treaty that was concluded with a celebratory toast. Soon after the toast, one hundred Indians lay dead from poisoned drinks served by Tucker and his company of attendees in retaliation for the year-earlier killings and for the Powhatan having kidnapped, after the killings, many white settlers as hostages. The captives were held by the Indians for about one year and released in connection with the well-publicized, mutually-agreed-upon "peace treaty."

Given all this, it was in the best interests of Virginia colonists if only a *Christianized Indian* lived and worked among them—one engaged in merchant activities profitable to both local Indians—never mind that *this* Indian was from faraway Southeast Asia and England too. He would be introduced to all as a model servant, one whose public profile should be emulated by all Virginia Indians who resisted Christian conversion. A teenage boy totally dependent on white adults like Crowshaw and Captain Tucker and the young white Christian workers on Tucker's plantation, the Virginia Indian-looking field worker, trader, and hoped-for evangelist could still be molded into the kind of Christian who would serve one of the most important concerns of Virginia's white planters: turning Virginia natives into Christians.

The reverend was, according to the *Virginia Magazine of History and Biography*, "a strong [Christian]" and ordained evangelist,[173] but he was equally convinced that the Virginia heathens should be Christianized not by the sword but only through engagement in willing, normal, colonial merchant activities with England.[174] As an esteemed member of the Virginia Company, the reverend never forgot, however, his number one reason for agreeing to serve the enterprise. He was there to help the corporation be profitable. If Virginia natives could be convinced to become Christians and trade with the colonists, then sustained profitability of the enterprise, he thought, was all but guaranteed. Given that he was an ancient planter and investor himself in the Virginia Company enterprise, Captain William Tucker agreed. The company's short history of generating solid losses for investors must be reversed into one of sustained profitability. All but the colony's native Virginians thought likewise.

On the eve of famous Virginia governor-to-be Lord Delaware's departure for the colony on February 21, 1609–10, Reverend Crashaw preached to him a London sermon, which concluded:

> Remember thou art a . . . general of Christian men; therefor principally look to religion. You go to commend it to the Heathen . . . make the name of Christ honorable, not hateful unto them.[175]

On the same topic, Reverend Crashaw declared to the general audience that night:

> The Israelites had a commandment from God to dwell in Canaan; we have leave to dwell in Virginia; they were commanded to kill the heathen; we are forbidden to kill them, but are commanded to convert them.[176]

For Puritans like Reverend Crashaw then, to enable God's plan calling for the English to bring salvation and prosperity to a ready population of heathens in the land of Virginia, there remained "the need to populate the New World with people of sober and godly deportment who would set a proper example for the 'savages'"[177] and live side by side at peace among them.

In his poem titled "On the Baptized Ethiopian," Reverend Crashaw's famous poet son Richard was just as confident as his father that any peaceably baptized native heathen could be molded into an instrument to open God's preordaine path among Virginia's own heathen savages:

Let it no longer be a forlorn hope
To wash an Ethiop:
He's wash'd, his gloomy skin a peaceful shade
For his white soul is made:
And now, I doubt not, the Eternal Dove
A black-faced house will love.[178]

The English believed that if only they could gain control of the Indian children, then the colony could raise the future generations to be good Christians. In 1618, Tucker and the company planned a large residential university-college at Henrico to educate and Christianize young Indians. Construction funds were provided by England's East India Company whose merchants later brought the future William Crawshaw to London's Puritan reverend. The Powhatan uprising in March 1622 killed that idea. The violence also killed the company official sent from London to Virginia to launch the project. After the uprising, Virginians lost all interest in trying to Christianize the Indians. Even before the disturbance, colonists displayed little interest in converting the natives, as funds dedicated to the college's construction costs were never spent for that purpose. Instead, these funds were dedicated to what the colony considered important projects.

"From under the World" (Early Seventeenth Century)

Life in Virginia was to take a different turn for all who lived there after 1624.

In England, after the 1622 Virginia Powhatan upset, Reverend Crashaw's utopian contingent among the Virginia Company's executive membership lost influence with the venture's decision-makers. Even before then, any sincere commitment on the part of its London membership to encourage colonists to reach an amicable, Christian-like settlement with the Indians did not command overwhelming support in the company. When William Crawshaw was sent from London to Virginia to help stimulate trade with the natives—to plant, weed, hoe, and pick tobacco for the colonists and see if, just maybe, he could perform evangelical miracles too—he was effectively a lone sheep being sent among a pack of wolves. It was sometime after his indenture had ended that he realized his predicament. Between 1625 and the 1646 final peace treaty with the Powhatans, whether he desired it or not, William Crawshaw's fate in Virginia was cast to be part of a society with whom there was a most natural fit: Virginia's new freedmen, its stunted population of angry and increasingly sickly Indians, and a small but growing chorus of recently arrived field Negroes, as well as the even newer but also growing population of amorphous mulattoes.[179] Although he was declared free, his rank in the social hierarchy of Virginia was not unfamiliar.

The 1622 Powhatan revolt caused hardship, bloodshed, and anger among Virginia colonists and servants. Additional investment in the Virginia Company dried up. Few English citizens were interested anymore in traveling to the colony in the period immediately following the attack. Given the circumstances, young workers like Crawshaw were increasingly relied upon in the aftermath of the attack to continue needed work in the tobacco fields. Given the dire situation, King James I of England undertook what he called prudent measures to ensure the long-term viability of England's Virginia experiment and the profits it promised to bring to his court. The king canceled the company's original private charter, effective May 24, 1624. The young colony thenceforth became responsible directly to the English monarchy and his privy council. They, in turn, continued to cater to a coterie of elite friends who owned Virginia property and friends who would do anything to bring themselves and the king all the wealth that Virginia promised it could deliver, even if the profit taking meant complete obliteration of the colony's "savages". The new arrangement would lead to some unfortunate changes in how the growing young colony treated the territory's indigenous peoples and those unlucky white colonists who openly favored them. William Crawshaw and his progeny would not go untouched by these changes.

After the first of Virginia's English settlers arrived and following the 1622 Powhatan War, publicly recorded reference to William Crawshaw could not be found again until, obliquely, 1656. If English adventurers inadvertently or otherwise aided the young East Indian's escape from the treachery of Dutch slavers more than one generation ago, their role in his life now and in the lives of his descendants was to take on a more complicated—even ominous—cast. And between mention of him in the 1624/25 muster and a darkly sidelong reference in the Virginia of 1656, still more had changed in the English colony.

Hatred of the Indian, fed by fear, affected most white Virginians after the uprising; and the more it grew, the less likely it became that any white servant would wish to flee his servitude, however severe, to live free among the Indians. Moreover, the policy to erase anything Indian made foolish—even dangerous—future attempts to exist among them. Still, some white servants thought it worth the risk. Most, however, were caught in Virginia's tightening labor discipline, to be bought and sold as their masters pleased and to hoe tobacco for however long as they were likely to live.[180]

Upon termination of his own work agreement, Crawshaw sought to minimize entrapment in the "labor discipline" (i.e., servitude) of his day. It was not unusual then for postindentured servants to establish their own farms, trade networks, and other related livelihoods to avoid, or at least minimize exposure to, the tightening labor discipline that was then customary.[181] The young Afro-Asian was no exception in all this. As the stories handed down through the Howard family all indicate, William Crawshaw's later life was spent mostly as a sprung-from-the-Virginia-soil native and as part of the colony's slowly rising population of Southeast Asian Indians. Crawshaw's lifestyle was not typical of the lives spent by most ex-indentured servants of his day. Relegated by white Virginia to a style of life that entailed living among Virginia's most hated—the savages—rendered the indigenous-Indian-looking Crawshaw unworthy to most English eyes.[182] While life with the Indians brought welcomed freedoms from constraints imposed by the colony, it also marked Crawshaw for the rest of his life and cost him aplenty, as the events of 1656 demonstrate below.

Whenever land was appropriated as part of a former servant's severance agreement back then, it was not uncommon for the property to lie on or near the border that separated the colony's planter class along with other elites living in the area from less-desirable property on which lived England's immigrated poor and recently freed servants (called freedmen).[183] While nonpoor freedmen lived there too, the area was also known for its indigenous habitués.[184] Typically, this less-desirable land consisted of unimproved parcels on which lived many unmarried males who had concluded their indenture contracts and sought ways to earn a living.[185] All who lived near this border were armed against the wild animals that dwelled there and against imminent Indian attacks, real and imagined. They armed themselves against the European predators that lived amid themselves too. Theirs was wild and—for the average white man living out there by himself—disquieting territory.[186] It was with such a place that William Crawshaw was associated in 1656 Virginia documents.

Meanwhile, Virginia's population of Negroes, as Africans and African Americans were called then, increased compared to 1625 (just one year after William arrived) from less than two dozen to roughly 300 in 1650.[187] The number of European colonists also increased during the period despite devastations spewing from the Indian-settler violence of 1622. Ignoring agreements with Virginia's natives not to do so, the increased number of colonists pushed indigenous peoples off their lands. In the process, most local Indians died after exposure to European diseases, warfare, and a diminishing amount of territory available to tribal people on which to live, hunt, and plant corn. The Beaver Wars[188] of the 1640s and 1650s caused a major upset in the distribution of tribes who traversed the Blue Ridge Mountains and lived in Virginia's Piedmont and elsewhere in the southern colonies. In the Ohio River Valley, just to the west of Virginia's Piedmont, there occurred a vicious struggle among various tribes to supply their West European customers with a declining supply of beaver pelts in trade for guns and ammunition. As the number of beavers farther north around the Erie Valley were slaughtered for their pelts, native groups in the area moved south in search of replacement beaver populations. As they did so, native groups who were indigenous to that area either defended their territory against encroaching groups or, as in most cases, moved to other areas, where they warred with a different group of tribes, causing further native peoples' displacement. As if the Beaver Wars were not upsetting enough, in eastern Virginia's Tidewater, where the colonists initially settled among the increasingly disadvantaged Powhatan Indians, the land had become more crowded, and the area provided less opportunity for the white colonists to become instantly rich.

To the early-1600s Englishman, colonial Virginia was the new frontier, a land that offered him the most likely chance for prosperity. The successful marketing campaigns of the London Company encouraged hundreds of Englishmen and a few of their families to migrate to the colony's Tidewater region. By the first half of the seventeenth century, the richest, and otherwise lucky, of these settlers who managed to stay alive had taken from the Algonquians the most sought-after tobacco-growing lands, pastures, and valuable riverfront properties, making it impossible for the displaced Indian and any less-affluent Englishman to plant his stakes there. Beyond the 1640–46 third Powhatan War, those who still had not found their fortune—ex-indentured servants, landless, and poor males—looked westward to Virginia's Piedmont area as their only opportunity to stake a claim in the disappearing El Dorado. But to do so, they would have to contend with the area's various Siouan-speaking natives and the Sioux's most recently arrived enemies who had their own designs on the area: the Iroquois.

Between the pressures imposed on aboriginal people by colonists and the effects of the Beaver Wars, in 1654, a group of Indians were run off their traditional Piedmont lands along the Rappahannock and Rapidan Rivers. These Indians fled east to the Virginia Fall Line along the James River to a point just outside of present-day Richmond. The area was on the border of what the colonists claimed was their legitimate territory.

In his out-of-print 1935 account of the situation, David I. Bushnell, Jr. writes:

> As so often told in history, sometime before the spring of 1656, a large number of Indians, probably an entire village with all of their possessions, "sett downe neer the falls of James River, to the number of six or seven hundred." They had come as friends to seek a new home, not as enemies, and desired peace, not war. Later they were attacked by the Colonists in the endeavor to expel them from the colony. The English had as allies Totopotomi and his Pamunkey warriors. In the encounter that ensued the English suffered great losses and their allies were routed and driven back. The Indians against whom the combined attack had been directed probably retired up the James and were lost to history.

> It is now believed the Mohocks,[189] who had come from a distance, were a village or group of Manahoac who had been forced to abandon their country to the northward, along the Rappahannock and the Rapidan.

The pressure exerted by enemy tribes from the north undoubtedly caused the dispersal of the Manahoac from the region they had occupied in 1608. The movement might have begun soon after the middle of the century, at a time when the Iroquois were waging a relentless war against the Erie, thus leaving the tribes to the south of them free to act on the offensive (Bushnell, 12–13).

The incident referred to in Bushnell's slightly inaccurate description is related to Virginia's 1656 Battle of Bloody Run.[190] It was in 1654 that Shackaconia Indians of Virginia's Manahoac Confederacy[191] fled their traditional territory in Virginia's Piedmont at the confluence of the Rappahannock and Rapidan Rivers.

There was more than one immediate impetus offered to explain why the Shackaconia left their riverine Piedmont home. But the ultimate cause can be traced to the Beaver Wars referred to above and the westward expansion led by the pioneering English. The year 1656 was not the first encounter between the Manahoac and the English. In August 1608, English explorer John Smith of Pocahontas fame led a team of European men to the upper reaches of the Rappahannock when they encountered a Manahoac hunting party. These Manahoac were said, even by their Powhatan Indian enemies, to be formidable and "very barbarous, living of wild beasts, fruits, and [roots]." Smith claimed to come seeking their "love and peace," but the indigenous tribal hunters that day were having none of it. From the forest branches above, the Manahoac rapidly rained arrows on the surprised Europeans. Asked later why they resisted their first-ever encounter with the English, Smith was told by a lone wounded captive, Amoroleck, that his people heard that "you were a people who come from under the world to take our world from us."[192]

Targeting the Shackaconia and other Indians living nearby, the Virginia Assembly—in a 1659 *order*, which was based on that official body's 1641 *act*—fed the speculative urges of a majority of Tidewater Virginia's English planters by granting exclusive patent rights to settlers who possessed the financial capital of those like one Francis Hamond and his associates whom the order said could:

> discover, And shall enjoy such benefitts, profitts and trades for fourteen yeeres as [he] and his associates . . . have found or shall find out in places where no English ever have been or discovered or have had particular trade . . . And take up such lands by pattents (proving their rights) as they shall think good, not excluding others after their choice . . . from takeing up lands and planting in those now new discovered places. (Hening, 548)[193]

Much of this Virginia Northern Piedmont property consisted of lands hunted on and inhabited by the Manahoac. The Manahoac was a confederation of one-half dozen or so Siouan-speaking tribes, but some say the Manahoac was a tribe unto itself under a Monacan Confederation. According to the first idea, though, Shackaconia was the town in a confederation tied to the Battle of Bloody Run incident described above—that is, in addition to the Nahyssan, an allied kindred people, plus an unrelated third Native American group who reached the same area, but later in the period leading to the 1656 battle.[194] The latter were members of the Iroquois Nation and were the reason for the 1656 battle. Referred to by several names, most frequently, these Iroquois were called Richahecrians, Rickohocken, and Westo Indians.[195]

It was among the Shackaconia, though, that my story picks up from where we left off with William Crawshaw in 1625. But first, a paraphrase of one eyewitness's account of the 1656 Battle of Bloody Run given by Lionel Gatford—Puritan, like William Crashaw, writer of epistles to Cromwell, and friend of Lord Baltimore (note: Mahocs here refers to the Manahoac [or Mannahoac]). I have interspersed my own words to elucidate the seventeenth-century written account that, at points, can otherwise be confusing:

> The Mahocs had been just outside of the border that separated the Colony from the hinterland since 1654 before the arrival of the Richahecrian Indians, who came by 1656. The Mahocs came to the area outside the colonists' settlement because "The Planters have turned some of the Indians out of their places of abode and subsistence."

Gatford[196] goes on to recount:

> After that (i.e., "heathenish inhumanity" on the part of the colonists) the [Manahoac] Indians have submitted to the Colony, and to their government, and have taken up their own lands, after the custom, used by the Colony. These Mahoc Indians assumed that the recently-arrived Indians (the Richahecrians/Westos who had not submitted to the Colony as had the Mahocs) were enemies of the Europeans, and came to Richmond "to do mischief" to the Colony.[197] Already having been treated by the colonists in a "very unchristianly requite," (repayment), thinking that he was understood by the Colonial soldiers to mean good, "one of the Indian Kings" [Mahoc Indian chief] did adventure too far with his own Indians, in the pursuit of those other Indians, and thereby lost his life in that action as some report, though others thought him to be taken alive by the enemies.[198]

The king's wife and children:

> were by him at his expiring, and they were "recommended to" put themselves in the care of the settlers and planters for their own safe keeping (it was certain that "King" or Chief Shackackonia's assumed customary "tributary" service to the Colony merited kind treatment by the Colonial officials of the wife and children. The wife and children followed the recommendation), but they "were wholly neglected, and exposed to shift for themselves."

> According to some, a grievance before the court was that land had been taken from the King before his death by "an English colonel." But in his own defense the accused colonel countered, and it was "stoutly asserted by some," that the only reason the King said such things was because the King had been "affrighted, and threatened into that acknowledgement."[199]

Referencing a transaction consummated in the same year as the Bloody Run Battle of 1656, a Virginia document for the first time revealed the name of William Crawshaw's son. York County, Virginia, records (1665–1672) show that "on July 1, 1665, Joseph *Croshaw* to William Calvert, for £24, sells one Indian boy called Benn, which he bought of Maj. Gen Hammon in 1656."

Ben ("Benn") was the son of William Crawshaw. Even though full-blown slavery technically did not yet exist in 1656 Virginia, York County files make it clear that young Ben's time did not belong to him or his people. Despite its laws, Virginia's custom rendered the unbaptized young Indian a slave for life.[200] Ben's mother was one of the "children" of the Shackaconia chief killed in the Battle of Bloody Run,[201] and as Indian war captives, both mother and son were effectively unfree[202]—or, more politically acceptable at the time, made "servants." As part of some mysterious machinations, Ben fell into the hands of one of the militia's colonels.[203] He was one or two years old.

At the time when it was recommended that the Shackaconia chief's family entrust their welfare to the English, among Virginia's Indian policy pronouncements occurring weeks later was a March 1656 edict that urged *free* Virginia Indian families to release their young children to the care of white families so that these children would not grow up to be heathens.[204] Under the law, hurriedly passed after the time of Virginia's massacre, suspicious Indian families were promised that their children would be taught to read and write English, they would be taught a trade, and they would be made Christians. It was promised that each *free* Indian family could select a white caretaker and that the children would not be turned into slaves. But everyone knew that Indians were already being bought and sold as servants and slaves. Records from the period indicate that the promises made in the March law were rarely kept. Most native tribes who learned about the declared policy believed none of it. The confused Shackaconia captives, however, would have jumped at the opportunity had they not already been, by law, war booty. Among the confused crowd of colonists surrounding the misplaced bunch of equally confused, bedraggled Indians, there was a colonel who, with one extended hand, bade the family a sympathetic welcome while, with the other, he quickly sized up one boy child who would soon answer and come running when called Ben by his master. Virginia records document that young Ben (no surname, implying he was unbaptized)[205] had become the war trophy of the English colonel identified below.

The Crowshaws (relatives of deceased reverend William Crashaw of London) continued to play a role in the life of the East Indian after his indenture ended. On this occasion, it was *the child of William Crawshaw* who had become the center of the Crowshaws' attention. Written history makes no further reference to William Crawshaw after the infamous 1656 battle. Joseph Crowshaw, to remind the reader, was the son of ancient planter Raleigh Crowshaw. The East Asian might have been originally indentured to the senior Crowshaw, and it might have been he who had ultimately financed the young native's London-to-Virginia voyage.

In 1656, lifelong enslavement of Africans was technically illegal. Not so the native peoples. In Virginia, it was the custom to enslave Indians, especially if such indigenous people had participated in or were otherwise linked to such conflicts as the 1656 battle. Had Joseph Crowshaw not prevented young Ben from being swallowed up in an *international* slave market spearheaded by the likes of Virginia, it is likely that the child would not have survived in the colony for very long, and I'd not be writing these words today. Joseph Crowshaw's 1656 purchase, it turns out, helped preserve a memory of what soon became today's Howard family.

Major General Mainwaring Hammond,[206] business partner of Joseph Croshaw and an Indian fighter like the latter's father, was a close friend of Virginia governor William Berkeley. Hammond was also associated with the 1656 massacre, but unlike the governor, some in his family were documented land speculators in the Indian areas that lay in Virginia's Piedmont region. These speculators were anxious to remove the Indians who used these lands to hunt, fish, grow corn and other vegetables, and reside. The general's brother, Francis Hamond, who was one of the earlier-mentioned land speculators covetous of the valuable Indian properties, would soon be granted patent rights by the Virginia assembly to a large tract of remote and supposedly "vacant, unowned" land, which, in fact, the Shackaconia chief said planters had recently chased him away from. Virginia records reveal that it was in 1656 that Hammond acquired the Indian baby, later called Ben. As we already know, Hammond quickly profited from the sale of William Crawshaw's baby to friend and fellow soldier Raleigh Crowshaw's son, Joseph. Major Joseph Crowshaw was a local government official, an attorney, a prominent planter, and an owner of a large estate. No doubt, one of the recent additions to this estate was Ben's indigenous Indian mother. She herself was made a servant (read slave) after the Battle of Bloody Run. Those "recommendations" that were made to her family were perhaps instigated by or on behalf of Hammond and associates.

Major Joseph Crowshaw, Major General Mainwaring Hammond, and their well-placed English friends were in league with the Richahecrians, or the Rickohocken as more lately known. But could it have been Major Joseph Crowshaw's son-in-law, Colonel John West, that the above "Virginia Carolorum" quotation mysteriously implies as the "English colonel" who took "the King's Land"? If yes, as I once concluded, then Colonel West was an item for the history books for another reason as well. After the Battle of Bloody Run, West left his wife, a daughter of Major Joseph Crowshaw, and the couple's five children to live with the widow of the Battle of Bloody Run's slain Pamunkey Indian chief Totopotomi. The adulterous couple had a son from the infamous affair. He would later rise to prominence in the English colony, thanks to the political craftiness of his widowed mother, "Queen" Cockacoeske.[207]

Colonel West and his descendants, inheriting deceased father-in-law Major Joseph Crowshaw's Indian properties,[208] would go on to become major investors in the lands close to where the dying "king" (i.e., Chief Shackaconia) and his native ancestors once lived and hunted. Today, that land is a part of the Virginia counties of Stafford, Spotsylvania, and Culpeper. Without ever having seen the unexplored territory, exiled English king Charles II—in a 1649 royal decree, followed by another one shortly thereafter—had awarded 5.2 million acres of the expanse to seven of his loyal English supporters. Henceforth, the area became part of Virginia's so-called Northern Neck Proprietary, also known as the land grant.[209] Major Crowshaw was an investor in the related Poplar Neck.[210]

But the "English colonel" who, according to Gatford, defended himself against the allegation that he was a member of the group of colonists who chased Shackaconia off his territorial lands was a different colonel. The true colonel would later be known as Major General Mainwaring Hammond, and as pointed out above, he was the brother of land-patent grantee Francis Hamond. At the time of the Battle of Bloody Run, Hammond was still an English colonel.[211] He had arrived in Virginia around 1649—that is, soon after the beheading of English pro-Catholic king Charles I. As one of the English cavaliers who fought in England on the side of the defeated king, the cavalier colonel Mainwaring Hammond fled to Virginia to save his own head after Cromwell and the English Parliament overthrew the king. Even then, Hammond was a friend of Virginia governor and Royalist William Berkeley. After King Charles's beheading, Berkeley (pronounced like *BARK-LEE*) lost the governorship. He was restored to the office, however, after the son of Charles I, Charles II, was made king around 1660. It was then that Governor Berkeley promoted his friend and Royalist supporter Colonel Mainwaring Hammond to the office of major general, said to be the second highest government office in Virginia (just beneath the title of governor). One of Hammond's sons, John, eventually married a Catholic Howard in the pro-Catholic colony of Maryland.[212]

The brother of Francis Hamond, Major General Hammond, who himself held government-sanctioned land patents on Shackaconia property, joined Joseph Crowshaw as an officer of the powerful Rickohocken organization. Indeed, as of 1662, Hammond listed his address as Riccohocke [town].[213] White Rickhohocken members sought to increase their wealth by removing indigenous Indians who lived west and south of Virginia's Tidewater, including the indigenous confederation of which Shackaconia was a part, from their traditional lands. These Virginia Indians were not the only victims in the scheme, but so were those throughout the Colonial South. The white Rickohocken, with their Indian allies, continued to kill such indigenous peoples and then take title to the abandoned properties. Hammond and Crowshaw were attorneys for the Rickohocken organization that committed such deeds.[214] Because of the work of the organization that enlisted Westo Indian allies to help carry out their plan, hundreds of Indians in Virginia and in the Colonial South were eventually driven off their lands, enslaved and removed elsewhere in the South, shipped to the Caribbean, or slaughtered.

These Westo Natives were the same Richahecrians against whom Shackaconia "with his own Indians" aimed to defend the English and consequently lost his life during the 1656 Battle of Bloody Run.[215] Aside from greed, much of the group's Indian removal ideology and planning came out of the anti-Indian sentiments, which sprang up from the 1622 Powhatan-English war.[216] Crowshaw could not escape the consequences, including the Battle of Bloody Run.

The Battle of Bloody Run was not his first time being a military target. The most important occasion, of course, was when he and his brother became victims of the Dutch-English military blockade of Manila Bay. From the time when he was old enough to occasionally play those war games with boys his age amid the mangroves lining the slippery banks on Manila's Pasig River and the days when he raced brothers and cousins through the coral-fringed deep waters encircling his island homeland—it was since his boyhood back home in the islands that an unknowing Pasco had long been in training for the 1656 violent misunderstanding, which led him to fight alongside the chief of Shackaconia to defend him and his own burgeoning family in the Battle of Bloody

Run. Indeed, it was a patriotic call to honor and his duty, cloaked in his most recent claim on fatherhood. It was not in the makeup of Pasco, a.k.a. William Crawshaw, to ignore this call to battle in defense of the Indian chief.

Now, the logic of Virginia's westward expansion required that everybody in the Battle of Bloody Run have a part to play in the drama. The Richahecrian Indians profited from the battle by subsequently joining forces with Virginia's most powerful white planters to expand the lucrative fur trade not only throughout the remaining western and southern parts of the colony but throughout the American South too—killing, enslaving, and stealing the lands of thousands of aboriginals in the process. For the poorly executed role he played on that infamous day, Edward Hill, the colonel, was censured and fined for all too briefly leading his colonial soldiers and Pamunkey Indians to a quick defeat, to death, and, according to some, to his unforgivable disgrace. But that was only for show, according to some, for it was a short time thereafter that the same colonel found himself resurrected in the plans and ventures of the Virginia Colony's most powerful men: generals and the planters. After that, Hill boldly but quietly reclaimed his wealth and stature as though nothing untoward had occurred.

But lo to Shackaconia and those warriors who accompanied him on that wintry-turning-to-spring day in 1656! The Battle of Bloody Run marked the tribe's beginning of the end, as well—and the last time that any published reference was made to William Crawshaw.

But should we pity William Crawshaw[217] too? Thanks ultimately to the well-intended plans of our Puritan reverend from London, and joined by the defeated liberal faction of the Virginia Company's ruling membership, the baptized, foreign-born Indian did indeed disappear amid a confused crowd of pitched-angry voices emitted by hundreds of English soldiers and their Pamunkey allies. He disappeared against the ultimately victorious Shackaconia, the Nahyssan, and the Richahecrain Indians too, as they all vanished amid the dead and the wounded and among the three Siouan tribes who retreated up the James to the territory of their Monacan cousins.[218] Now joining these indigenous natives as they quickly retreated up the James, William Crawshaw finally found the freedom he thought that Pasco would gain with the wily Dutch back in 1622, only to be hijacked back then and brought here to Virginia. Just imagine all that dust, confusion, the unending assault of arrows, and gunfire as William struggled that day on the side of alleged heathen Indians, defending Christian soldiers against heathen invaders from the hills while being an object of all that ungodly hate, tribalism, and colonial theater so typical of those times.

Some of today's historians question just who the Shackaconia really were. Perhaps a small collection of seventeenth-century natives (said to total no more than one thousand heathens by the midseventeenth century) who lived in a town of Siouan-speaking Indians within a larger Manahoac settlement? It was on a March 1656 day that Chief Shackaconia dared come between the colonists and the bunch of unfamiliar Indians called Richahecrians. For this and for daring to lay claim to lands much desired by both, he was made to pay the dearest price, leaving behind a daughter, grandchildren, and other family to the whims and fancies of uncaring, westward-gazing planters.

According to some, the Battle of Bloody Run counted for progress in England's first frontier colony. It counted for "progress" for two reasons. For one, the conflict helped pave the way toward the economic development of the budding English Empire's Canaanite land of plenty. For future Virginia society, the battle rid the territory of a major part of its indigenous population, subjecting the few "legitimate" ones to tributary status on special reservations—to what some termed just another form of slavery.

For William Crawshaw, it bought freedom.

A Manahoac tribesman sketched by sixteenth century Captain John Smith, the explorer.

Frances, Race, and the Howards (1665–ca. 1798)

On July 1, 1665, Joseph Crowshaw "sells one Indian boy called Benn," about eleven years old, to William Calvert for £24.[219] The Calvert family was a staunch Catholic clan—founders of the Catholic-centric English colony of Maryland. Calvert was a good friend and neighbor—evidence suggests kin too—of the pro-Catholic wing of the Howard[220] family. In fact, John Heyward (Howard) died on February 1660, and by 1661, his widow, Margaret, had married her probable cousin William Calvert.[221]

William Calvert's July 1666+ last will and testament left "one Indyan boy called by ye name of Ben" to his son, by his previous marriage, named Robert Calvert. Shortly thereafter, Ben, descended from Southeast Asian and Virginia Indians, became the "Indyan boy" of Margaret Howard-Calvert's son, Henry Heyward (Howard).[222]

Indian Ben was last recorded by name and ethnicity on October 8, 1675. It was then that Benjamin the Indian filed a legal complaint against one "master Dunn." Between 1654 (his approximate birth date before 1656's Battle of Bloody Run) and 1675, when Ben was twenty-one years old and probably argued he was thus legally eligible to be freed from Master Dunn's servitude, much had changed in the colony of Virginia.[223] But given the political winds, such pleas would prove meritless.

Just months after Ben filed his legal action against Master Dunn, an English-born, prosperous Virginian named Nathaniel Bacon declared that he had had enough. Bacon is described as a brilliant but troubled in-law of then-governor William Berkeley. Bacon used his charisma to become a backwoods Virginia rabble-rouser.[224] It was within a short span of time that Bacon's charisma and the social movement it helped spawn would come to define the contours of Virginia's race relations and social class system, which were to have important implications lasting well into twenty-first-century America.

By 1676, social classes had become baked into colonial Virginia society. At the top of the social heap targeted by Bacon were men like Governor William Berkeley, along with his colleagues and personal friends who lived on and otherwise owned valuable property in Virginia's Tidewater. This group included the Rickohocken organization's upper-class whites, mainly wealthy planters. These Rickohocken investors used the Westo Indians and other native tribes to clear Indian territories that lay to the west and south of Virginia's Tidewater of their traditional owners so that these elite European men could, in accordance with the law, declare the land abandoned. The price of these "abandoned" properties was then set at a high-enough level to guarantee that only certain wealthy whites—like Berkeley, his friends, and the Rickohocken—could afford the purchase. Those who were shut out included, but were not limited to, men at the bottom of the social-class heap. These were the white and black poor and otherwise relatively humble men who became Nathaniel Bacon's followers. In addition to owning their Tidewater tobacco properties, the elite who were targeted by Bacon owned a monopoly on the lucrative Indian fur trade, further angering lower-class frontiersmen, small black and white farmers, and former indentured servants, all of whom were legally prohibited from participation in this trade with the Indians. None of the latter could afford to buy and cultivate major Tidewater-area farm property since it had all been taken up by the likes of Berkeley's prosperous white friends.

In the spring of 1676, Bacon came to represent a class of disgruntled backwoods men, ex-servants, and small property owners who were left on the outside of any opportunity to improve their economic lot. The Bacon mob began by focusing anger on local Indians—any Indian—for Bacon's response to claims that only certain Indians deserved blame was that all Indians were the same to him and his followers and that "the only good Indian is a dead Indian."[225] The rebellion claimed the lives of many uninvolved native peoples and culpable Europeans. Before the rebellion ended at the end of the summer of 1676, Bacon had died from nonrebellion causes. Governor Berkeley, Bacon's biggest adversary, was called back to London to face King Charles II, who demanded answers about the killings and other allegations lodged against him. An aged and bitter Berkeley died soon after, never returning to Virginia.

Following the rebellion, race relations in Virginia were never the same. Bacon's Rebellion was largely a class war on the way to concretizing social castes of freed and indentured Europeans and blacks who together acted against Berkeley and a privileged caste of Englishmen who owned all the good land and monopolized the fur trade. But while the violence was a class- and caste-based affair, it was mingled with race hatred because caught unfairly in the middle were the Indians. They were accused by Bacon and his supporters of being under the protective wing of Berkeley, who repeatedly refused Bacon's requests to order the militia to march against the natives. However, Berkeley was no friend of the Indians. He and the rich friends who lived in Virginia's Tidewater did not want to upset their profitable trade with Virginia's natives. It was mainly for this reason that the governor remained a staunch enemy of Bacon and, therefore, deftly tiptoed around the issues leveled against him by Bacon's followers. At the end of the affair, King Charles II and the post-Berkeley Virginia governor promised to investigate the claims of injustice, but they quietly shuddered at the prospect of any mass uprising consisting of a multirace alliance against them and the power that such a coalition represented.

After 1676, Virginia moved away from permitting any kind of racial alliance such as there had been under Bacon's Rebellion. Instead, Tidewater and accessible portions of its frontier became a society of rich *and* poor white men against everybody else. It was the Indians and, by 1680, Virginia's blacks who were the "everybody else" lumped together as nothing more than the faceless dark-skinned inferiors of all the territory's whites, and they were regarded as needing to be corralled and carefully monitored. By 1676, most Indians and blacks in Virginia had become a caste enslaved to a newly formed, once-mutually-antagonistic class of strategically aligned rich *and* poor whites.

After 1705, a Virginia statute declared that imported Africans, their progeny, and categories of the progeny's mixed-race variants were the *sole* source of the colony's slave population—a population owned by rich and low- and moderate-income whites alike. Eastern Virginia–born Indians, however (as opposed to "those foreign Indians" who lived in the Blue Ridge Mountains, its foothills, and beyond), could no longer be made slaves after the 1705 statute. Whereas under Bacon, all Indians were subject to attack and enslavement by gangs of frontier and recent indenture-freed whites and their black friends and neighbors, by the early eighteenth century, Virginia law allowed that only such whites and their upper-class black cohorts could be slave owners. Indians, Africans, and most blacks could not own slaves.

Bacon's Rebellion paved the way for undisguised racism[226] to serve as an acceptable basis for public policy that became codified in both the colony of Virginia and, soon after, in America. In its embryonic stage, the policy grudgingly acknowledged the existence of merely three kinds of people residing in its jurisdiction: white, colored (or Negro), and an amorphous mixed-race "other," labeled mulattoes. By the late seventeenth century, natives throughout the Southern colonies had noticeably paired with black paramours to produce mixed-race offspring. Even though many of these offspring identified themselves as Indian and continued to live within the cultural milieu of their nonwhite forebears, court records and public documents from the period called progeny of such people mulattoes. After the 1790 federal census, "Indyan Ben's" descendants were listed as members of these mulattoes or, more specifically, as "other free persons" or simply "free persons."[227] After the 1676 rebellion, Virginia declared there were no more *real* Indians left in its colony, except for a few wealthy natives, the many who fled west beyond the frontier's border, and the few others confined to reservations.[228] Virginia's people of color (blacks, Virginia Indians, Southeast Asian Indians, and mulattoes) all had been turned into one caste by itself.

The year 1675 was the last time that I found any public record that identified Ben's ethnicity as Indian. Indeed, in his 1711 last will and testament, a dying white Henry Heyward (Howard), who inherited the "Indyan boy" from his half brother Robert Calvert, declared, "I give unto my son Francis Hayward four negroes by name Gravesend, Ben, Hannah, & Will ye wch Negroes I give unto my sd son Francis . . . but if it should please God . . . ye sd Negroes return to be divided between my Two sons William & John Heyward."[229] All subsequent wills in at least this branch of the white Howard family referred to the family's bequeathed servants—be they aboriginals, Africans, African Americans, or any combination of these three groups of peoples—as Negroes.[230] In a 1692 court hearing (described below), reference to the nonwhite once called Indyan Ben was by then designated a Negro,[231] which was also the way that Virginians at that time referred to East Asian Indians[232] and all captive people who were not labeled white.

In 1700, Ben was still claimed as the property of Henry Heyward (Howard) in New Poquoson County, Virginia (in 1692; the name was changed from New Poquoson County to Charles Parish).[233] Recall that Henry was the oldest son of the first white Howards to come over to Virginia from England. When his parents, John and Margaret, died, Henry inherited their 600 acres of land. By the time of his own death in 1711, Henry Heyward (also Hayward) was rich, owning some 1,780 acres and several nonwhites, including the services of Indyan Ben, who, post-Bacon, had become by then one of the estate's Negroes.

By 1711, Ben was the father of Ann Howard.[234] On December 6, 1758, Spotsylvania County Court records show that Ann was the "free mulatto" mother of nine children.[235] Ann's mother was white English indentured servant Frances Haward, the illegal paramour of Indyan Ben.[236] Just months before the union of Ben and Frances, Virginia law in 1691 banned all interracial sexual relationships—that is, in- and out-of-wedlock relationships involving whites, blacks, and Indians in any combination.

Frances Haward was born in Dunstable, England, in the county of Bedfordshire in 1665.[237] She was christened in the arms of a godparent,[238] as was the custom in her day, beneath the ancient chancery screen inside the twelfth-century priory of St. Peter.[239] The christening occurred on April 9, 1665.[240] She was born to a household of seemingly yeomen or tenant-farmers. France's father was William Haward,[241] whose own father was also named William. They could trace their family's roots to the English Middle Ages aristocrat named William Howard and to a time even before the Norman Conquest of England in 1066.[242]

Despite having upper-class roots in Middle Ages England's Norfolk County, 1642 found William Haward in Bedfordshire when he married Ann Tommes on October 22.[243] The two were the parents of Frances Haward.

As outlined in *The Howards of San Juan Hill*, a considerable number of white English Howards were members of the world's aristocracy: queens, nobles, and gentlemen—part of the Plantagenet, for example. The large English Howard family includes two wives of King Henry VIII: Ann Boleyn (her mother was Lady Elizabeth Howard) and Catherine Howard. England's Queen Elizabeth I was the daughter of Ann Boleyn and Henry VIII. All the dukes of Norfolk, starting with Sir John Howard, friend and commander of the forces defending Richard III in the Battle of Bosworth during the War of the Roses, were also English Howards. The Duke of Norfolk was once the second most powerful office in the kingdom.

However, ancestor Frances Haward, later the English paramour of Ben who was the son of William Crawshaw, was of that country's nonroyal line. Her father's relationship to the royal Howards is through the 2nd Duke of Norfolk, His Grace Thomas Howard, and his son Sir William Howard, 1st Baron Howard of Effingham.[244] Sir William Howard's descendants included two famous Frances Howards. Both were rich women of considerable intrigue and alleged beauty; but most interestingly, each—in succession, of course—was the wife of the dashing, aristocratic Sir Edward Seymour, 1st Earl of Hertford, who died at a young age. It was after one of these two aristocratic Frances Howards that Frances Haward was given her Christian name.[245]

> Both Frances Haward and England's Queen Elizabeth I were descendants of Sir Thomas Howard, England's second duke of Norfolk. Frances Haward was also the descendant of one or possibly two of this duke's heirs, each of them named William Howard.

Frances Haward was born in the final year of England's disastrous string of plagues that, in 1665, killed in London alone over 68,500 people. In 1666, the year following Frances's birth, the Great Fire of London destroyed 80 percent of the city proper but miraculously took six lives. Although London is about thirty-five miles south of Dunstable, most of the plague bypassed its small population.

Dunstable was a village of about 1,000 inhabitants when Frances lived there, and at least by the middle 1700s, it was a regular stop on the increasingly popular stage-coach route that linked the area's towns. In those days, there were plenty of inns in the village. The village of Dunstable was also famous for its markets and the priory where Frances and her ancestors were christened. It was in 1533 at the Dunstable Priory (a.k.a. St. Peter) where King Henry VIII divorced Queen Catherine of Aragon. He immediately thereafter married Ann Boleyn, daughter of Countess Elizabeth Howard-Boleyn, and replaced the Catholic Church of England with his newfound Anglican faith.[246]

Not so well-known today, Dunstable traces its roots to the infancy of Christianity and to the second-century Roman town called Durocobrivis. It was then that the Romans built a road called Watling Street, which crossed the pre-second-century Icknield Way. That intersection still exists and is where the center of Dunstable stands today.

For the Romans, Durocobrivis was a posting station where travelers could change horses. Dunstable, even for the Romans, served as an important transportation hub for travelers, much as it did when Frances lived there in the late 1600s.[247]

The Roman Empire left England during the fall of the Western Roman Empire in AD 410. Present-day Dunstable lay dormant for hundreds of years after that until King Henry I built a new town on the site in 1109, followed by a priory in 1123. The present-day Priory of St. Peter (originally Catholic, now Anglican) traces its origin to 1132.

Though baptized Anglican, certain Howard family members after King Henry VIII remained recusants. The humbler Haward family (viz Howard) would not have been able to defy the church laws of England so boldly, and so they settled for being Anglican-though-secretly-Catholic sympathizers, as the adult Frances might have been. By the time of England's Glorious Revolution of 1688 to 1689, young Frances—with the help of one nephew of a well-to-do ancient planter, William Taylor—was in Virginia. Her reasons for leaving Dunstable are not clear. Frances probably left Dunstable before the end of 1686.

Having financed her passage, the Taylor nephew then received his entitled headright compensation of 50 Virginia acres upon Frances's arrival. Besides England's political turmoil culminating in the Glorious Revolution, Dunstable's economy was undergoing fundamental change when Frances set sail.[248]

For as long as anybody could remember, during England's Middle Ages, the name Haward and some of the country's open areas were inseparable on account of England's extensive manorial system.[249] Such rustic spaces were tied to the grains and livestock that gave sustenance to families. Tradition has it that the Haward family was the protector of these fields and livestock as caretakers and guardians of the fences that encircled them.[250] In the late 1600s, the county of Bedford's long-standing dependence on wool for hat making—and the sheep that provided this piece of clothing—began a long, irreversible decline.[251] These sheep and their wool had been an important mainstay of the Dunstable economy for a very long time, and they were an important underpinning of the household economy of the Haward family. When the production of hats, a major item of commerce for Dunstable, became less dependent on the wool from which they used to be made, it had ripple effects on the economy of the Haward household. The Haward family was made less well-off, as hat making switched from its reliance on wool to a reliance on straw or plait making.

As if this was not bad enough, economic conditions in the family were not helped by England's slow-moving land enclosure policies.[252] Enclosures meant open land was no longer available for rearing sheep and planting vegetables and other foods for the Haward family table. Instead, the land was chopped up, and individual sections fell into the pocket of profit-seeking landlords who charged high rents when such lands were offered to local modest-income households at all. Most often, such land was consolidated under the ownership of a private, profit-seeking landlord.

The decision to move to the Virginia Colony was, for young Frances and her family, a desperate if not even a somewhat hasty one. The decision perhaps carried with it dreams of one day soon owning land on the frontiers of Virginia that young Frances might secure with the financial assistance of William Taylor. Nephew of the religiously liberal[253] William Taylor, he could be relied upon to not frown on the Haward family's furtive sympathies for the Catholic Church. Taylor's Virginia connections were impressive. Men like him could help young Frances achieve her dreams. Like William Crawshaw before her, Frances would repay her benefactor by performing the years of hard work required by the terms of an indenture contract. But as was so often the case with dreams, Frances's future would tell a different story.

Frances's voyage across the Atlantic was not without risks. Take, for example, the experience of one Mary Lee aboard the ship *Charity* in 1654:

> The ship left England, for Virginia. The voyage was stormy, and two or three weeks before the vessel entered Chesapeake Bay, the sailors whispered that a witch was on board. Mary Lee a little, and quite aged woman, was the suspected one, and it was demanded of the master that she should be examined, which the captain at first refused to consent to, but as the sailors continued clamorous, after consulting with Henry Corbin, a passenger twenty-five years old, and Robert Chipson, a merchant, he yielded to the demand. Two seamen searched her body declaring they had found the sought-after witch marks. During the night she was left fastened to the capstan, and the next morning it was reported that the marks "for the most part were shrunk into the body." Corbin was pressed to examine her, and at last, the terrified woman said she was a witch. In opposition to the captain, the crew then hung her, and when life was extinct, tossed her body in the sea.[254]

Frances survived her ocean journey, according to Virginia public records dated October 5, 1692:

> Frances haward servant to Captain Wm Taylor being brought to the court tonight for having a mulatto bastard during her time of her service to Capt.Taylor. The court orders servant woman Frances Haward to pay Capt. Taylor for all charges and trouble master invested in her mulatto child, to assign mulatto to church wardens of [illegible] Parish, and servant after her assigned five years – ordered to pay £10, and to serve Captain William Taylor or his assigns for one year after her time, being fine for committing the sin of fornicating with a Negro.[255]

Furthermore, in 1691, just before Frances's Richmond court appearance and as part of the post–Bacon's Rebellion era, Virginia passed a strict anti-miscegenation law labeled ACT XVI, declaring that

> whatsoever English, or other white man or woman being free shall intermarry with a negro, mulatto, or Indian man or woman bond or free, shall within three months after such marriage be banished and removed from this dominion forever, and that the justices of each respective countie within this dominion make it their particular care, that this act be put in effectuall execution.[256]

In 1682, the Virginia Colony passed two acts combining Indians and Africans into a single caste called "*negroes* and other slaves" (emphasis added). As one chronicler of the period put it, "by lumping Indians, mulattos, and Negroes in a single pariah class, Virginians had paved the way for a similar lumping of small and large planters in a single master class."[257] Never again would Virginia allow in its midst an interracial kind of class warfare such as the Bacon's Rebellion; and Indyan Ben—according to the October 5, 1692, Richmond court[258]—was now a Negro. During the period, there are several examples of interchangeable usage of the words Negro and Indian in Virginia's legal disputes.[259]

Permanent banishment from Virginia County after such miscegenation was just too harsh a punishment for any labor-starved Virginia county to suffer. Such a punishment would render implementation of the policy impractical, according to local planters and their county justices.[260] Cross-race sexual unions in parts of Virginia were not exceptional then. Rather, they were not uncommon in poor counties.

> Assisi and Heinegg report that between 1675, when Ben was last identified "Indian" in Virginia's public records, and 1692, when Frances was found guilty for having committed the sin of fornication with a Negro, Virginia's Southeast Indian population—who, by then, was mostly ex-indentured servants or, in smaller numbers, slaves—were referred to in the public record as Negro. Indeed, by the late seventeenth century, Indians from anywhere in Asia quietly had blended into Virginia's growing African American community and had disappeared as a distinct race of people. Later, many were ignorant of any Asian past.

To forever banish participants in such unions would "deprive [any affected] county of a potential laborer (or two),"[261] with devastating effects on the welfare of local communities. Arguments like this were a common criticism heard from local white farmers and plantation owners such as "George Ivie and others" who, in 1699, sought repeal of the "Act of Assembly."[262] The original 1690 act was watered down in 1705.[263] Such banishments were eliminated from the Virginia codes after that year, but the further appearance of Frances in the records of Virginia could not be found after 1692.

While it is unclear just where Frances permanently resided during the period following her October 2, 1692, court appearance, it is clear that Ben continued to live in Virginia as late as 1711 or 1712.[264] In the March 17, 1711/12 Charles Parish, Virginia, last will and testament of white Henry Hayward (Howard), Ben was listed as one of the four Negroes being left to Hayward's son Francis Hayward.[265] It was not much later than 1707 that daughter Ann was born to Ben and Frances.[266] By 1711, Ben was about fifty-seven years old, and Frances was forty-six.[267]

Before making further reference to the couple's daughter Ann, mention should be made here that ample evidence indicates, as described in my *San Juan Hill Howards*,[268] that both Catholic and Anglican (Episcopalian after 1783) white Howard families in Maryland and North Carolina welcomed Frances Haward—even named their children after her—and that she might have intermittently settled among them although Maryland soon after Virginia's 1690 act also banned mixed-race marriages. In fact, as detailed in my 2015 book, the northern North Carolina counties of Granville and Halifax, where lived white Howards who were clearly in close communication with Frances Haward and some of her descendants, were extraordinarily accepting of blacks and mixed-race marriages.

For example, it was on November 9, 1762, that "many of the leading residents of Halifax County petitioned the Assembly to repeal the discriminatory tax against free African Americans";[269] and in the January 5, 1832, issue of Halifax County's *Roanoke Advocate*, the editor wrote:

> It cannot be denied that free negroes, taken in the mass, are dissolute and abandoned—yet there are some individuals among them, sober, industrious and intelligent—many are good citizens; and that they are sometimes good voters we have the best proofs . . . We do think that too much prejudice is excited against this class of our population . . . —but, at the same time, there is a class of white skinned citizens, equally low and abandoned, whose absence whould (*sic*) be little regretted.[270]

No wonder that in an 1810 count of the population, free African Americans comprised more than 18 percent of the free population of Halifax County, North Carolina.[271] Among these free coloreds were the descendants of Ben and Frances Haward.

Frances Haward appeared in a Richmond, Virginia, court for having violated the terms of her indenture in 1692; and as part of her punishment, the court might have ordered her expulsion from the colony effective a year or so later. Regardless, her and Ben's daughter Ann was born in Maryland or in Virginia[272] between 1707 and 1711, in which latter year white Henry Heyward (Ben's master) died in Virginia and willed Ben to his son Francis Hayward and to Francis's heirs should he die.[273] Between 1707 and 1711, when Ben was in Virginia as part of the Howard family estate, it is likely that Frances was there too because it was then that the couple's daughter Ann was born.

Virginia's Spotsylvania County records list Ann and her nine children as residing there in December 1758. But the father of Ann's children was not identified. In fact, none of the male partners of Ann or her servant daughters was ever publicly identified in colonial Virginia records for at least two reasons. First, as part of a May 9, 1723, law, Virginia mandated that "all free negro, mullatto, or indian" married couples in Virginia pay twice as much tax as a free white married couple (Hening IV). As a North Carolina act—following the example of Virginia—explained in 1723, "an additional tax [has been imposed] on all free Negroes, Mulattoes, Mustees, and such Persons, Male and Female, as now are, or hereafter shall be, intermarried with any such Persons, resident in this Government." Proslavery factions of both legislatures maintained that such policies were necessary to curb the growth of free people of color already living in colonial Virginia and moving to North Carolina. The tax heavily burdened affected families, especially the poor, who, as a result, faced the prospect of being driven into enslavement. To escape the tax and certain prosecution for committing the unholy crime of fornication and adultery, nonwhite parents avoided living together as married couples or in the same household.

Second, Ann, her daughters, and their mulatto children were caught up in a multigenerational web of bound-out servitude that began with white ancestor Frances Haward's 1692 alleged sexual indiscretion. Mixed-race, out-of-wedlock children like young Ann were, upon their discovery by the county, immediately bound out to the church, who then placed them with white masters until the age of thirty-one (up to 1765) and until the age of eighteen thereafter. During these years of servitude, the laws forbade such females to have children and marry. The law often left free families of color in servitude for generations, while the fathers generally escaped unmentioned.

Ann and her Virginia descendants remained a free people even as they pursued a life that was poor to middling hard. Home to them was in the Virginia counties of Spotsylvania, Stafford, Botetourt, Middlesex, and Campbell and in the independent city of Fredericksburg located on the Fall Line of Virginia's Piedmont. Significant to my research conducted on behalf of this narrative, I found that all but Middlesex County were traditionally lands of the Manahoac and the Monacan, whose confederation included natives now known to us as the Tutelo, Saponi, Nahyssan, and the Occaneechi tribes. All are members of the Sioux Nation; and traditionally, they intermarried, hunted, and traded with one another.[274] The aforementioned counties are part of the region to which William Crawshaw retreated up the James River at the end of the Battle of Bloody Run. Long before 1758, the Manahoac and Nahyssan (allied combatants in Bloody Run) ceased to exist.[275] Today, they are simply known as extinct tribes.

From 1705 until the early antebellum 1800s, Virginia records identified adult members of the Howard family as free mulatto, other free, free, or mulatto complexion.[276] For people like these Howards, such terms were inclusive of the legal and federal census definitions for persons of mixed Indian, African, and white descent.[277] As explained above, court records reveal that their so-called out-of-wedlock children living in households headed by the mother continued to be forcibly bound out[278] by the county to the local parish church, which indentured them to a master until the age of legal majority. While in bondage, these freeborn unwed mothers of color, a category that included Ann and those of her daughters who had reached single parenthood, not only lost custody of their children, but until the children became old enough to be released from their indenture, the mothers were deprived of any economic benefit attributable to their children's labor. Instead, the court transferred custody of these allegedly "female head of household" children, as well as the economic benefit of their labor, to the legal guardian, whom the court designated as the children's master and the one who controlled the mother's physical contact with her children. In effect, colonial and early antebellum-era Howard children living with their mothers (and discreet fathers) were, by law, indentured and thereby required to be "trained" oftentimes away from home for almost their entire youthful years in order, it was said, to teach them a job skill and make them productive citizens of the state.[279] Meanwhile, already frustrated by successful results of proslavery lobbyists on state legislators that forestalled their attempts to learn how to read and write—until their children were old enough to be released from court-ordered indentures, thus enabling them to contribute to the welfare of their mothers—"poor to middling hard," freeborn mothers of color remained stuck on the lower rungs of the economic ladder in Virginia society.

Some of the twenty-first-century descendants of Ann Howard living in North Carolina spurned efforts of the Halifax Historic Office to recount their history of the area's free-Howards, strongly arguing that their ancestors were always slaves. This response, while sad, was not unlike those cited in Heinegg's own research. He reports that in the mid-1800s, "life for free African Americans in North Carolina must have been truly oppressive," since many immigrated to allegedly better conditions in the states of Indiana, Illinois, Ohio, and Michigan—and even to Africa's Liberia. "By 1870, many of those who remained behind were living in virtually the same condition as freed slaves" (Heinegg, p. 17).

Mandated indenture laws helped meet the extraordinarily large demand of white masters and churches in Virginia for farm labor and represented one more antebellum instrument that controlled the lives of colored people. One of their aims was to curtail race and class uprisings, especially any that would confront privileged white power. Such measures were outlawed after the Civil War.[280] In effect, during the antebellum 1800s at least, the Howard children were trained and employed in skilled trades (the girls were limited to domestic trades) even while their mothers stayed economically challenged.

Ironically, in twentieth and twenty-first -century America and Europe, residential jobs-skill training programs were—and sometimes still are—considered not only good community economic development policy but also necessary to exert social control over the community's restless young men and women of color.

For instance, the largest of these programs in the United States in recent times is the 60,000-clients-per-year Job Corps Program. At an expected cost of some $1.7 billion in 2014, the Job Corps Program serves about 50,000 sixteen- to twenty-four-year-old black and Hispanic men and women per year. It was formed in 1964 during the war on poverty.

During the years when I ran social and economic development programs for low-income people of color who lived on Chicago's desperately challenged West Side, the Chicago Job Corps Program sat on a 33-acre campus located in the city's West Side South Lawndale Community. Some of that center's skills training would not sound strange to my second-great-grandfather Robert Howard, who was born in the 1820s. Training programs in both eras include bricklaying, painting, and carpentry. Not surprisingly, among recent Job Corps' critics are those who characterize the training there as one big babysitting venture that has failed to keep up with the times. More silently (for understandable reasons), many nineteenth-century, nonwhite Virginia parents of children forcibly removed from the home to be placed for half their lives in mandatory parish-training programs opined the same.

Miles (ca. 1799–1857)

The name Miles comes from white Miles Smith, who claimed to have owned my third-great-grandfather until 1811.

Miles's father, John, was the eighth child of Ann Howard, and he (Miles) was white indentured servant Frances Haward's grandson. Born in Botetourt County, Virginia, in 1799, his enslaved mother was Sara. His father, John Howard, was the free mulatto child of Ben and said Frances.[281] Miles later became a prosperous barber, wealthy property owner, farmer, and musician in the important river town of Halifax in North Carolina. When taken to Halifax at the age of eleven, he was enslaved. There, a prominent white lawyer, Thomas Burgess, purchased him as his personal servant, freeing him seven years later, then deeding him valuable land and property.[282]

Contrary to my mother's enslaved ancestors, all indications suggest that most male descendants of William Crawshaw, like Miles, died free tradesmen. Just after the midseventeenth century, Virginia law (as did the laws of other Southern English colonies) declared that the free or slave status of any nonwhite child like John Howard and his son Miles was the same as that child's mother.[283] More on Miles Howard below, but first, some interesting snippets about his freeborn son Robert (a.k.a. Bob), my second-great-grandfater.[284]

On June 14, 1848, a Halifax job application listed Robert Howard as "24 years old, 5 feet 7 inches tall, of bright mulatto complexion . . . mole on his forehead [and with] right little finger crooked."[285] Between 1848 to the early 1850s, Robert, as

Isaiah was born between the years 1848 and 1853 to unmarried Robert Howard and black enslaved Margaret Peggie. She was enslaved by white Samuel Smith of Granville, North Carolina. Samuel's father was related to the white Miles Smith described above. Up to 1845, it was illegal for free coloreds and slaves to socialize and marry. But in that year, the state's legislature approved an act that, with the consent of the slave's master, allowed the two classes to marry. Robert, by choice or otherwise, later married free Indian Antoinette Meacham. They were the parents of two daughters. Margaret Peggie Smith went on to marry Jordan Thorp, who died twenty years later. Margaret, a mother of two herself, later disappeared from the public record.

required of all young free males of color in North Carolina, entered an apprenticeship, where he learned brick masonry. Rooming with his cousin Wesley Smith in late 1840s Granville, he had what was until 1845 an illegal—but what was still for a long time, thereafter, socially unacceptable—liaison with a slave. Enslaved Margaret Peggie gave birth to their child Isaiah.[286] Born enslaved, Isaiah went on to apprentice as a blacksmith.[287] The Civil War occurred when Isaiah was a boy. When the war ended, such apprenticeships ended too. About twenty-five years later, Isaiah's lengthy career as a smithy came to an end as market demand for the once-popular services of the blacksmith professional had ground to a halt. But whether smithy or commercial cook (which records show he later became), Isaiah was also the owner of Franklin, North Carolina land and houses, and on one of these lots sat his family home.[288] Prosperous Isaiah was my grandfather's father. Curiously, when he was still a boy, my unhappily reared granddad only lived with his handsome, by-then-twice-widowed-thrice-married father, at best, intermittently.[289]

Some of the Howard girls were identified as apprentices too. However, whenever their trade or skill set was identified in the records, it was invariably that of a seamstress or homemaker or some such domestic position. But unlike any of their brothers, these females were not educated in the 3*R*s. Miles's eldest girl, Frances, an obviously take-charge leader, was illiterate.

Miles Howard's life spans the entire spectrum of social spaces that the English had pushed Africans and African Americans into since starting the colonial era, including enslavement, servitude, and *free persons of color*. Miles was antebellum America's quintessential man of color. As he used the system to his advantage, it was by sheer self-confidence, willpower, and luck that he was able to climb the social ladder, starting from being enslaved to temporarily enslaving close family members to rescue *them* from the pernicious enterprise.[290] Then, he went on to become a barber, property owner, landlord, and musician while bowing to convention and church law only when no better alternative seemed within reach. In the 1830 Halifax County Census, he was a landowner who headed a household of nine, including two enslaved relatives: an elderly female (possibly his or Matilda's mother) and a nephew or cousin, Soloman. (Solomon was enslaved by white Solomon Smith of Halifax before 1840, and by the 1840 census, he was free.)[291] In the county's 1820 census, the propertyless young "colored boy," Miles, who was merely three years out of slavery, did not warrant even a modest mention in the official records of his day.

But a reliance on stubborn persistence, self-assuredness, and nonconformist stratagems to buck the system were Howard-family character traits not confined to Miles alone. In 1675, twenty-one-year-old Ben filed a court complaint against the man for whom he worked at the time, i.e., a "master Dunn," says a Virginia document.[292] In 1771, Miles's uncle and aunt Peter and Eliza, respectively, sued white James Tutt for detaining them as servants.[293] Years later, a young child of then-deceased Miles Howard was assigned a white guardian by the court to administer his share of the estate awarded to him by his late father. Later, young John II sued in court, and won, to have his unscrupulous legal guardian replaced by a more trustworthy one.[294] Then there was the *Howard v. Howard* county superior court decision when Miles and Matilda's children felt they had been treated unjustly, so they appealed that outcome to the state's Supreme Court. All these incidents demonstrate that Miles and generations of Howard family members before and after him were not shy about fighting a system they argued brought them injustice.

Miles's life alone displayed to me circumstances that I thought only happened in other family histories. But tracing him through a variety of records, including when he was an enslaved eleven-year-old, I couldn't believe that for years, I'd seen his image hanging on my grandfather's vestibule wall in a daguerreotype portrait. By the late 1850s, the formerly enslaved ancestor died a free man and well-to-do property owner who earlier baptized himself along with his wife, Matilda, and their children as Catholics in an area of the antebellum South where essentially there were virtually no other black Catholics to be found. Adding to my surprise, as explained below, his survivors became willing plaintiffs and defendants in a North Carolina Supreme Court case that gave new definition to the legal limits and the "rights" of both slave marriages, or "unions," and legally accepted marriages of free coloreds. Through further research, I learned later that free people of color did not constitute a scientifically or even a legally, clearly defined group of people; rather, they were a mixture of people informally connected by their neighbors' and their own memories and perceptions of lineage and status (Milteer Jr., p. 21). This was just one more reason why his community could label him Indian.

Only once can I remember giving serious attention to that daguerreotype portrait of Miles and his wife, Matilda, that hung on a wall in my grandfather's New York apartment in the fifties and sixties. I was a restless teenager in the sixties, one with lots of more "important" priorities to get on with one Friday night. The daguerreotype featured a coiffed man, one whose handsome face included a manicured, full mustache and straight black hair. He wore a double-breasted suit with a pocket watch chain running to his torso. Matilda, my great-great-great-grandmother, sat with Miles's hand resting on her shoulder. Both looked stern, austere, and prosperous. Neither of them smiled. The daguerreotype photo was taken around the time that the technology had first come to America—during the era of so-called Daguerromania—say, 1840–1845.[295] Matilda died at the end of that period.[296] I declared to my granddad when I first studied the portrait that I did not know we had white people in our family. Today's cloudy memory tells me that the middle-aged couple did not look white, but their tawny features and straight hair did not indicate to me then that they were average-looking African Americans. My memory reveals that they otherwise did not resemble me, my grandfather, or anyone else in the Howard family that I knew. But I remember Granddaddy emphatically declaring, "They are Indian. They're my people." US census records seemingly supported the claim, as mention of the family in such records that I would research long after my grandfather's death, with the few exceptions mentioned shortly after the Bacon's Rebellion, described them as mulatto or other free, which is how the aboriginals, mixed-race, and Southeast Asian natives living in Virginia and North Carolina were recorded during an age when hypergamy[297] was not uncommon. Realistically, however, *all* nonwhites were less than free. Even up to my grandfather's generation, the descendants of Ben and Frances married men and women whom *custom and the law* recognized as their own kind. Guided by the laws of endogamy, the Howard members of their caste married *one another*, calling themselves, as my grandfather did, Indian.[298]

Grandpa was proud of the elegantly framed portrait that disappeared after his death. He wanted me to know that the handsome couple was his *real* family. I can't remember if he told me then or later that his mother, Betty, disappeared (records imply she had died) shortly after his birth and that he was raised in a different household[299] than the one headed by his biological father, Isaiah, after her disappearance.

Importantly, during one visit, Grandpa told me that the people "who raised me were mean." Asked who they were, he told me one name: Paris. According to 1900 US census records, Paris Howard headed a North Carolina household that included my fifteen-year-old grandfather Charlie Howard. This household lived in the town of Lower Conetoe in Edgecombe County. In 1900, Paris and his wife, Rebecca, had a biological son, and they named him Charlie too.[300] It was probably my grandfather's biological dad, Isaiah (related to Paris), who gave him the daguerreotype portrait. Paris had been enslaved by the white Catholic Howard family from Maryland. Although these Howards did not live in the same part of North Carolina as did their white Protestant cousins, the two families were neighbors in Halifax in the 1820s. Initially residing in Maryland, many of these Catholic Howards moved on to Tarboro, the county seat of Edgecombe, where they became prominent, rich citizens in that eastern part of the state. Paris told a 1910 US census taker there that his other name was Pasco.[301] Giving added importance to the name, he told the census taker that one of his sons was called Pasco too.

I remember when Granddad first boasted to me about an Indian lineage. I had remarked to him our ancestors were slaves. He responded his Indian ancestors were never enslaved. Later, I learned there were Indians living in the county where he grew up who said a true Indian could never have been a slave. So when he exclaimed "These are *my* people!" as we stood before the portrait of his great-grandparents Miles and Matilda, Grandpa wanted me to share his contentment that these Indian ancestors were always free.

Two of his great-grandfather's milestones occurred in 1836 and 1838, as we will see. Miles Howard had been a free person of color since his second so-called master, a prominent white attorney named Thomas Burgess, emancipated him in 1818. Matilda's master, William Burt, though giving his consent for her to marry eighteen-year-old Miles, would not free her as Miles requested. Miles, living along Halifax's Underground Railroad and no longer Burgess's personal servant, purchased Matilda as his slave. The marriage of the free-person Miles and temporarily enslaved Matilda was performed, according to the courts, "in the manner that slave marriages were typically celebrated in those days."[302] Theirs was an illegal union. Nevertheless, Matilda's freedom was purchased by Miles before the birth of daughter Frances, the couple's third living child, according to records. The fact that the children were born to a mixed-slave couple whose union was never formalized inside a state-approved institution such as the Episcopal Church was destined to cause legal problems in the future.

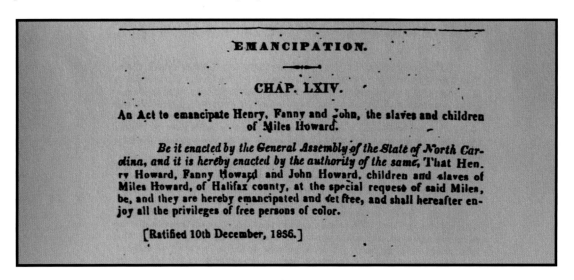

Emancipation of Miles Howard's enslaved children, official document
issued by the North Carolina legislature in 1836

Before 1839, the never-before-baptized couple had some eight or nine children in the household: Henry, seventeen; Robert, nine; Thomas, eight; Miles, seven; Charles, six; George, four; Frances, fourteen; Mary, nine; and Carolina, two (estimated ages). There was one other child, John, who died around the date of his emancipation in 1836. At least three of these children (Henry, Fanny, and John) and perhaps a fourth, Mary,[303] were born enslaved. After several legal pleas, the state of North Carolina emancipated children Henry Howard, Fanny Howard, and John Howard on December 10, 1836,[304] after much work on the part of Miles and after the intervention of his former master and later friend, business partner, and benefactor Attorney Thomas Burgess.

On June 19, 1838, Miles baptized the entire family into the Catholic Church[305] when 600 Catholics represented less than 1 percent of North Carolina's total population, virtually none of whom was colored. Begun by Irish immigrant Michael Ferrall, the growing population of Irish religionists was not especially favored in Carolina during the era. Yet Miles boldly chose to worship alongside these few Irish Catholics who settled in Halifax. Though Miles's decision was not popular, it was deliberate. Why did he do it?

The highly unusual baptism *seems* to acknowledge the religious sympathies of ancestor Frances Haward, the furtive Catholic leanings of the many white Howards whom Miles and his family were intimate with, and the nominal Catholicism of some of his Portuguese, Filipino, and other Asian ancestors. But by 1838, it appears that Miles had had his fill of the state church and its parish-level surveillance and restrictions placed on the lives of people of color like himself and his colonial ancestors. Before knowing anything about the family's ancestral connections to Portuguese-Catholic Kongo and Angola and to Asia, especially to the Philippines and Pasco, in 2015, I wrote,

Miles grew to disparage the power of any state-level apparition to exclusively determine for him what should constitute a legitimate and proper marriage. After all, it was because of such authority in the first place that his forebears [had been] condemned to a lifetime of servitude and poverty and labeled "bastards." And so, too, would he have remained—poor and enslaved—had it not been for a benevolent so-called master-turned-friend. For Miles, his and Matilda's marriage was already sanctioned by his own community-of-preference—by their immediate family, by their Halifax friends and relations, and by the Howards of Granville County—and it was rooted in a folklore that he and Matilda and their joint-community best understood and accepted. It can even be said that perhaps it was Miles's familial, African interpretation of the sacraments that for him properly ritualized, and therefore legitimated, marriage—at least more than any ill-intended state law did. Even to Miles's 17th-century ancestors in Angola, the Church preached that marriage was not a human institution, but instead an indissoluble arrangement granted by way of the sacraments to the baptized from God. And so, he refused to remarry—to re-do what he and Matilda had already done in a way that had satisfied them both, as well as their community. So [according to the Courts] he refused to remarry on purpose, and instead he elected to receive and comply with the sacraments of [his] Church . . . His marriage was rooted in Church Law which to him always trumped the state.[306]

Neither the Catholic leanings of Frances Haward nor that of his great-grandfather William Crawshaw was ever given official recognition and acceptance in Virginia and North Carolina, whose worship favored the English Anglican Church (Episcopalians after the Revolution). Before considering the information outlined below, today, some might marvel at the thought that Miles knew anything of the long history related to the Catholicism of his non-American ancestors. But some of the oldest of these ancestors, mixing their inchoate Christianity with long-held indigenous and political beliefs, eventually came to accept the Catholic Church as an essential part of their spiritual beliefs. As devoted to the faith as some of these Christian ancestors might have considered themselves, there were European Catholics back then who would not take seriously the new religion of Miles's Christian ancestors. Later, Dutch colonizers even believed the Catholicism of Asian natives was mere "superstition" that had to be eradicated as quickly as possible!

If, at the time of their 1692 liaison, Ben considered himself and Frances as existing in an actual or otherwise acceptable Christian union, Virginia law thought otherwise. Enslaved Ben was apparently never considered legitimately Christian; but even if he were, after 1682, the colony passed two anti-Indian-related acts, one of which said that whether Christian or heathen Indians, such Negroes were to be enslaved for the rest of their lives.[307] Slave marriages were not upheld by the courts.

Eighteenth-century census records show that members of the Howard family left Virginia after the late 1700s and resettled primarily in the counties of Halifax and Granville, North Carolina. However, the Virginia legacy was one that the North Carolina Howard family would never forget. Both Frances and Ben might have known that in many Catholic churches of their day, their union would have been legitimate, assuming, of course, that Ben had been secretly, or otherwise, Catholicized at all.

It may seem that any or all the foregoing help explain the unusual Howard family baptism in the Protestant Upper South. But among the most intriguing of *these* possible explanations has to do with the Catholic legacy of Miles's Manila Bay ancestor, Pasco. Still, Miles might have had more concurrent and otherwise practical reasons for the baptism.

For much of colonial North Carolina's history, Catholicism was a banned religion. When the colony was founded, adherents were not permitted to travel from England to settle in Virginia. During Miles's day, practitioners were still likely to be persecuted. Reluctantly, throughout non-Spanish colonial North America, Catholicism was confined to just a few territories, including Maryland, which was home to many Howard family members in contact with John Howard and his son Miles, as well as Louisiana. To Miles, then, the Catholic religion was a more appropriate faith compared to the establishment-based Anglican Church and to the more moderate Methodists, Baptists, and Presbyterians. The less-exotic but experienced abolitionist-Quakers, to Miles, could have been a choice worth considering, but that faith was not his preference. In nineteenth-century North Carolina, the religious faith of the relatively unpopular Catholic Church was an attractive alternative to at least one free-colored head of household. Why?

The North American Catholic Church's nineteenth-century pronouncements on the slave issue were ambiguous enough to have left the impression that the institution was antislave trade, if not antislavery. And yet, from the standpoint of slavery's proponents, the church's position could be seen, at worst, as ambiguous. In fact, the church's pronouncements at the time *seemed* to have condemned the Atlantic trade while also upholding, or at least not condemning, the institution as it already existed in North America. Why? During the first half of the nineteenth century, the church sought to strengthen its roots in North America, and it did not want to jeopardize its chances of recruiting candidates to the faith. Accordingly, the Catholic Church attempted to play on both sides of the then-important and controversial issue of American slavery.

John England (September 23, 1786–April 11, 1842)[308] was the first Catholic bishop of Charleston, South Carolina. At the time, South Carolina included the present territory of North Carolina. In 1833, England was appointed apostolic delegate to Haiti. This was the first important diplomatic mission given to a prelate in the United States. Despite his efforts, he was unable to secure a concordat.

England believed that the best way to refute racist ideology was to educate the persecuted,[309] thus helping to defang the opposition. In 1835, he attempted to establish a Catholic school for free blacks in Charleston but was rebuffed by public opposition almost to the point of violent confrontations.

To Miles, these credentials were impressive, even if only strategically.

And then there was the Catholic William J. Gaston (September 19, 1778–January 23, 1844),[310] a distinguished North Carolina politician and jurist. He was a prominent, articulate champion of black rights in nineteenth-century America. His most important accomplishment on the North Carolina Supreme Court, which he helped to establish, was the 1834 case of the *State v. Negro Will*, in which he ruled that a slave had the right to defend himself if his master attacked him without justification and with intent to kill. In the 1838 case of the *State v. William Manuel*, Gaston ruled that manumitted blacks were citizens of the state and thus entitled to constitutional guarantees. Gaston was a strong advocate for the continued suffrage of free blacks. In North Carolina, property-owning free blacks lost their right to vote in 1835, a decision that Gaston did not support. Among other not-so-popular opinions he expressed was the declaration that Protestant religious standing should not be a requirement to hold public office or serve on the bench in North Carolina.

The public opposition of the prominent white Catholic jurist William Gaston to state laws disfavoring the rights of coloreds could not help but further embolden an already-discontented Miles.

When Catholic bishop England visited New Bern in May 1821, he celebrated with a mass held in the parlor of Gaston's house. Since there were then no Catholic cathedrals in the state, Bishop England authorized Gaston as one of five who could hold services in his parlor in lieu of a cathedral or in the local St. Mark's Episcopal (later Catholic) Church. Services like those in Gaston's parlor were conducted in the parlor of Irishman Michael Ferrell's house in Halifax. Miles Howard and his family attended mass there, led by visiting Catholic clergy. Several of Miles and Caroline's children were baptized Catholic at St. Mark's.[311] Gaston remained an abolitionist until his death, at which time he owned some 200 slaves.[312]

This mildly favorable political climate aside, Miles's actual reasons for joining the Catholics are presently unknown, but I am not at a loss to suppose why. Submission to the church after his family's 1836 emancipation relied on what Miles knew of his family's history. An awareness that his "new Christian" ancestors were repeatedly compelled to dispel links to Jews while proving a sincere Christian devotion are not things a family easily forgets. Because so many others doubted their faith, as conversos, these ancestors were persecuted and starved. They often lost everything they owned and even knew death. But while in the Spanish Empire, these converso ancestors were shielded from the worst by Catholic missionaries. Encouraged by the missionaries, Pasco escaped his evil overlords and fled to London, leaving behind a history of atrocities from pogroms to vandalas.[313] To Miles, his family's salvation had always rested on the grace of Catholics. Having won his family's emancipation in 1836, in 1838, he followed the trail made ready for him by his fathers. By the 1830s, Michael Ferrall had opened the parlor of his house to the small number of servants and other would-be Catholic worshippers living in Halifax County.

Before his death, Miles had become a prosperous man of color. By then, he owned an impressive estate, including cash, receivables, and real estate in the important Roanoke Riverfront town called Halifax in North Carolina and in that town's adjacent farm country. Matilda died sometime after the 1842 birth of Thomas. On May 6, 1846, Miles and Afro- (or Anglo-) Indian Caroline Valentine, a free woman half his age, concluded wedding formalities that complied with the laws of North Carolina.[314] Like Matilda (whose DNA included the white Howard family) and her children, this second family too was baptized by a Catholic priest. The couple's child, John, was Miles's second child so named. In the 1860 US census, this John was listed as the second wealthiest free Negro property owner in Halifax County.[315]

Between 1853 and 1856, just before the Civil War, Miles sold about a third of his real estate to white and colored neighbors F. S. Marshall, Henry J. Hervey, David Reynolds, Henry Archer, and William Pope. His holdings briefly included the law office and home of his friend Thomas Burgess, Esquire, according to at least one source. Then, on July 1, 1857, the father of thirteen died without leaving a will. Caroline's death preceded his, before which Caroline and Miles had four children: Nancy, John II, Andrew, and Sarah. Besides inheriting some of his father's estate, records show that in manhood, John II decided to become the proprietor of J. H. Howard & Co. Groceries in Weldon, North Carolina.[316] The court of equity had divided and sold the late Miles Howard's land, distributing the proceeds to Caroline's young children. John II was awarded farmland appraised in 1860 at $2,500. The court appointed wealthy white farmer George Barnes, a Miles Howard family neighbor, to be John's guardian until the ward turned twenty-one. In the interim, Barnes promised the court to teach his ward about "the mysteries" of farming.[317]

The court of equity's decision was contested by Matilda's children, who claimed that they, as plaintiffs, were "tenants in common" with the defendants, which is to say that they had rights to their father's estate equal to those of Caroline's children. Caroline's children protested, so with the consent of all the children, the matter was appealed to North Carolina's Supreme Court.

In *Howard v Howard*,[318] the court found for Caroline's four surviving children because Miles and Matilda's domesticity was a so-called slave union, not a real marriage in the eyes of North Carolina law. Deceased Henry and deceased John I were born to a woman who was enslaved, rendering them enslaved too, and enslaved children had no legal rights to the free Miles Howard's estate. Also, these two children and lead plaintiff Frances were born when Matilda and Miles had not married in a "proper" church ceremony. For this reason too, none of Miles and Matilda's children could claim their parents' estate. Besides, the court's reasoning continued, Miles had "refused" to remarry after Matilda's emancipation, after which they "ought to have married according to law." If they had not ignored the law, then the court's decision might not have been so harsh to all the plaintiffs. Because the free couple refused to redo what they called their marriage in accordance with the laws of North Carolina, they did so to the "misfortune of their children,"[319] the court wrote. Miles had bucked the system, but his children were made to pay the price.

Howard v. Howard became another historical landmark for North Carolina's people of color in that it established a legal precedent for defining the limits associated with so-called slave "unions" versus the rights associated with Christian marriages of free people of color. The legal precedent, however, was short-lived. It became moot upon the conclusion of the Civil War.

Exceptional in life, Miles was buried outside of town in a cemetery reserved for the county's blacks.[320]

As with most pre–World War II African American families, Howard households named the children after their ancestors. This Howard tradition began after William Crawshaw, their declared *Catholic Indian* ancestor, came to Virginia in 1624. After his son Ben, each Howard generation had its share of Williams and Bens—often in combination with other first names. Howard-family girls assumed a more varied set of names, including Frances, Ann, and Elizabeth (the latter perhaps the name of Ben's Siouan mother). Robert named one of his daughters Matilda. But prominently missing is the name Miles.

Doe on demise of FRANCES HOWARD v. SARAH HOWARD, et al.

Supreme Court of North Carolina, Nov 30, 1858 51 N.C. 235 (N.C. 1858)

Miles Howard, a free man of color, died intestate in 1857, seized in fee of the premises in dispute.

About the year 1818, he being then the slave of the late Thomas Burgess, Esquire, without other ceremony, took for his wife, by consent of his master, and a Mr. Burt, *Matilda*, a slave of the latter, and was immediately thereafter duly emancipated. *Miles* then bought his wife, *Matilda*, and by her had issue, the lessor Frances, when the said *Matilda* was duly emancipated. After this event, they had other issue, to-wit: the lessors, Robert, Eliza, Miles, Charles, Lucy, Ann, Thomas, when the said Matilda died.

In a few years afterwards, the said Miles took another wife, a free woman of color, and had issue, the defendants, Sarah, John, Nancy, and Andrew. The latter marriage was performed with due ceremony, the former was celebrated in the manner usual among slaves, and the parties lived together ever afterwards as man and wife, and kept house together as such.

In 1836, the lessor, Frances, with other children, who died before the intestate, Miles, was emancipated as the children and slaves of the said Miles Howard, by an act of the Legislature.

The plaintiff's lessors claimed to be tenants in common with the defendants — which the defendants denied, and claim to be the only legitimate children, and sole heirs of their father. The Court, upon consideration of the case submitted, gave judgment in favor of the defendants; from which the lessors of the plaintiffs appealed.

PEARSON, C. J.

A slave, being property, has not the legal capacity to make a contract, and is not entitled to the rights or subjected to the liabilities incident thereto. He is amenable to the criminal law, and his person (to a certain extent) and his life, are protected. This, however, is not a concession to him of civil rights, but is in vindication of public justice, and for the prevention of public wrongs. Marriage is based upon contract; consequently the relation of "man and wife" cannot exist among slaves. It is excluded, both on account of their incapacity to contract, and of the paramount right of ownership in them, as property. This subject is discussed in *State* v. *Samuel*, 2 Dev. and Bat. 177, where it is held, that the *status* of a child born while both parents were slaves, and lived together as man and wife; for the relation of master and slave is wholly incompatible with even the qualified relation of husband and wife, as it is supposed to exist among slaves, and the idea that a husband may own his wife as property and sell her, if he chooses, or that a parent may own his children and sell or give them away as chattels, and that the wife or the children, are, nevertheless, entitled to any of the civil rights incident to those relations, involves, a legal absurdity. The relations are repugnant; and as that of master and slave is fixed and recognised by law, the other cannot exist; and it follows that the lessor, Frances, does not take as one of the heirs of her father.

The other lessors are in a condition still more unfortunate; for, while relieved from the incongruity, which is involved in the case of their sisters, by the fact, that their mother, at the time of their birth, was free, yet, that circumstance caused them to be unlawfully begotten. Their parents, having become free persons, were guilty of a misdemeanor in living together as man and wife, without being married, as the law required; so that, there is nothing to save them from the imputation of being "bastards."

Our attention was called by *Mr. Moore* to *Girod* v. *Lewis*, 1 Cond. Louisiana Rep. 505, where it is held that, "a contract of marriage, legal and valid by the consent of the master and moral assent of the slave, from the moment of freedom, although dormant during the slavery, produces all the effects which result from such contracts among free persons." No authority is cited, and no reason is given for the decision, except the suggestion that the marriage, being dormant during the slavery, is endowed with full energy from the moment of freedom. We are forced to the conclusion, that the idea of civil rights being merely *dormant* during slavery, is rather a fanciful conceit, (we say it with respect) than the ground of a sound argument. It may be, that in Louisiana, the marriage relation is greatly affected by the influence of religion, and the mystery of its supposed dormant rights, is attributable to its divine origin. If so, the case has no application, for, in our courts, marriage is treated as a mere civil institution.

To the suggestion, that as the qualified relation of husband and wife between slaves is *not unlawful*, and ought, in fact, to be encouraged, upon the ground of public policy, so far as it comports with a right of property, emancipation should be allowed to have the effect of curing any defect arising from the non-observance of the prescribed form and ceremonies, and the absence of a capacity to contract, as there is plenary proof of consent, which forms the essence of the marriage relation; the reply is:

The relation between slaves is essentially different from that of man and wife joined in lawful wedlock. The latter is indissoluble during the lives of the parties, and its violation is a high crime; but with slaves it may be dissolved at the pleasure of either party, or by a sale of one or both, dependant on the caprice or necessity of the owners. So the union is formed, and the consent given in reference to this state of things, and no ground can be conceived of, upon which the fact of emancipation can, not only draw after it the qualified relation, but by a sort of magic, convert it into a relation of so different a nature. In our case, the emancipation of the father could not draw after it the prior relation, because the mother was not then free, and, in fact, afterwards became his a slave is a competent witness for or against another slave, towards whom she sustained the relation of wife, in a certain sense of the term, on the ground that the relation was not that of "man and wife" in its legal sense, and did not embrace any of the civil rights incident to marriage.

In *Alvaney* v. *Powell*, 1 Jones' Eq. 35. It is held where a mother and children are emancipated, a child begotten and born while the mother had no husband, was entitled to the same share of her estate, as the children who were begotten and born while she had a husband; on the ground "that in regard to slaves, even after they become free negroes, there is no necessity growing out of grave consideration of public policy, for the adoption of the stern rule of the common law. "A bastard shall be deemed *nullius filius;* to have no parents, and not even be considered the child of the mother who gave it birth; and in contemplation of law there is no difference between the case of slaves who enter into the qualified relations of "man and wife" by the express permission of their owners, and that of those who "take up" with each other, from a mere impulse of nature, in obedience to the command, "multiply and replenish the earth," for the law does not recognise either relation so as to give to it any effect in respect to civil consequences. On the other hand, there is in moral contemplation, and in the nature of man, a wide distinction between the cohabitation of slaves, as "man and wife," and an indiscriminate sexual intercourse; it is recognized among slaves, for as a general rule, they respect the exclusive rights of fellow slaves who are married. Such marriages are permitted and encouraged by owners, as well in consideration of the happiness of the slaves and their children, as because, in many ways, their interests, as masters, is thereby promoted. Hence a married couple is permitted to have a "cabin and a patch off to themselves," and where they belong to different persons, the man, at stated times, is allowed "to go to his wife's house." The relation is so far favored in the administration of the criminal law, as to allow to it the effect of drawing into application the rule, that when a person finds one in the act of adultery with his wife, and instantly kills him, it is but manslaughter, because of the legal provocation. This result, however, is not attributable to any civil right, growing out of the relation, but to the fact that, to a certain extent, it has its origin in nature; and a violation of the right which is peculiar to it, in that respect, excites the *furor brevis*, whether the relation was entered into with or without the legal capacity, and the ceremonies and forms necessary to make a marriage valid for civil purposes. This is assumed to be the law in *State* v. *John*, 8 Ired Rep. 330, and has been so held upon the circuits.

Thus far the line is established by these three cases. We are now to run further, and fix another landmark. In *Alvaney* v. *Powell, supra*, the Court was not called on to decide whether the children, after being emancipated with their mother, were to be considered as legitimate, or illegitimate; the purpose of the case being answered by holding that they all stand on the same footing; because, in either view, they were entitled to succeed to their mother and to each other, both, according to our laws, and the laws of Canada. Nor are we now at liberty to decide it, because the facts of this case do not present it. Both parents were slaves when the relation was entered into. Afterwards, the father was emancipated, and bought the mother, and *held her as his slave*, at the birth of the lessor, Frances. This presents a question, in many respects, different from that of slave. So the relation was not connected with the *status* of the parties in a way to follow as an incident. Suppose, after being free, the father had married another woman, could he have been convicted of bigamy, on the ground that a woman, who was his slave, was his wife? Or, after both were freed, would the penalty of the law have attached, if either had married a third person, living the other? Certainly not; because the averment of a prior, lawful marriage could not be supported, and yet, if the marriage followed the emancipation as an incident, it would present an instance of a marriage relation, which either is at liberty to dissolve at pleasure.

The parties after being freed, ought to have married according to law; it is the misfortune of their children that they neglected or refused to do so, for no court can avert the consequences.

PER CURIAM, Judgment affirmed.

At first, the omission appears odd to my generation, given Miles Howard's remarkable climb from slavery to freedom and his accomplishments after that. To this day, he remains a familiar figure among the older set in his hometown of Halifax, North Carolina. I have visited the town several times. He was a prominent property owner in his home county and a businessman and business partner of the white attorney who manumitted him when he was eighteen. Miles was a musician too. But we might suppose that to the family he left behind, such achievements were overridden by less-flattering events, for instance, the tragedy that soon after his death befell his daughter Frances.

These less-flattering events also seem to have been associated with his second marriage, after the death of Matilda, to a woman who was the same age as his daughter Frances. At least for a time, both Frances and Caroline and Miles's other children were still at home, and his new children apparently all lived in the same Halifax house located on the northwest corner of the intersection of Dobbs and Prussia Streets.[321] Such a situation could have led to friction in the crowded household. The fact that his estate left no inheritance to Matilda's children could not have helped matters.

Howard v. Howard was the straw that broke the camel's back—a straw that might have come after pleas from daughter Frances to her parents to redo their union in the local St. Mark's Episcopal Church,[322] a ceremony more likely to stand up under the law. In any case, by the time of her father's death, she and most of her marrying-age sisters had all wedded skilled men, and her full-blooded brothers were already economically secured in their skilled trades and in farming. By this time, Caroline's children maintained in court that their stepsiblings were not entitled to their deceased father's property.

North Carolina's Supreme Court was not at all reticent in reminding the losing plaintiffs how their father's failure to prepare a will now made it impossible for any of them to win a share of his estate. But what might have been particularly galling to Frances was that her father was now so careful to comply with the marriage laws of the state *this time* when the unconventional old man chose to wed a young local girl, now known to all in the community as her new stepmother.

Upon the death of his father, and as the equity court mandated, nine-year-old John II went to live with his court-appointed white guardian George Barnes. In 1868, when John was twenty, he sued, won, and replaced George Barnes for misappropriation of funds.[323] Subsequently, John chose and the court approved another wealthy white neighbor, merchant H. J. Hervey, to replace Barnes. Guardians of free colored children, in compliance with the law, needed to demonstrate a capacity to teach their wards long-term survival skills. Hervey later helped John to set up his grocery store in Weldon, North Carolina.[324] Both Barnes and Hervey were familiar with the family as both had engaged in land transactions with Miles.[325] The Hervey-John Howard guardianship worked fine, as John's 1916 death certificate listed his occupation as a "retired merchant." The fact that Matilda's children played no obviously supportive role in all this is one more reason to suspect that at least some of them were not pleased with the estate-related court decisions resulting from their father's death.

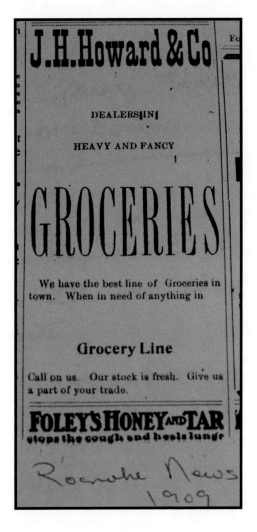

J. H. Howard & Co. Grocers. The proprietor is the son of the late Miles Howard.

Of interest here is the political environment in which both enslaved and free Howard family members lived on the eve of the Civil War during 1850s Carolina. Even before 1850, Miles and his family went about the business of living despite the threat of an always-present minority of white proslavery extremists whose aims were to enslave them all or send them packing to Liberia. Some extremists carried out random kidnappings and more. In 1850, Congress passed the Fugitive Slave Act. Among the act's consequences was that neither captive nor free people of color could give testimony in court, much less legally challenge any white citizen. In 1857, the year Miles died, the court declared in the Dred Scott decision that slaves and free black people were not citizens within the meaning of the Constitution. But as can be seen here, after the Civil War, none of this stopped the Howard family from carrying on with their lives after their father had formed legally sanctioned business partnerships with white neighbors, continued to accumulate wealth, and inherited properties from his white lawyer-friend and white neighbors. During Reconstruction, Miles's youngest son, John II, sued and won court cases against his white guardian as he became Halifax County's second wealthiest Negro property owner.

That Miles had not willed property to Matilda's children was deliberate. As far as the county court was concerned, the final distribution of the Miles Howard estate satisfied local law-abiding defendants and their community while holding in check rebellious plaintiffs. The losing sons, after all, were grown by 1857 and had begun solid careers. Miles had arranged for their apprenticeships in lucrative trades: barbering and brick masonry. If the disappointed daughters were to be achievers, they would have to marry men as promising as their skilled brothers. Mary had done so when she wedded carpenter John Wilkins in 1849. Shortly after her father's death, young Lucy Ann married wheelwright Thomas Saunders. Even strong-willed Frances, at the matrimonially not-so-appealing age of thirty-three, married farmer James Henry Bird in August 1858. He was six years younger than she. But Frances was dead before the Supreme Court's November 30, 1858, decision was officially revealed.[326] To Miles's way of thinking, his younger children, which is to say Caroline's, needed his wealth more than Matilda's already-grown children did. And he was confident that his potentially contentious plan to provide for Caroline's children alone after his death would be carried out even without a will through the reliable court of equity. So why bother to prepare the contentious document?

As of the early nineteenth century, the lots that comprised Halifax's Prussia Street were owned by Miles Howard, having been acquired through purchase and otherwise deeded to him by his friend Attorney Burgess.[327] Among these parcels was the Burgess bequest: "To my worthy and excellent friend Miles

Howard the barber two lots in Halifax, now occupied by said Miles."[328] This neighborhood was in a more affluent newer location, away from the bad health effects of the mosquito-infested, flood-prone, and otherwise-unpredictable Roanoke River. The Howard house stood on one of these lots at the northwest corner intersection of Dobbs and Prussia Streets, near the new Wilmington and Weldon Railroad, which, in 1840, was the world's longest railroad line, running 161 ½ miles.

Burgess's wife resented the gifts that her late husband had bestowed upon his colored friend and declared that he had not awarded her enough. She sued to halt both bequests. On the eve of the Civil War and upon passage of the Dred Scott decision, the matter went to court. There, the affair was worked out to the satisfaction of both parties, including Burgess's wife, Sarah.

To learn more about the everyday tastes and habits that further distinguished the man and his family, I researched items found among Miles's personal papers.[329] In 1839, I found that neighbor James Halliday had died. Sifting through Halliday's estate papers, I discovered that Miles purchased from the Halliday estate sale 32.5 yards of calico, 3.5 yards of "cotton velvet," and two yards of "domestic"—all no doubt to be used by his seamstress wife, Matilda, and purchased for a total of $5.72. From the 1835 inventory of white Aquilla Wombie, Miles bought a chest for $1.40 and three pairs of sheets for $3.00, among other items. At the 1836 A. A. Litchford property sale, he delighted himself and the family to some treats when he purchased a bag of walnuts for $0.05.

At the Halifax library, I read an essay about the town's free blacks written by a local African American in which she concluded that Miles Howard was a prominent free black businessman who owned two slaves for reasons of "economics." In research related to *William to William*, the two slaves were identified as a fifty-five- to one-hundred-year-old female and a ten- to twenty-four-year-old male, according to the 1830 Halifax County–Northampton Second Regiment Census. The first does not appear to have been one of Miles's *economic* assets, and the second seems to be Soloman, a likely relative—one who became a free colored, still living in the Northampton household of white Solomon Smith, according to the 1840 federal census of the two adjacent communities. That said, records collected by Monica Moody (Historic Halifax State Historic Site) show that in August 1839, Miles sold "one negro girl" for $550 to Willie Eppes of Virginia "to permit Martha Marshall to receive Mary and use her," according to a note written by Martha's husband (see deed book 30, p. 254, of Monica Moody papers). Parties to this transaction were intimates of Miles, and the transfer seems meant to enable untutored Mary to be taught a skill. Subsequent census recordings do not list any slaves in the Miles Howard household after 1839.

Regarding his relationship with daughter Frances, history tells me that Miles and Frances each soldiered in the same struggle for justice. Each said that the Old South's centuries-long system of statutory and customary law regarding its low regard for people like them was absurd and primed for change. Their struggle continued from more than 250 years before when carried on by their Afro-Asian ancestor's resistance to the Spanish Empire and later in 1656's *Bloody Run*.

Young Charles's San Juan Hill neighborhood in New York City was as much the grimy asphalt jungle as Miles Howard's Halifax was a country town idyll. Motivated by his father's stories about the Howard family's rags-to-riches success, by 1909, the bellman had married while residing at 54 West Ninety-Ninth Street in Manhattan. By 1910, the couple moved downtown to one of the borough's few segregated neighborhoods open to the flood of colored immigrants fleeing what was, for them, an economically depressed, violent South.

Grandpa had only a few years earlier left an unhappy childhood spent near Halifax. Like the young Howard men who preceded him, he was determined before turning thirty to begin making something of his life despite San Juan Hill's well-earned reputation for poverty, crime, and slum landlords. He returned to his southern roots only once. That was because of the 1911 death of his father, Isaiah. Still, the neighborhood's brand-new Phipps Apartments, located on West Sixty-Third and Sixty-Fourth Streets between Amsterdam and West End Avenues, were a good place for him and newly wedded Janie to begin their family.

Despite San Juan Hill's reputation for crime, poverty, and slum landlords, the Phipps Apartments were then New York's banner opportunity for "negroes" to enjoy unprecedented niceties such as ensuite steam heat and private toilets with bath. Other conveniences included nearby public schools like PS 94 and Commerce High School, the new Riverside Public Library on Sixty-Ninth and Amsterdam, access to shopping, and proximity to the African American Episcopal and West Indian Anglican Chapel of St. Cyprian. Public transportation to Harlem, the boroughs, and downtown was excellent given the new Interborough Rapid Transit (IRT) Subway Line with neighborhood stops at West Fifty-Ninth, West Sixty-Sixth, and West Seventy-Second Streets.

But the area was also prone to heavy police violence perpetrated against its nonwhite residents, and parts of it were downright dirty, often vermin-infested, and gang-plagued. Leonard Bernstein's fabled *West Side Story* was based on the community's all-too-frequent turn-of-the-century gang wars mainly between Puerto Rican, Irish, and Italian toughs. Three of my father's siblings suffered early deaths in San Juan Hill, one in infancy and two others from TB while young adults. But even during the thirties' Depression, Charles Henry was never without work, he and Janie maintained their tiny apartment for decades, although grandma died in 1949.

While the family was one of San Juan Hill's more fortunate, their top-dog status was buttressed by grandpa's wins from playing the policy numbers. Most of my late-afternoon or early-evening visits to his apartment found him with a magnifying glass at the kitchen table hunched over any number of sources for potential three-digit winners taken from the green-colored dream book, double-entendre newspaper cartoons, or listings of the winning numbers at the track. Whichever one of these was the source, the selected three digits—or another "combination"— were played first thing the next morning. Because the numbers racket was illegal, he and his neighbors were forever watchful of the vice squad's surprise raids carried out by the "bulls."

As I reflect on all this, I also recall that it was more than just two generations that separated the lives of prosperous Miles Howard and grandpa. One was a Catholic, the other Episcopalian. One was affluently rural, the other resided in a turn-of-the-century Manhattan tenement. But grandpa was also the grandson of what some called the spurious union of a mid-nineteenth enslaved woman and her freeborn mulatto lover, a union that was not unlike the parentage of Miles. But differences like economic status, the categories of men and women each called his friend and his associate, and the times in which each raised their families seem to have relegated my grandfather to a different caste than the one his age-wise superior belonged to.

Yet in the daguerreotype of Miles and Matilda that hung in the vestibule of grandpa's apartment when I was a teen, they were his equal. He called them "my people." It was as if he wanted me to know that alleged differences of a larger nature did not matter anymore. They were of one lineage now.

"Your Road is Orula" (2015)

The Bandas is an archipelago of ten small islands plus a volcano located in the Banda Sea 600 miles north of Australia, south of Ambon, and west of Irian Jaya (now part of the province of Papua). Their total landmass does not exceed 40 square miles.

Among these islands is an even tinier one called Rhun (Run). It was not until 1667 that the English finally relinquished all claims to the nutmeg-rich Rhun Island in exchange for a Dutch island called Manhattan, located thousands of miles away. The Dutch had paid the Indians of Manhattan the equivalent of $24 for their long piece of land surrounded by water. By the end of the seventeenth century, the Dutch East India Company was finally in complete control of the world's only supply of nutmeg. But by the 1790s, the company had dissolved in bankruptcy, while Manhattan went on to become the richest piece of real estate in the world. In a bitter piece of irony and an interesting twist of fate, we Howards, descendants of a people who once traded with inhabitants of the Banda Islands, profited nicely over the years from investments in a Manhattan Island real estate that the Dutch East India Company calculated as an inferior investment compared to an island filled with spice.

Charles Howard moved to New York City's Manhattan about one hundred years after the Dutch East India Company went bankrupt. He called the once-Dutch-owned island home some three hundred years after fellow Uli-Siwa clan member and rich *orang kaya* of Labbetácca Senen Wattimena was tortured to death by the Dutch in 1621. It was in Manhattan where I was born, and my dad was born there thirty-two years earlier.

Ancestors of my grandfather were not the only Afro-Native American Howards in the family. His wife Janie Miller-Howard, my grandmother who died when I was four, was born on October 6, 1882, in South Carolina to descendants of ex-African slaves mixed with Irish and Native American aboriginals. Janie Miller's grandmother was Dianna Scaif, and she lived in South Carolina's Union and Chester Counties, once associated with the now-extinct native tribes known as the Waxhaw, the Westo, and the Sugeree.

Staying with this Native American connection, it was only a short time before Dianna Scaif was born that these Chester and Union Counties were Cherokee hunting grounds. The 1850 slave list of local white slave owner Charner Scaif includes three or four unnamed mulatto female slaves. On the list, an approximately thirty-six-year-old enslaved woman appears to be Dianna. A daguerreotype photograph of Dianna Scaif taken in the 1840s presents a mixed-race woman. While Dianna Scaif's African features might have been muted, mtDNA findings confirm the African origins of her female ancestors. Researchers at africanancestry.com defined the haplogroup of her female ancestors as L3b1a. Janie and Dianna's most distant detectable female ancestor was Yoruba with possible links to the Hausa people of West Africa.

But my Yoruba ancestry extends beyond the paternal chain. In my personal genetic makeup are the Oyo-Yoruba chromosomes of my mother's mother's father. The most prominent and well-researched of them is Filorí, one of the many grandsons of late-eighteenth-century Oyo emperor Abiodun. Filorí arrived in North America more recently compared to my paternal Howard ancestors. He reached 1800 Charleston, South Carolina, aboard the *Charlotte*—some two hundred years after William Crawshaw came to Virginia.

Filorí is a Yoruba affectionate name meaning "cap of the head." Oyo elders said when Filorí's soul knelt before the potter, this unseeing soul was lucky because the choice then made was a good head. Filorí's destiny rests at the tip of his head, says the oracle. Wearing his spiritual cap, Filorí was destined to stand head and shoulders above all the rest in front of the crowd—always in the lead, especially of his family.

After the 1789 death of Abiodun, Yorubaland descended into a violent civil war that lasted for one hundred years.[330] Thousands of Yoruba were then sent into the Atlantic slave trade, an enterprise begun by the Portuguese. Although a number of these victims, like Filorí, became slaves in North America, most were sent to South and Central America and to islands in the Caribbean. Among these islands was Cuba, where, according to 23andme, descendants of these African ancestors in my family continue to live even today. I did not learn of my genealogical connections to Cuba until after my two visits to the island.

My first visit to Cuba was in 2014. The most memorable part of that visit was the time I spent with a Yoruba-Cuban family. I was part of a small National Geographic tour group on that occasion, and our time spent with this Yoruba-Cuban family was filled with traditional Afro-Cuban singing and dancing, together with enjoyable conversation.

Filorí and Flora were enslaved blacks who married in a nineteenth-century white Christian church called Ghents Branch located in the vicinity of present-day Denmark, South Carolina. One of their descendants, my cousin Carrie Hightower-Sojourner Simmons, served as mayor of Denmark from 2002 to 2009 and was otherwise a leading civic figure there. Filorí and Flora—he Yoruba and she from Kongo—were called by their master William Hightower and his family "husband and wife" to the chagrin of many members of their white community. What a contrast were they and the other enslaved African ancestors of my mother's family as compared to the so-called free-born indentured servant-ancestors who preceded my father! Anyway, the enslaved-for-life Christian couple called their first child by the Yoruba praise name ola me de (or Lande for short), meaning "my honor has come." They had seven sons, but something was odd about the last one. His praise name was Kola wole, meaning "bring honor [back] to this house." Someone added the name Bacchus, name of the Greek god of drink and excess pleasure. About the time that Kola was born, William Hightower's only son, Henry, left for Georgia under mysterious circumstances. He later died there. About fifty years after he was born, Kola too was found living in Georgia, where he had established himself as a free servant, living with his wife and son. By then, he no longer used his no-doubt too-African-sounding-name Kola. Instead, he called himself Bacchus Hightower, and was listed in the 1880 U.S. Census as a mulatto. Bacchus and his wife had only one child: a son named Henry.

In 2015, I visited Cuba again. I hoped to see the Yoruba-Cuba family once more on this second trip; instead, as luck would have it, I visited a priest steeped in the traditions of the Yoruba orisha. Although he spoke no English, he and I understood each other very well.

The priest's small home was filled with dozens of altars to the orisha. There were altars to the orishas Ogun, Oya, Oshun, Yemoja, Aganju, Dada (an important ancestor-king among my mother's mother's father's Yoruba ancestors), and others. But among them was one that cried out for my attention. To those who knew nothing about the traditions of the orisha, this altar might have seemed simple, even crude. Beautifully yellow and green bananas, with symbolic touches of more yellow and yet more green, encircled this altar. There could be no doubt as to whom the altar was devoted. This was Orisha Orula's space. The Yoruba tongue is famous for its elisions; to the Yoruba in Africa, the Orisha Orula is called Orisha Orunmila.

Yoruba tradition says that there are 401 orishas, symbolizing the apparently infinite number of variations in human nature—variations that, in the Afro-Cuban religion of Santería, are correlated with a myriad of personalities, tales, and colors unique to West Africa's individual orisha. Among them, according to the Yoruba of Africa and Cuba, it was this orisha who was present when each guardian soul blindly chose its head of destiny. Orunmila (Orula in Cuba) witnesses everybody's creation, knows everyone's true nature, and is a keeper of the family's origins and secrets.

The priest asked one of us to volunteer for a ritual he wished to demonstrate. He wanted to throw sacred kernels and use their fallen pattern to help discern the volunteer's fate and destiny, with some help from the Yoruba oracle. I was encouraged by the others to step forward. Reluctantly, I did.

After he had tossed the shells and then studied the pattern into which they had fallen, the priest first consulted my translator and then confided to me:

La vía para tí eres Orula

Sire:

Your Highness has favored us by writing that we may request by letter anything we need, and you will send it. After God, the peace and well-being of our kingdoms depend on our own longevity. Yet, because of our age, we continually suffer many illnesses that debilitate us to such an extent that they have brought us to the verge of death. Our children, relatives, and countrymen also suffer from these illnesses due to the lack of physicians and surgeons with the knowledge to administer true remedies to these ailments and the lack of medicines and potions to treat them more effectively. Because of this, many of those who have already learned the ways of our Lord Jesus Christ have perished.

This great tragedy should be prevented. It would be wrong not to help because, after God, all the good we possess, as well as the medicine to heal us, have come from Your Highness. We beg Your Highness to grace us with the favor of sending us two physicians, two apothecaries, and a surgeon with their medicines and tools because we are in dire need of every single one of them . . .

In addition, Sire, our kingdom faces another obstacle, which is of very little service to God. Many of our countrymen capture and sell many of our free people to satisfy their immense greed for the goods that your subjects (living on Sao Tomé Island) bring from your kingdom. They often abduct noblemen and their children as well as relatives of ours and sell them to the white men in our kingdoms. As soon as the white men buy these captives, they brand them with hot irons, and our guards find them while they are waiting to be shipped out. The white men claim they purchased them but cannot say from whom. We must do justice by those who were free persons and restore their freedom, for that's what they cry out for.

In order to put a stop to this great scourge, we decreed by law that every white man staying in our kingdoms who purchases slaves by any means must first notify three noble officials from our royal court whom we trust . . . They will determine whether these slaves are royal captives or free persons. Therefore, there will be no doubt whether these slaves should be traded, and they may be taken away by ship. If the slaves are not captives, the traders will forfeit them. We grant the favor of continuing the slave trade to Your Highness because of your stake in this trade and because you earn a lot of profit from the slaves shipped from our kingdom. Otherwise, for the above-mentioned reasons, we would not authorize it. We are informing Your Highness of all this so that you know the truth when you are told lies that persuade you from giving us the care that we need for the service of God. We would be grateful to hear from you by letter.

Sire, we profusely kiss your Highness's hands.

In the City of Kongo, written by João Texixeira on the 18th day of October of the year 1526.

> Signed: His Majesty King Dom Afonso
> [Letter sent to Portugal's King Dom João III]

From: John K. Thornton, Afonso I, Mvemba A Nzinga
King of Kongo (Indianapolis/Cambridge: Hackett Publishing, 2023), 212–213.

With their East African roots having been planted tens of thousands of years in the past, it was during the AD early second millennium that Bantu speakers continued migrating south from West Africa's Nigeria and Cameroon Cross River region. Traveling south along the Atlantic coast, the group formed small villages on the north side of Africa's second longest river, the mighty Congo. Bantu villages emerged there among the native San and other indigenes into the rich Kingdom of Kongo, whose early wealth was based on the mining, consumption, and distribution beyond its borders of domestic iron and copper. By the thirteenth to early fourteenth centuries, the kingdom expanded even farther south into territory occupied by fiercely independent Kimbundu-speaking chiefdoms. These Bantu-based chieftaincies were settlements located inside the Kongo Province of Mbata,[331] more than 200 miles east of the Atlantic.

Young San hunter kindling a fire.

Portuguese Diogo Cão and explorers fifteenth century first landing in Angola.

Kongo's Mbata Province included the northernmost reach of Kimbundu speakers long governed by chieftaincies living not only to the south of Kongo but also to Mbata's northwest, including land that became Kongo's capital city called Mbanza Kongo (now San Salvador). This Kimbundu-Kongo area of Mbata had come to be called Hungu.[332] As the Kongo Kingdom expanded south, its migrating citizens married local Hungu daughters.[333] The children of these marriages spoke a blend of the Kongo and Kimbundu languages (called Hungu) as some became assimilated within Kongo culture, even becoming members of Kongo's ruling elite. Eventually, the unassimilated who lived in the more remote areas outside Mbanza Kongo were simply called Mbundu by the Kongo people. These Mbundu—along with prisoners of war, foreigners, and criminals—could be enslaved according to Kongo custom and laws.[334] But so long as the people of Hungu paid agricultural tribute to their superiors (ultimately including the

Kongo king) and otherwise complied with minimally invasive Kongo customs, most were left to live as they always had.

The Portuguese came to Kongo in the early 1480s, bringing with them an ultimate desire to find wealth creation opportunities and baptize the heathens. Shortly after arrival, there developed a mutual interest in the other's culture and commercial trade.[335] The overall comparative economic development of the two countries was about equal but with a bit of an edge in Kongo's favor. The Portuguese immediately took an interest in Kongo's metals and high-quality fabrics made from the Africans' raffia plant, which was said to rival the most sought-after Italian cloths of the day. Kongo's royals quickly volunteered to join the Catholic Church as they learned Portugal's laws and language. They aggressively sought the medical, architectural, and arms technologies of these Europeans. For a while, such exchanges were mutually satisfying. Some members of Kongo's royalty were educated in Lisbon's monasteries, with a smaller number becoming Catholic bishops, even establishing relationships with Rome. Elite Kongo citizens adopted Portuguese royal titles such as duke (called soba by the Mbundu), viceroy, noble, and the like. But by the 1520s, mutual affections began to sour. Instead of respecting Kongo's restrictions Regarding the enslavement of freeborn locals I's 1526 letter[336] to Portugal's King Dom João III made clear, private Portuguese traders based on the island of nearby Sao Tomé, plus medical and technical consultants to Kongo and soldiers too all illicitly—more to the point, illegally—began to enslave the local freeborn, including members of Kongo's royal family. Especially vulnerable were the Mbundu, including residents of Hungu.

Jovette Raimundo Eduardo

Pedras Negras de Pungo Andongo

The Kalandula Waterfall is Africa's second largest. It is on the
Lukala River, part of my ancestral homeland.

It was incredible to recognize someone I had never seen before. The closest recognition that came to mind was my paternal grandfather, who died in New York City in 1976. He never visited Africa. Such were among my reflections on the afternoon of August 23, 2023, when introduced to yet one more Mbundu soba. I had gone to the area with my translator-guide and our driver after spending a considerable part of the day elsewhere in the region of Malanje Province, including its famous Pedras Negras de Pungo Andongo (Black Rocks at Pungo Andongo). Up to then, I had been introduced to several Mbundu sobas (a hereditary title earned by village chiefs) who, by turns, either quietly or enthusiastically introduced me to their village domains and highlights of their people's customs and histories. Toward the end of the day, we drove about thirty to forty minutes to the village of Hunga, whose appearance was deceptively simple and unassuming. I learned Hunga is a very old village. At the time, I erroneously assumed that the name Hunga was a variant of the word Hungu.

But there was something different about Hunga's soba. I recognized him. Unlike the others I had met that day, this soba—Jovette[337] Raimundo Eduardo—bore what I later realized was a Filipino first name. He insisted that I was a son of his own lineage – a lineage now associated with Pedras Negras. Although at the time I did not understand the alleged connection between me and him, I knew he was not without important qualifications enabling him to make such a claim. As the hereditary chief[338] of the Mbundu lineage who settled in the area a long time ago, he stood at the head of a line of men thought to have encyclopedic knowledge of his village kinfolk – their ancestry and their migrations. Leaders like him – together with his traditional priests and other advisors – could be depended upon to lead the family to secure times ahead. But our lineage came into existence centuries ago on the banks of the Lukala River before moving to Pungo Andongo, where my ancestor left Africa for Europe 500 years ago.[339]

Soba Jovette Raimundo Eduardo, like so many lineage heads with roots in the upper Lukala, carried with him the *lunga*. The important stick-like symbol of the soba's military and political authority was emblematic of the lands over which leaders like him ruled. It manifested the spiritual, political, and military boundaries that encapsulated not only the head of the lineage but his ancestors and offspring too. It was the soba and his lunga, along with the spirits and priests, who brought forth the rains, made the soils fertile, and the crops grow to sustain his lineage who resided on the land ever since the earliest villagers and their ruler arrived behind palisades separating the village from outside threats. In the past, such threats included not only human perils but the wild animals too, which lived on the savannah and in the nearby forests. . Traditionally, it was the soba, along with his vassals, who protected the family against invasive diseases and violence and ensured harmony within and between his village and outsiders. When necessary, sobas raised armies and went to war to extend their territorial limits, defend their family-based kandas and provinces, or at the behest of the king. Under an ancient form of patrimonialism, the soba collected tribute from his villagers, ultimately satisfying the king. Later, during the slave trade, he may have tried to meet the demands of Portuguese overlords as well. Before the Portuguese came, such tribute consisted of farm and forest products. In 1658, however, the Portuguese demanded instead that *their* tribute be paid to them solely in the form of human bodies, a change that profoundly buttressed the Atlantic slave trade, affecting all Mbundu. Today, a few Mbundu sobas still carry the lunga.[340]

We were introduced while standing among the ancient rocks at the top of Pedras Negras. Jovette searched among the stones while I prepared to photograph him and the area. After a few minutes, he brought me one of the area's ancient rocks, called me before him after placing the stone in my hands, then asked me to kneel as he prayed. I placed the rock on the ground and offered a prayer to my father as the soba asked me to, then to the ancestors. Jovette insisted I keep the rock as a blessed memorial to the ancestors we shared and to our one day together.

Author's grandparents Charles and Janie Howard and the wedding
of parents William and Albertha Howard.

It was not until I returned to Chicago that I began to grasp the importance of Pedras Negras, located in what once was called the province of Ndongo, in its southeast corner.

Likely image of my father's fathers

Jovette's physical resemblance was remarkable. I was especially amazed to notice how much he resembled my grandfather Charles Howard. The familiarity of his facial features – especially around the mouth – was striking . His physique, though thinner, otherwise matched that of my grandfather. Upon my return to Chicago, I read reports of scientific findings concluding roughly 66 percent of children inherited their father's philtrum, the area of the face between the bottom of the nose and the mouth, through genes. It was this area of Jovette's visage, along with his lips, that most resembled my grandfather's face, and to a lesser extent, even my own. Mention has been made of the philtrum in

Jewish mystical tradition, fairy tales, Icelandic folklore (huldufolk), the book *Prince Ombra* by Roderick MacLeish, and Philippine mythology's enchanted creature known as *diwata*.

Physical similarities aside, the genealogy testing service known as 23andme reports that among my sister Linda's autosomes (her nonsex chromosomes) are generations-old genes from people whom 23andme labeled Kongo and Mbundu. Meanwhile, africanancestry.com showed me my Y-chromosome came from one Mbundu male who lived between five hundred and two thousand years ago. These chromosomal patterns were consistent with what I later learned about Jovette's own background. Eventually, it was obvious that my sixteenth-century Mbundu ancestor called Jovette's lineage our own.

Statue of Queen Njinga, 17th century ruler of Ndongo and wife of Kituxi whom she married and declared king. Kituxi is an ancestor of Jovette Raimundo Eduardo.

My father's African ancestor left the continent around the eventful times that Kongo king Afonso I complained about in his 1526 letter to Portuguese King Dom João III. When my Mbundu ancestor left the land, locals—often children—were kidnapped off the roads, taken from their homes, or never returned from the fields. I increasingly wondered how the lineage whom my sixteenth-century Mbundu ancestor left behind experienced Angola after this ancestor left the continent for Lisbon. DNA and historical accounts now show that from Lisbon, at least one mixed-race descendant (part converso) sailed with sixteenth-century Portuguese explorers to Melanesia's Spice Islands in today's Indonesia. At least one of *his* descendants, the mestizo called Pasco, was born to a woman living in the nearby Spanish Empire's Philippine Islands in the early 1600s. From the Philippines, Pasco escaped to London, leaving behind a seventeenth-century Dutch-English food blockade of Manila Bay, only to reappear in the 1624/25 muster of Elizabeth Cittie, Virginia, as "William Crawshaw, a baptized Indian."[341] Over the next eight generations, sons of the lineage—Ben, John, Miles, Robert, Isaiah, Charles, my father William, and I—moved from Virginia to North Carolina, New York, and then Chicago. Only recently did I begin a search to find out what became of my Mbundu lineage remaining in Africa after the early sixteenth century.

Mention to some Americans today of my plans to visit West Africa as part of my search for an answer sometimes elicits responses far removed from any reality: "Oh, so you're going to see jungles filled with monkeys and apes and tigers and lions and elephants and hyenas and tribes upon tribes of people with paint on their faces—how wonderful and adventurous!" First, there are no tigers in Africa. True, there was once a time when images otherwise like such descriptions were common in West Africa's forests and savannahs. But such peoples, fauna, and flora have largely disappeared. My visit to north-central Angola during the country's cool, dry season of 2023 revealed miles of dry savannah country. I saw vast areas devoid of people and, seemingly anyway, wildlife.

But I could not escape the poverty. Lots of it. I was struck by how few songbirds, butterflies, and flowers I saw. Was their absence due to the fact I visited Angola during the country's winter season? I wondered. The 217 miles I witnessed between Luanda and Malanje was largely barren prairie with no antelope, no baboons, or any other visible evidence of animal wildlife compared to all that I had seen, for instance, in nearby Botswana's Okavango Delta and in the country's Kalahari Desert. Minus the snakes, I believe they started disappearing with the arrival of the Portuguese and the Dutch, with their guns, warfare, and, most of all, the Atlantic slave trade and the strife that caused. The area's long civil war did not help. By contrast, the remote and richly endowed Okavango and Kalahari went largely untouched by any European slave trade or major civil war.

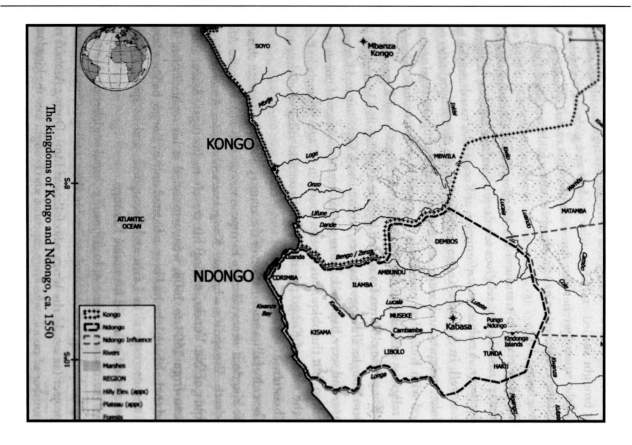

Map of the Ndongo Kingdom as it was in 1550 (Heywood 2017, p. 5)

In contrast to what I saw in 2023, before Angola's seventeenth- and twentieth-century civil wars, the Mbundu village was typically located some distance from its nearest Mbundu neighbor. This allowed for enough family-tended fields planted with millet, sorghum, tubers, and wild vegetables to feed households, provided there had been adequate rainfall to help ripen the hoped-for harvest. During the dry season, when I visited the country, produce from these fields and forests would have been supplemented with meat yielded from game captured in surrounding forests. Fowl and local fish were other supplements.

Centuries-long slave raids and warfare brought an end to such early circumstances, and the results were plain to see during my 2023 road trip to Malanje. For example, villages had become smaller and moved closer to one another for enhanced security and economies of scale. Today, it is hunger—even famine—and unemployment and sickness that help define the limits of population size, as the lucky ones flee the village to attend school and search for work located in distant cities and towns. Too often, schools train the young for nonexistent jobs. What is often apparent in today's Mbundu village is a material misfortune that too easily masks the upbeat spirits I enjoyed in my one-on-one interactions with the people who live there.

Until 1671, sobas paid the *baculamento*, historically an honorary tribute collected from villages comprising the large ancestral Kingdom of Ndongo. As far as anyone can remember, the *baculamento* was gratefully passed up to Mbundu kings in the form of produce. By 1658, however, Portuguese colonists mandated that instead of an honorary tribute, a tax had to be paid to them in the form of enslaved human bodies living inside every soba's domain.[342] Each soba was thereafter ordered to collect the tax, which was then forwarded to the colonial Portuguese governor. If the soba did not comply, severe penalties meted out by Portuguese authorities and enforced by his soldiers would follow. The soba's own enslavement and that of his family, their exile to Brazil, and even death were the usual costs of noncompliance. Sobas who could not round up the requisite number of healthy men, women, and children, or who simply refused to pay, were known to run away, joining forces with enemy renegades. Still, at least one Mbundu regal—the one-time queen of Ndongo and, more latterly, queen of nearby Matamba Kingdom, Ngola Njinga, half sister of Ndongo's king Philipe Hari I—answered no to Portuguese demands for the *baculamento*. This instantly made her and the large number of sobas who supported her enemies of the Portuguese and a powerful, persistent thorn in the side of the colonialists. Pedras Negras de Pungo Andongo harbored a number of these rebellious sobas and bore witness to it all until 1668 when Ngola (King) Philipe Hari I was succeeded by the Ngola's son Ngola João Hari II, who, upon assuming office, quickly protested the Portuguese *baculamento*. In 1671, João Hari II not only refused to pay it but also refused to send any more slaves to the Portuguese. He declared his Kingdom of Ndongo henceforth independent of Portugal.

João Hari II's defiant declaration of independence could not have happened at a worse time as far as Portugal was concerned. In 1580, Spain and Portugal had been forced into an unpopular royal union—a shotgun marriage many called it that relegated Portugal to second-tier economic status within the Spanish Empire. It was only in 1640 that a relatively subdued Portugal escaped the union, only to face a long, hard struggle to make up for the years of economic decline it endured during the sixty-year partnership. It was during this long period of economic struggle for Portugal that another son of my lineage, Pasco El Meztizo of the Philippines,[343] jumped into the Sea of Manila as he fled the harsh economic circumstances of his Spanish-Portuguese serfdom to begin his daring second chance as a relatively free person in England and Virginia. It is easy to understand then why Portugal was in no mood to tolerate what it viewed as João Hari II's treacherous attempt to sever its vital economic lifeline to recovery, i.e., the Atlantic slave trade.

Meanwhile, Portugal sought to increase the number of slaves it thought necessary to sustain its profitable sugar plantations located on the small Atlantic islands of São Tomé and Principe, as well as in its new overseas territory of Brazil. In the early seventeenth century, the Portuguese tried unsuccessfully to enslave more war captives from Ndongo citizens they falsely claimed were unwilling Christians or heathens. When caught by Christians, heathens became *legal* captives—workhorses and currency—in a "just war," meaning they could be legitimately enslaved by the Portuguese. But traditional Ndongo law insisted that escaped war captives from any battle were entitled to remain free. Adhering to tradition, Njinga Mbande, then the controversial and unconventional queen of Ndongo after the 1622 suspicious suicide of her brother King Ngola Mbande, refused Portuguese demands to deliver these captives to the Europeans. By 1626, the Portuguese realized that Njinga would never give them the slaves they wanted or accede to their other demands. Therefore, they organized a campaign against her, declaring that a woman was not fit to lead the Kingdom of Ndongo. They hastily displaced Queen Njinga by arranging a rigged royal election, installing a pliant Philipe Hari I, Njinga's half brother, as the propped-up sovereign of Ndongo against the wishes of the kingdom's villagers, Njinga herself, her family, and those sobas associated with Jovette Raimundo Eduardo's family.

It was also in 1626 that the Portuguese began to try enforcing the *baculamento* in Ndongo, now that Njinga had been removed. Ndongo was now ruled from Pungo Andongo by the puppet king Philipe Hari I. Philipe Hari I seemingly accepted the tax at first, even as he protested, saying that as the king (rather than the soba he used to be), he should not have to pay it. It was only in 1658 that the already-unpopular sovereign openly submitted to Portuguese demands to pay the *baculamento* tax. His displaced royal half sister Njinga, now queen of nearby Matamba, continued to refuse to pay or otherwise endorse it. By 1658, the puppet sovereign was even more unpopular with the villagers of Ndongo, disgraced in the eyes of his own Hari royal family, and his relationship with the Portuguese had soured. He died in 1664.

João Hari II's declaration was too much for the Portuguese. Their response was swift, as the colonial power feared the contagion would spread even further, thus destroying its profitable empire forever. The

Portuguese had already made plans to link the trade in Pungo Andongo all the way to Africa's east coast, to Mozambique, and João Hari II's declarations upset such potentially lucrative designs. He had to go.

João Hari II was seized by the Portuguese, having been turned in by trusted familiars. Also seized was King João Hari II's formidable military leader brother. The sovereign, along with his wife, was captured, turned over to the Portuguese, and beheaded. Just to make sure that he and the Hari legacy were gone forever, João Hari II's head was forbidden to be buried in the soils of Africa. Instead, his head was shipped to Portugal and disposed of there. Decapitating an enemy, according to the Portuguese following traditional Mbundu religion and politics, was to appropriate that enemy's power.[344] It is said that João Hari II preferred death to playing any future role in the Atlantic slave trade or otherwise extending Portuguese control over his kingdom.[345] The rest of the Hari royal family was banished from the African continent and, by 1672, exiled to Brazil and Portugal as politically sensitive "prisoners of war."[346] The Pungo Andongo fortress commanded by the Hari royals was destroyed by the Portuguese and their African allies, and a Portuguese fortress was constructed in its place. Pungo Andongo's days as the throne of the Hari family and it's military fortress were over.

Portugal's war in Ndongo caused two thousand deaths and took many prisoners,[347] a tragedy that did not go unnoticed by Jovette's contemporary ancestors. The difficulties also served as the springboard for yet one more revolution, one whose aim was not only liberation from the Portuguese yoke but also an end to the Atlantic slave trade entirely. Its leader, an abolitionist who sprang from the soil of Africa and preceded the first European and American abolitionists by some one hundred years, was a son of the Hari family, one named Lourenço da Silva Mendonça,[348] a prince said to have been born in Pungo Andongo. Like Soba Jovette Raimundo Eduardo, he too had bloodlines going back to the kings of Kongo and Angola, including to *kiluanje kya samba*,[349] even to Hungu itself, and links to conversos and the Portuguese as well.[350] He was determined to erase the shame and disgrace brought upon the Hari family since his grandfather, Philipe Hari I, had been made a puppet king by the Portuguese.[351]

Prince Lourenço da Silva Mendonça was born around 1650 to Dom Ignacio da Silva, son of King Philipe Hari I, and to an unknown mother.[352] In 1671, a young Mendonça—along with his brothers, uncles, aunts, and cousins—was exiled by the Portuguese as a political prisoner to Brazil's San Salvador in Bahia. The breakup of the royal family included exiling to Portugal King Philipe Hari I's son, Dom Philipe Ngolamano, and the king's uncles Diogo Cabangua, Dom Antonio, Dom Sebastian Don Deonizio, and Dom Ignacio, Lourenço da Silva Mendonça's father. Had the Portuguese allowed the royals to continue living in Angola, it was feared their presence would ignite a rebellion—one demanded by the locals and even by other regional kings and sobas. Their breakup and exodus to different parts of the world and their removal from Mbundu historical accounts were meant to render the family's inherent political powers impotent.

But exiling the royals had unintended consequences. Their exile enabled younger family members like Mendonça to travel among free and enslaved militant Mbundu separatists, part of the Quilombo dos Palmares. Subsequently, in Portugal, Mendonça met more free and enslaved Mbundu. He formed alliances with other Mbundu, Africans, and Native Americans in both places. He allied himself with national politicians and Catholic Church higher-ups as well. Importantly, Catholic Brazilian and Portuguese exiles enabled Mendonça to forge relationships with the confraternities of Our Lady of Rosary of the Black Men, a respected institution in Portugal and in other Catholic European countries. It was composed of free and eligible-to-be-freed enslaved Catholic Africans who, in contrast to formidable fugitive slave colonies such as Palmares, were given voice and *constitutional rights* honored by the countries that housed them.[353] Accordingly, with legal and financial support, all enslaved members of confraternities were constitutionally entitled to seek freedom.

By the end of a thirteen-year exile, Mendonça had been sent by the Portuguese crown to stay at the convent of Vilar de Frades Monastery, where he likely studied law and theology[354] and later sought an end to the suffering, inhumanity, and homicide and the denial of freedom visited upon enslaved Africans and Native Americans. As part of his campaign for universal human rights, Mendonça also sought an end to the persecution of conversos (Jews converted to Catholicism). Mendonça argued that they were all Christians, after all, whose baptism supposedly guaranteed their unqualified humanity before God and man. Yet the church and the kings and minions of Portugal, Spain, and Christian Europe denied them the freedom and humanity the blessed shield of a Christian baptism promised. Rome was especially culpable, Mendonça argued, because since fifteenth-century pope Alexander VI, the church had issued papal bulls sanctioning the enslavement of non-Christians while turning a blind eye to the same *Christian* slaves it declared had been saved from such a fate. As the international attorney representing both the enslaved and freed members of Our Lady of Rosary of the Black Men of Europe and Brazil, Mendonça personally presented his court case to Pope Innocent XI and the pope's Propaganda Fide tribunal of Rome in 1684.[355] Pope Innocent XI was known for the stress he placed on "Christian education, social justice, and public decency." He was in fact a charitable pope to the needy. So taken by his evidence, presentation, and credentials were the potentates of Spain and Portugal that Spain's King Carlos II appointed Mendonça international attorney[356] for the Brotherhood of Our Lady of Rosary. The kings of both countries endorsed Mendonça's recommendations and followed the pope in pursuit of their implementation:

Rome accepted the evidence of Mendonca's case, and acting on what had been presented to them, accepted the solution proposed by African descendants from the different confraternities. The ministers of justice from the Propaganda Fide demanded that Spain and Portugal change their treatment of enslaved Africans in the Atlantic region. Rome sent warning letters to the nuncios in Spain and Portugal to ask both countries to abide by Rome's decision. The Spanish and Portuguese authorities were expected to instruct their respective governors overseas to stop the cruelties associated with slavery and were warned that they would be punished if they did not do so . . . Christianity was expected to provide protection to enslaved African Christians from abuse by the sugar cane mill masters and slave-traders.[357]

But instead of an unprecedented abolition of the Atlantic slave trade, which Mendonça's court case had argued and legitimately won before the Pope's Propaganda Fide tribunal, Portugal and Spain subsequently promised a kinder brand of the same old program—a continuation of the Atlantic slave trade but one that would now be gentler and nicer to the enslaved than before. In the end, despite the continued struggle pursued by the brotherhood and Mendonça, despite endorsements won from the kings of Spain and Portugal, and despite the approval of Pope Innocent XI himself, the recommendations were deemed impossible to implement. Advisers to the pope and the courts of Spain and Portugal convinced potentates that the long-term viability of Portugal's Atlantic slave trade was at stake. Its profitability would be destroyed if Mendonça's recommendations were carried out, so they never were.

It was good to be back in Angola. I was greeted at Luanda's Quatro de Fevereiro Airport on July 14 by the driver who escorted me last year, José Mateus, and by my new guide and interpreter, José Tomás. Though ill from the food poisoning I picked up apparently at Chicago's O'Hare Airport the day before, I was determined to return to Angola. In the country's Malanje Province, I was to have my second meeting since 2023 with Jovette Raimundo. The date had long ago been arranged. I wanted to speak with him about the Hari Kingdom, where I presumed his and my ancestors lived, and find out more about what happened to the lineage who stayed behind after my Mbundu ancestor left Africa in the sixteenth century. As a result of my 2023 visit, I researched likely ties between the lineage Jovette said I was a member of and my father's American ancestors. I had no intention of letting an illness or any other manageable disaster interrupt my plans to meet with Jovette.

Since my 2023 visit, a voluminous, heavily documented research study was published by the Cambridge University Press. *Lourenço da Silva Mendonça and the Black Atlantic Abolitionist Movement in the Seventeenth Century*, authored by José Lingna Nafafé, is a 468-page tome concentrating on the sociopolitical history of the sobas and Hari family linked to Pedras Negras de Pungo Andongo. Most of the book's discussion had never been published before 2022, and it is presented within the context of freshly discovered colonial political facts and oral history through the 1600s. The publication answered many of the questions I had formulated after my 2023 visit, but it raised many more. Long before finishing the book, I made up my mind to revisit Jovette.

Jovette looked different in 2024. He no longer wore the military cap and uniform he was in when we met in 2023. Out of uniform, the sixty-four-year-old appeared less formal, and he showed a full head of surprisingly straight and wavy hair, displaying even more evidence of a genealogical link to my fathers—to my grandfather especially.

My first 2024 conference with Soba Jovette Raimundo Eduardo in my hotel lobby in Cacuso.

Jovette and author in the hills of Pungo Andongo.

Jovette was glad to see me, telling my guide and interpreter that after our 2023 meeting, his children had posted our photographs on Facebook for friends and family to see. They said Jovette and I looked like brothers. Before we took an afternoon hike through Pedras Negras, Jovette and I sat down in the lobby of my hotel located in the commune of Cacuso.

Jovette told me his earliest named ancestors go back to *kiluanje kya samba* who lived on the upper Lukala River in the early fifteenth century.[358] Like the Hari family who also descended from *samba*, Jovette's earliest ancestor-fathers who lived in the fifteenth century were apparently non-royal rulers. What is clear is that Jovette's ruling ancestors were "landowners whose estate covered an extensive territory including many vassals."[359] These sobas carried the lunga as a kind of badge and certification of their prestigious landowner status. Jovette's ancestral rulers were nobles, according to Western historians (fidalgos, according to the first Portuguese). They were called sobas by the Mbundu and by the Kongo Court of Afonso I, and they exercised tremendous power over their villagers and territory. Each belonging to different categories of sobas—the Hari family and the Njinga family—later became competing *ngolas* (kings) behind whom different nonroyal sobas threw their political support. Royal families were supposed to define the political and military functions of the kingdom. They were dependent upon the sobas to execute these policies and military requirements.[360] Despite their distinctions, both sobas and ngolas were nobles, and they were bound together administratively and by marriage. They were blood relatives who often quarreled.[361]

Road sign announcing the village of Hunga, founded as a refugee village 353 years ago.

Footprint said to be that of Njinga or her king.

Jovette and his line of male ancestors were hereditary sobas. Since the seventeenth century's second half, they were descended from the founder of Hunga Village located near Pungo Andongo. The settlement had been created by a Jovette ancestor, a man known as Grandfather, founder of the village itself.[362] Hunga was first founded as a refugee camp in 1671 after the Portuguese had destroyed the Pungo Andongo residences and fortress in the Portuguese-Pungo Andongo war of that year.[363] Those Pungo Andongo victims who were not killed or enslaved and sent to Brazil and São Tomé fled to Hunga. In 2023, Jovette told me Hunga was among the largest sources of slaves sent to Portugal's expanding Atlantic slave trade.

I began my 2024 meeting with Jovette in the Cacuso hotel lobby by asking him about Ndongo's royal family who lived at Pedras Andongo. "What can you tell me about our lineage's relationship to Ngola Philipe Hari I and his son João and—" Suddenly I noticed a puzzled look on Jovette's face. He interrupted my interpreter to ask who I was talking about. He had never heard of the Hari family. "Who were they?"

On the Kwanza River, Angola's longest river. It passes near Pungo Andongo before emptying into the Atlantic Ocean.

Serious questions regarding the proper role of the Hari family in the affairs of Pungo Andongo did not begin with my August 2024 sit-down with Jovette Raimundo Eduardo. Before the sobas were besieged by Portuguese and African soldiers in 1671, for instance, many were manipulated into electing Philipe Hari I as the new king of Ndongo in 1626.[364] Throughout his long reign headquartered at Pungo Andongo and lasting until 1657, the new king Ngola Philipe Hari I never did win the full support of the kingdom's sobas, who argued that his installation was not part of any legitimate Mbundu tradition but merely a creation of the Portuguese that served their selfish colonialist ends. Many of these sobas believed Queen Njinga Mbande was the rightful ruler despite the fact that this ruler was a woman. Among her backers were Jovette's contemporary ancestors.

After the deaths of Njinga's father, brother, and the brother's young son, the heir apparent, whom some say was murdered by Njinga, the Portuguese governor and allied Mbundu sobas did not want to install Njinga as queen of Ndongo, declaring no woman could legitimately rule Ndongo. With no luck in challenging her political enemies, a determined Njinga followed a more radical course in her efforts to seize what she maintained was rightfully hers. If her enemies and conservative Mbundus wanted a king, then she would give them one. Njinga was known to keep a large harem of males and females in her quarters. In 1624, she married her "chief male concubine," her favorite, naming him king after declaring to one confidant that the young man "was much loved by her."[365] King Kia Tuxi (Kituxi) was allowed to fulfill his largely ceremonial role while enabling Njinga to hold the real power as queen of Ndongo. The only problem was that Kituxi died not long after becoming Njinga's beloved king.

After his death, Njinga married Ngola Tombo, another arrangement that did not last. Subsequently, she took other dependent husbands, but she did not call any of them king. Some maintain that to ensure her power, she continued to marry dependent men.[366] But these men were not enough to convince her enemies. Therefore, she embarked on an even more radical course designed to ensure the longevity of her regal power.[367]

By the 1640s, she declared herself a man, ruling Ndongo as its king.[368] Dressed in men's clothing, she called her male concubines her wives, taking several at the same time, making each of them dress in women's clothes.[369] Njinga moved her throne to nearby Matamba and continued to outmaneuver her Portuguese, Mbundu, and Imbangala (violent, landless marauders) enemies for years. She engaged in some dramatic escapes, often under the cover of darkness. In one instance, at the age of 50, she climbed down the side of a mountain to escape enemy soldiers in hot pursuit. She died peacefully at the age of eighty-one in 1663.

Jovette Raimundo Eduardo was born sixty-four years ago to Ndumba and Dibeto Kituxi, his mother and father, respectively, at the beginning of the Angolan War of Independence (1961–1974). Since the Mbundu people have a matrilineal society, kinship is passed from one generation to the next through the female line, meaning the mother. Until 1961, Jovette told me, the family used their traditional Kimbundu surname inherited from a female ancestor. Kituxi was a name bestowed by a female ancestor descended from Njinga's "much loved" concubine king.

But in 1961, Jovette and his family were baptized into the Catholic Church. Jovette's father's name was then changed from Dibeto Kituxi to Raimundo Eduardo. Prior to the baptism, the family's religion was "traditional," a religion whose supreme leader is the creator god Nzambi. But after baptism, Jovette's elders renounced the traditional surname Kituxi, and any family member who continued to use it was declared a "sinner."

When Jovette was born, Kwanza Norte and the province of Malanje, where the family lived, were in the beginning stages of a violent invasion, which led to a war instigated by the Union of Peoples of Angola (UPA) under the leadership of Holden Roberto based in the Belgian Congo. After March 15, 1961, Roberto launched an invasion into northern Angola that killed 6,000 people, including women and children, and destroyed houses, farms, roads, bridges, and related infrastructure, causing panic and chaos throughout the northern part of the country. The Portuguese offered assistance and civil guarantees to the indigenous peoples living in impacted areas of Malanje and Cuanza Norte, where Jovette and his elders lived.

It is my conclusion that these unsettling circumstances contributed to Jovette's family's decision to join the church, as they hoped to receive protection from the Catholic Portuguese. Relying on the Portuguese and otherwise becoming even more assimilated in a Christian society necessitated that they adopt Portuguese first and last names and lifestyles, as they turned their backs on their own traditions. By doing so, Ndumba and Dibeto sought a better future for their children, themselves, and the Hunga village they helped establish.

"Jovette," a variation of "Josette," is usually a female first name having French roots. Others say Jovette is of Hispanic origin, where "Hispanic" includes Spain but not neighboring Portugal. A more likely source of Jovette Raimundo Eduardo's first name is to be found in the Philippines. The name probably was brought to Angola, I estimate, between 1618 and 1648 during the Thirty Years War. It was then that Portugal rebelled against the yoke imposed by the Spanish Empire in 1580 – an allegiance forced upon the Portuguese which they never ceased to resent. To complicate matters, the Dutch, warring against both Spain and Portugal, sought control of profitable Filipino domestic and international trade markets controlled by the two Iberians, and the Dutch occupied a portion of Portuguese Angola as it became the powerful ally of Queen Njinga in her efforts to overthrow the Hari alliance and its Portuguese backers in Pungo Andongo. The Dutch were also an ally of Kongo in its contentious relationship with the Portuguese. This network of colonialist intrigue provided ample opportunity for Mbundu soldiers and traders to develop cultural links with the Hispanic-controlled Philippines just as Afro-Portuguese Pasco and his father had in the 17th century and before.

If I have learned nothing else in this so many years-long project during which I've only scratched the surface covering the roots of my paternal ancestors, I have come to appreciate that the history of my father's fathers is practically without end. The project that I call a history in my bones is a multi-headed hydra – one that will continue to teach me and command my attention for the rest of my life.

On the border of Angola and Kongo. In the background is the Atlantic Ocean, conveyor
of more than 12 million enslaved Africans to the Americas and the Caribbean.

Endnotes

1 Giving names to her children was exclusively a responsibility of the mother in this society. Traditionally, surnames, when individuals used them at all, of pre-Christian natives of the land where Pasco was born were not necessarily consistent even among siblings in the same family or remained the same throughout any individual's lifetime. Before Spanish colonization, most native Filipinos carried just one name. When surnames were used, "people were identified through their children, as in 'the mother or father of so-in-so,'" according to Paul Morrow ("Claveria's Catalogue," *Philipino Express*, vol. 2 no. 18, 2006). Separately, Google lists San Francisco's professor emeritus Penelope V. Flores's account of how Filipinos acquired surnames. In her 2016 "Positively Filipino" article, Flores tells us that traditionally, Filipinos formed surnames after the area where they lived (e.g., by the seashore or river); based on the name of a grandfather and, upon this grandfather's death, the name of his son, i.e., of one's father; or a unique physical characteristic related to the individual. The seventeenth-century name Pasco might have been sourced after my first American ancestor's *maternal* grandfather. DNA evidence and refereed academic journal and book research all indicate that he was born to a Filipina. Today, I am told (by Filipinos in Chicago) that Pasko is the Tagalog name for Christmas; these Filipinos were not familiar with the spelling Pasco. However, according to Google's "Surnamelist," accessed on December 20, 2019, "[t]he last name *Pasco* is most frequently held in the Philippines where it is borne by 16,036 people, or 1 in 6,313." The website mentions that Manila is still one of the Filipino locations where individuals with the surname Pasco can be found today. When I visited Manila in 2020, the name Pasco did not sound strange to two men living in Manila with whom I discussed the subject. In fact, one of them said his own surname was Pasca. When asked how his family came by the name, he said that in the days when Spaniards ruled the islands, they assigned the surname to his ancestors. That is because the family's Filipino surname was unpronounceable to the Europeans. The other Filipino I talked to said that he understood the name as bearing some relationship to two Christian holidays celebrated in the Philippines: Easter (or Passover) and Christmas. He said Pasco was not an unfamiliar name in the Philippines.

2 Ibid.

3 By 1572, the conquest by the Spanish Empire of Pasco's Asian homeland was "virtually complete," according to William Lytle Schurz's *The Manila Galleon* in 1939. It was not until after the early 1580s when more Catholic missionaries arrived that Pasco's maternal ancestor was baptized into the Augustine (Augustinian) Catholic Order. Author Bernadette Soto provides interesting background information on the topic of Catholic baptisms and the setting when Pasco was born.

4 Suburb.

5 These early Portuguese traders and soldiers (except for "Viera" and "Lima") first settled in the Maluku Sultanate of Ternate, marrying there into local families including descendants of the Sultan. The Portuguese pronunciation of Pascoal is *Pas-squow* and in the English Isles, it is pronounced *Pasco*, as among the Spanish and in the Philippines.

6 James C. Boyajian, *Portuguese Trade in Asia Under the Habsburgs, 1580-1640* (Baltimore and London: Johns Hopkins University Press, 1993), 316.

7 This ancestor descended from the Mbundu male accompanying an adventurer from Africa to Portugal, then – *at least two male-headed generations later* – to SE Asia. Though his skin color would forever mark him and descendants as *sem limpeza de sangue* (born with unclean blood, i.e., not Christian), Portuguese policy told the world the mixed-race-African *converso* was a good *Portuguese* because he was now baptized; had *married* a local, Asian woman; been awarded land by Lisbon to begin a new life; and was engaged in (or about to enter) lucrative trading activity for himself and the Portuguese Court. He was therefore just what Portuguese colonization wanted: a *casado*, or a male who had "settled" into Asian society to spread the gospel of Christianity and engage in trade activity leading to spiritual and material gains for the Portuguese Court. Sometime before 1610 or so, this ancestor became associated with the Spanish East India Company which was based in Manila Bay, Philippines.

8 Seventeenth-century rich traders like *Pasco's* father, I was told by my Filipino guide in March 2020, typically received welcoming gifts from the hosting settlement's friar, whereupon such visitors were offered their choice of available Native women to become servants. Native servants often became concubines of the male head of household who was usually a prosperous trader – sometimes a foreign

one. Author Paulo Jorge de Sousa Pinto provides research evidence to support the claim. Pinto says that in 1500s Southeast Asia, situations like Melaka society, to take one example, saw miscegenation "progress more by way of concubines than by marriages." Paulo Jorge de Sousa Pinto, *The Portuguese and the Straits of Melaka, 1575-1619, Power, Trade and Diplomacy* (Singapore: NUS Press, 2012), 179-80.

9 Sources: *africanancestry.com* and *ancestry.com*. On April 2, 2014, *africanancestry.com* completed their analysis of the saliva I provided about 8 weeks earlier. They used the sample to examine markers on my Y-Chromosome, matching my Y-Chromosome polymorphisms with their large sample database that they had already collected in West and Central Africa. Based on the results of this test, I was matched with the Mbundu People of present-day Angola, which is the area where the pre-historic proto-Howards from Ethiopia's Omo Valley had moved by the first millennium AD. *Ancestry.com* traced my paternal lineage to haplogroup E1b1a. For my autosomal tests, I relied on *ancestry.com, familytree.com,* and *23andme.* The latter also completed another Y-Chromosome test on me, and beginning in 2016, *23andme* re-labeled haplogroup E1b1a to E-M263.2 – essentially a tighter measure of E1b1a.

10 Sources include an August 26, 2017 report on my paternal haplogroup's geographical origin and its migration across Africa as reported by the DNA research staff of *23andme.* Sources also include notes from my field trip to Ethiopia (including the Omo and Rift Valleys) from January 13 to January 26, 2016 with Walia Adventures, including a number of lectures and visits to the National Archaeological Museum in Addis Ababa; and *ancestry.com*; plus various online sites. For a timeline of Mbundu settlement in Angola, see the text below. Also, see Oliver and Atmore, *Medieval Africa,* pp. 166-67, below.

11 The first of present-day North America's Homo sapiens are now called American Indians. How long ago they reached these shores is controversial. Of these Aboriginals who helped form the proto-Howards were Siouan-speakers. The Sioux arrived in Virginia's Piedmont area, according to the Culpeper Museum of Virginia, about 15,000 years ago. This estimate is likely too low, however, based on more recent archeological discoveries.

12 As part of the Bantu Language Group, the Mbundu's migration out of the Cameroon-Nigeria area began roughly 3,000 years ago. The group is said to have reached Central Angola around 500 B.C: C. Ehret, "Bantu Expansions: Re: Envisioning a Central Problem of Early African History." *The International Journal of African Historical Studies* 34, 1 (2001): 5-41. According to many other sources

that I consulted, their migration to Angola started in the Middle Ages (ca 1100 A.D. to mid-1400s A.D.) and reached its peak between the 13th and 16th centuries C.E. "Ambundu," *Wikipedia,* last modified March 11, 2016, accessed August 28, 2016, https://en.wikipedia.org/wiki/Ambundu; for Roman, Israeli, Spanish history, see Yitzhak Baer, *A History of the Jews in Christian Spain*, Volumes 1 and 2 (Chicago: University of Chicago Press, 2008).

While my own genetic profile does not display a Jewish connection, according to *23andme,* a sister has Levantine DNA (i.e.,,an autosome chromosome). Moreover, Iberians believed to be 16th to 17th-century Cryptic Jews, according to retired Professor José Cymbron (formerly of Portugal's Universidade Lusófona de Humanidades e Tecnologias), were exiled to one of Portugal's penal colonies after the 1536 Portuguese Inquisition was installed. In my family's case, *maranos* and *conversos* of that period could have fled to Kongo/Angola and/or SE Asia to undertake trading. The Portuguese port of embarkation then was Lisbon-Belem. Other sources: John K. Thornton (1981 and 2018); and my March 2017 visit to Lisbon's special exhibit entitled *Jewish Experiences And Legacies in Portugal, 20 Mar-29 Apr 2017.*

13 Christopher Collier & James Lincoln Collier, *The Paradox of Jamestown: 1585-1700* (New York: Benchmark Books, Marshall Cavendish Corporation, 1998), 21, 22; Dr. Gayle Olson-Raymer, "The Europeans – Why they left and why it matters," accessed August 10, 2016, http://users.humboldt.edu/ogayle/hist110/expl.html. These represent the source data for material written in the rest of this paragraph.

14 Information in this paragraph relied upon Charles J. Reid Jr., *The Seventeenth-Century Revolution in the English Land Law*, 43 Clev. St. L. Rev. 221 (1995), especially pp. 258-260.

15 Brendan Wolfe, "Virginia Company of London," accessed August 10, 2016, http://www. EncyclopediaVirginia.org/Virginia_Company_of_London

16 Peter Wilson Coldham, *The Complete Book of Emigrants 1607-1660*, (Baltimore: Genealogical Publishing Co., 1988), xi.

17 The following statistics are found in: "Jamestown," page 17, accessed June 13, 2016, http://genealogical-gleanings.com/Jamestown.htm

18 See: "American Plantations and Colonies, Settlers living at 'Elizabeth Cittie' in Virginia, February 7, 1624/5." Sources: "Hotten's Lists" and "Adventurers of Purse and Persons," http://www.genealogy. com/ftm/s/e/e/Sylvia-See-AB/FILE/0052page.html

19 William Tucker represented Kiccoughtan (later Elizabeth Cittie) in the July 30-August 4, 1619 meeting of Jamestown's First Representative Assembly. George Yeardley was the Virginia Governor at the time.

20 Captain William Tucker was among Elizabeth Cittie's wealthiest residents, and he was a member of the Colonial Council. He was a Justice, a prosperous trader, and he carried the title of "Esquire." He was 21 years old (other sources say he was older) when he arrived in Virginia aboard the same ship as the famous Lord Delaware, after whom the present State of Delaware is named. See Rogers Dey Whichard, *The History of Lower Tidewater Virginia, Volume I,* (New York: Lewis Historical Publishing, 1959), Chapter V.

21 Some versions of the 1624/25 muster list him as "William Crawshaw an Indian Baptised." William Crawshaw was born in the Spanish East Indies, and his father had ties to Portugal's *Estado da Índia*.

22 Nell Irvin Painter, *Creating Black Americans: African-American History and its Meanings, 1619 to the Present (New York: Oxford University Press, 2006), 24.*

23 Joseph C. Miller, *Kings and Kinsmen: Early Mbundu States in* Angola (Oxford: Clarendon Press, 1976), 41-2; Roland Oliver and Anthony Atmore, *Medieval Africa, 1250-1800* (Cambridge: Cambridge University Press, 2001), 166-172. The remaining 6 groups were the *Ndongo; the Lenge; the Pende; the Songo;* the *Mbondo;* and the *Libolo.* See Miller, 41.

24 Oliver and Atmore, 166 and 170-1; Emma George Ross, *African Christianity in Kongo* (New York: The Metropolitan Museum of Art, 2000) – http://www.metmuseum.org/toah/hd/acko/hd_acko.htm (October 2002);"Catholic Church in Kongo," *Wikipedia, The Free Encyclopedia,* https://en.wipedia. org/w/index.php?title=Catholic_Church_in_Kongo&oldid=809928018 (accessed April 16, 2018).

25 John Thornton, "Early Kongo-Portuguese Relations: A New Interpretation," *History in Africa,* 8 (1981), 187-97. This article suggests my *Kongo-Mbundu* ancestor was taken from Angola to Portugal

by merchants\soldiers before 1526, p. 193, or, according to other sources, as late as around 1536 at the start of Portugal's Inquisition.

26 Linda M. Heywood, "Slavery` and its Transformation in the Kingdom of Kongo: 1491-1800," *The Journal of African History,* volume 50/issue 1 (March 2009): 1-22. Also see John Thornton's comments, "African Political Ethics and the slave Trade: Central African Dimensions," Millersville University (no date).

27 Ibid., 170-72.

28 See the discussion and Table I in Miller, 82-85.

29 Also spelled "Congo." See: "Mbundu." The Columbia Encyclopedia, 6th ed. . . *Encyclopedia.com.* (April 7, 2018). http://www.encyclopedia.com/reference/encyclopedias-almanacs-transcripts-and-maps/mbundu

30 Before signing the 1494 treaty of Tordesillas and its 1529 Zaragoza sequel, the world's two most powerful, maritime powers known then as Castile (Spain) and Portugal were in a fierce competition to claim trade monopolies for their respective Royal Courts in the as-yet unexplored, non-Christian ("heathen") lands of Asia and Africa. To keep from going to war, the two Catholic rivals bowed to the papal bull declared in Rome authorizing the treaty of Zaragoza which gave exclusive discovery and trade rights to the spices found in the heathen lands of Southeast Asia to Portugal, while Spain was given claim to resources found in the heathen lands to the west. In effect, rights of discovery and trade were assigned to Spain in the region of the Atlantic Ocean while Portugal commanded the same in areas of the Pacific. Exceptions were made, as evident by Portuguese Brazil on South America's Atlantic Coast and the Spanish Philippine Islands in the Pacific Ocean. Non-Catholic Courts and Muslim powers of the day simply ignored these Catholic treaties and the papal bull in their own quests to monopolize trade in vulnerable lands of the East and West.

31 After 1575, commercial quantities of clove cultivation would take place on Ambon Island, too. Quantities of the plant were brought to Ambon by the Portuguese after their 1575 expulsion from Ternate ordered by the Sultan.

32 According to author Stefan Halikowski Smith, one anonymous observer of the "political and moral status of 16th century [Portuguese] soldiery" wrote in the 1570s that "*Soldados* (soldiers) was actually a euphemism for a number of social undesirables effectively banished from the kingdom for crimes and misdemeanours [sp]. Many were simply escapees, individuals seeking looser straitjackets of social control. Smith quotes a song that went: 'I was banished to the Indies/But 'twas not for theft/ Was it because I hugged and kissed?/ Well, they do the same thing here!'" Smith concludes by writing: "Even amongst the crews that sailed to the Orient, there was over the course of the sixteenth century a marked deterioration in the quality of the personnel, their training and morale, even their physical state, and recruitment became ever more difficult." Published as: Stefan Halikowski Smith (2019), *Primor E Honra Da Vida Soldadesca No Estado Da India*: An Anonymous Late Sixteenth-Century Manual of Soldiery and Political Affirmation of the Military Frontier in India, Romance Studies, 37:1, 12-29, DOI: 10.1080/02639904.2019.1599565

33 According to one author, " . . . in about 1500, Melaka was one of the key nodes in Asian maritime trade, linked to China and eastern Indonesia, but also to Indian, the Persian Gulf and the Red Sea." See Sanjay Subrahmanyam, *The Portuguese Empire in Asia: 1500-1700* (Oxford and West Sussex: John Wiley & Sons Ltd, 2012), 15.

34 Pinto, 183-185, 225; Luis Filipe Reis Thomaz, "The Malay Sultanate of Melaka," in Anthony Reid, ed. *Southeast Asia in the Early Modern Era: Trade, Power, and Belief* (Ithaca and London: Cornell University Press, 1993), 80, 81.

35 Brigit M. Tremml-Werner and Angela Schottenhammer, "Communication Challenges in the China Seas; A survey of Early Modern 'Manila Linguists'", *East Asian Economic and Socio-Cultural Studies*, 12 (2014): 240.

36 Thomaz, 75.

37 We Howards have genes from the Portuguese, the Mbundu, and Kongo Peoples. My Y-Chromosome is Mbundu, and the Howard family's Iberian chromosomes come first of all from a Portuguese female who lived centuries ago in Portugal and was impregnated there by an Mbundu male (note: it was the Portuguese Iberians and not the Spanish who colonized the *Mbundu*). In those days, Portuguese women were not permitted to sail aboard explorers' ships to Asia. Early in my research it seemed that instead

of traveling first to Malacca and then to the Spice Islands, my proto-Howard ancestor may have entered Portugal's Asian territories through the Western India port of Goa, and from there traveled to China's Macao, where he took up trading with Southeast Asia. But later, I took Malacca and the Spice Islands as my ancestor's more likely port of entry. As author Roy Eric Xavier writes, the history of Luso-Asians in Macau reveal that their origins stem from "liaisons between Portuguese colonists and indigenous [Goa, India] women." In other words, Macau's "Portuguese" males came from mixed unions that generally occurred in Goa. There are no such genes in my Howard family. See Roy Eric Xavier, "Luso-Asian and the Origins of Macau's Cultural Development," forthcoming in *Journal of the Royal Asiatic Society-Hong* Kong, volume 57 (July 2017): 1-6. Sources of my own and my family's genetic trail are *23andme, ancestry.com,* and *africanancestry.com.*

38 Boyajian, 238-240. Especially important, see Etsuko Miyata, 68-70, whose publication is fully cited below.

39 *Casado* here is defined as a rich Portuguese trader: a man who has earned status in the eyes of his community and Lisbon because of his achievements, rather than by any birthright. He represents "an acceptable face of *mercantile* [emphasis added] activity" (see Subrahmanyam, 76, 230-34, and 236-43).

40 Ibid., Halikowski Smith. "Soldados" (soldiers) were always unmarried males, so obligated for military service.

41 Pinto, 40-45.

42 Ibid., 179-180.

43 Subrahmanyam, 271.

44 Ibid., 253-60 – especially 259.

45 To learn more about the lives of soldiers in 16th century Portugal similar to *Pasco's* father or the father's Black Portuguese ancestors, see Roy Eric Xavier, "Before Macau: Portuguese Colonialism and Early Transnationalism in Asia" (working paper of the Portuguese and Macanese Studies Project, Institute for the Study of Societal Issues, University of California, Berkeley, California, 2017), 9-14,

accessed April 5, 2020, http://www.academia.edu/146290/Before_Macau... Dr. Xavier is the Director of the Portuguese and Macanese Studies Project and a Visiting Scholar at U.C. Berkeley's ISSI. The description of *Pasco* and his family presented in this part of my narrative was largely based on Dr. Xavier's working paper and on sources cited elsewhere in this narrative.

46 Subrahmanyam, 185. Consistent with Howard family legend regarding the economic status of our Asian ancestor during the time *Pasco* lived near Manila, the author Sanjay Subrahmanyam informs us that the "Melaka-Macau-Nagasaki-Makassar-Manila network . . . sustained a good part of Portuguese private trade in the 1610s, 1620s, and 1630s . . . ." The Filipina wife's family were well-connected, prosperous traders; she may have been a concubine.

47 A number of citations support my view, including one E. Veen, "The VOC: FROM PRIVATEERING TO STRATEGY," Chapter 8 of his 2000 Doctoral Thesis submitted to Leiden University, accessed December 1, 2018, http://openaccess.leidenuniv.nl/bitstream/handle/...CHAPTER+VIII+THE+VOC.pdf?... The term "Black Portuguese" was used then to describe the issue of a Portuguese man and an Asian woman.

48 *Pasco's* father had likely commercial dealings in Makassar which in turn might have involved trade with Macao located just off mainland China's southern coast. But after 1592, it was through Manila instead of Macao that the Portuguese were able to conduct trade between mainline China and the rest of Asia, including with Spanish Manila (see Miyata, 4 and 23). Macao was a Portuguese enclave granted by China specifically to private Portuguese merchants – and not the Portuguese Court – in 1557. The Spanish were barred by both private Portuguese traders and by the Chinese Court from having direct commercial dealings with mainland China and its Macao enclave. Portuguese one-to-one, direct trade relations in Southeast Asia during the time that *Pasco* lived in Asia were superior to anything that the Spaniards were ever able to achieve in their Asia commercial activity. The Portuguese role in its trade with China was one of serving as an intermediary between this important Asian market and Japan along with the Spanish Empire itself. Spain depended on these independent Portuguese traders active in Southeast Asia for the Empire's commercial relations having to do with Asian kingdoms and sultanates who were neighbors of the Spanish Philippines. Manila in the Spanish Philippines was the Asian home of the Spanish Empire's economic workhorse known as the *Galleon* Trade – a subject that will be taken up later in this narrative.

49 It was the author James C. Boyajian (page 237) who first pointed out to me the Portuguese *casado* connection between the Moluccas and Manila. The Moluccas included a collection of small islands in present-day Indonesia. As reported elsewhere in this narrative, the Portuguese clove traders in Makassar moved there – after 1605 – from the southern Moluccas.

50 The only reason the Portuguese were ever on Ternate and nearby Islands was to try to capture and monopolize trade of the clove spice. See: Jacobs, Hubert Th. Th. M. (S. J.), *A Treatise on the Moluccas* (St. Louis and Rome: Jesuit Historical Institute, 1970), 271.

51 My future references to this man consider him to have been *Pasco's* father whom I call in the narrative *Pascoal*.

52 "During the last decade of the sixteenth century the Portuguese monopoly of Japan's trade and the Jesuit monopoly of the Japan mission founded by St. Francis Xavier in 1549 were alike threatened by the appearance of Spanish traders and missionary friars from the Philippines. These Iberian rivals caused the Portuguese considerable jealousy and concern, but . . . these activities did not . . . greatly reduce the profits of the Macao-Nagasaki trade. Despite [their union] in . . . 1580, the government at Madrid accepted, by and large, the Portuguese contention that Japan lay within their sphere of influence (as demarcated by the Treaty of Tordesillas in 1494) and that the Japan trade should be monopolized by Macao rather than by Manila," emphasis added). In other words, the Treaty of Tordesillas disallowed the Portuguese to establish any direct trade between Japan and Manila. The quote was taken from Boxer's "The Portuguese Seaborne Empire," 64.

53 Etsuko Miyata, *Portuguese Intervention in the Manila Galleon* Trade: *The Structure and Networks of Trade between Asia and America in the 16th and 17th Centuries as Revealed by Chinese Ceramics and Spanish Archives* (Oxford: Archaeopress Publishing LTD, 2016), 2-21. Also, see Schurz, 130-34.

54 *Pasco's* father or grandfather (by now a "Black Portuguese") was possibly – even likely – among these seven families and Portuguese soldiers. The Portuguese more-or-less dominated Ternate since 1512, and up to 1641 when Malacca fell under control of the Dutch. The Portuguese settlers' and soldiers' exodus to Ambon – ordered by the Sultan – occurred July 15, 1575. Until they were forced to exit Ambon on February 22, 1605, the Portuguese survived there by playing off against each other two rival factions of local tribes (the Lima vs the Siwa) – just as the Portuguese did in the Banda Islands.

(The box beneath the text contains separate text summarizing a quote taken from Willard A. Hanna & Des Alwi, *Turbulent Times Past in Ternate and Tidore* [Banda Naira, Indonesia: Yayasan Warisan dan Budaya, 1990], 92.)

55 When asked if our ancestor William was a slave, grandpa answered that our ancestor William was never a slave. His father was rich, said grandpa. "Slavery" as we know it in the modern era did not begin in Virginia until 1662. It was in that year that it was included in the Virginia statutes. Still, some argue that the Black indentured "servants" who landed in 1619 Virginia were effectively enslaved captives. While William may not have been such a captive (read "slave") neither did he enjoy freedom as we understand that term today.

56 See pages 15 and 16 of Noldus, P. J. M. 1984. "The Pattimura Revolt of 1817: Its Causes, Course and Consequences." Masters Thesis, University of Canterbury.

57 G. F. de Bruyn Kops, *Eenige Greepen uit de Geschiedenis der Ambonsche Schuttery.* Amboyna (1895), pp. 8-13 – see Noldus, 13. As to Portugal's control of clove exports to Europe, see Cynthia Gladen, "Cloves,"University of Minnesota Libraries, no date, accessed December 2, 2018, http://www/ lib.umn.edu> tradeproducts

According to Boyajian (237) and Miyata (4, 23), until the year 1592, it was difficult for Portuguese traders to participate in the *Galleon* trade except through Macao – much to the dislike of Manila Bay Spanish merchants. After 1592, Portuguese participation in the *Galleon* was allowed by the Spaniards only if the Portuguese traders employed agents in Manila. In the early 1600s (specifically, Boyajian quotes Portuguese trade statistics from 1611-20), private Portuguese traders controlled the major share of the cloves entering the China clove market. Boyajian tells us that "a secondary market for cloves developed in the Americas, via the Manila galleons. The developing Makassar-Manila trade axis also facilitated the exchange of American silver for South Asian cloth and spices from Ambon and the Bandas," (see Boyajian, 237). During this time when young *Pasco* was still in Manila Bay, I assume here that the boy's Portuguese father participated in the lucrative Chinese clove trade using agents in Manila, and that this period's clove trade involving China and Manila was a contributor to the wealth it was said he enjoyed.

58 Hanna & Alwi, 93. But according to another author, these same Portuguese were expelled from Tidore by the Dutch in 1606 (see the following endnotes and the Veen dissertation, page 6, cited elsewhere in these endnotes).

59 Schurz, 139-40.

60 John A. Holm, *An Introduction to Pidgins and Creoles* (New York: Cambridge University Press, 2000), 318-9.

61 Schurz, 139-40. Ermita was founded by a Spanish priest in 1591 according to Robert R. Reed, 63 (see the complete citation for this source in an endnote below).

62 Stephanie J. Mawson, "Philippine *Indios* in the Service of Empire: Indigenous Soldiers and Contingent Loyalty, 1600-1700," 63, no. 2 (April 2016): 387.

63 Another source tells us: "With 1423 Spanish troops and nearly 1000 Filipino auxiliaries [Pedro de] Acuna cleared the Dutch from most of the group and left a strong Spanish post on Ternate, whose fortifications were taken by storm." (See Schurz, 139) In any case, it does not appear that *Pasco's* father was among these soldiers, for it seems he was among the Portuguese trader-soldiers accepting the Sultans offer to remove himself along with a local woman – a Melanesian as documented by *23andme* – to Ambon, some 388 miles away. *Pasco* was not yet born.

64 Robert R. Reed, *Colonial Manila: The Context of Hispanic Urbanism and Process of Morphogenesis*, (Berkeley and Los Angeles: University of California Press, 1978), 59-63.

65 A Mexican Spanish-based creole with a Native Tagalog substrate. In the early colonial period, it was considered by upper-class Spaniards as vulgar Spanish, meaning Spanish spoken in poor taste by uneducated lower-class Filipino natives. In addition to Spanish, Chavacano was a Portuguese creole language – the two eventually forming an enriched creole after likely beginning as pidgin tongues. *Pasco's* father would have spoken Chavacano when communicating with traders, many of whom were foreigners from lands like other parts of Asia, the Middle East, and Europe. During Manila Bay's colonial period, Ermita had its own Chavacano known as Ermiteno which like all Chavacano creole was considered by Spaniards as street language or so-called kitchen language. See

"Chavacano," last modified April 25, 2020, accessed May 3, 2020, http://en.wikipedia.org/windex.php?title=Chavacano&oldid=953032661

66 Miyata, 14.

67 Reed, 33.

68 E. Veen. See the research study's "Summary." In the same year, 1605, the Dutch expelled the Portuguese from the Moluccan Island of Ternate. As a result, 400 Portuguese left Ternate for the Manila area. *Pascoal's* spice trade involved the Moluccas, Manila Bay and Makassar, and as a *casado* he may have had households in more than one of these three areas.

69 Schurz, 143; Boyajian, 237; Miyata, 16. This suggests that *Pasco's* Portuguese father – a trader – had business operations and partnerships in Ambon, Ternate, Makassar, and the Bay of Manila's Ermita and the nearby Port of Tondo as part of his merchant and distributor activities associated with cloves.

70 Jan Sihar and Karel Steenbrink, *A History of Christianity in Indonesia* (Leiden: Brill, 2008), 59-62. "In 1620, twenty-thirty Portuguese families are reported to live there" (in Makassar); and "A church with a priest for the Portuguese is recorded for the years 1617 and 1635" (in Makassar). These two quotes taken from: Herbert Jacobs, SJ, ed, *The Jesuit Makasar documents (1615-1682)*, (Rome: Jesuit Historical Institute, 1988), p. 6.

71 Partially explaining why *Pasco's* father was periodically away from his home in the Philippines.

72 Jacobs, 3.

73 Anthony Reid, "Pluralism and Progress in seventeenth-century Makassar," *Bijdragen tot de Taal-, Land- en Volkenkunde, Authority and enterprise among the peoples of South Sulawesi* 156, no. 3 (2000): 61.

74 New Christians were Jews forced to convert to Catholicism. They were called *conversos*.

75 This period during which Portuguese merchants (as opposed to representatives of the Portuguese Crown) dominated internal Southeast Asia trade is referred to by some as *Age of the Consados*.

76 In 1557, China permitted private Portuguese traders to act as intermediaries between its luxury porcelain and silk markets and the silver market in Japan (later replaced by Spanish America mines located in Peru and Bolivia). American Silver transported to Asia by way of the Manila *galleons* would not begin to replace Japanese silver until after 1565. These Portuguese merchant-intermediaries seem until 1592 to have been exclusively centered in Macao, located on China's southern coast. The Portuguese merchants (not its royal Court) at Macao played an essential role in facilitating the valuable *galleons* between Manila and Spain's colonies established in South America and Acapulco. Black Portuguese *Casados* like *Pasco's* father *Pascoal* – already successful in the Southeast Asia commercial trade – saw their wealth balloon because they assumed the role of intermediary-links in the *Galleon* Trade between Acapulco and Manila. To the extent that *Pascoal* participated as an intermediary in the Manila *Galleon* Trade, he likely did so from Makassar and Manila Bay, not Macao. But for more on the Portuguese of Macao (excludes *Pascoal)*, see Etsuko Miyata (pages 4, 23). For the Portuguese as intermediaries in the China-Manila trade, see Schurz, 130-31, and for evidence of their being essential to the *Galleon* Trade, see Schurz, 132 and Miyata, 68.

77 The Treaty of Tordesillas was the 1494 agreement between Spain and Portugal whose purpose was to prevent future conflicts regarding newly discovered lands like the territory recently explored by Christopher Columbus.

78 Schurz, 46-48.

79 Omri Bassewitch Frenkel, January 2017, "Transplantation of Asian Spices in the Spanish Empire 1518-1640: Entrepreneurship, Empiricism, and the Crown," A thesis submitted to McGill University in partial fulfillment of the requirements of the degree of Doctor of Philosophy. Also, see Schurz, 23 and 130 to 133.

80 Stephanie J. Mawson, "Convicts Or Conquistadores? Spanish Soldiers In The Seventeenth-Century Pacific, *Past and Present*, 232 (August 2016): 123.

81 Linda A. Newson, "Conquest, pestilence and demographic collapse in the early Spanish Philippines," *Journal of Historical Geography*, 32 (2006): 5.

82 Manila's indigenes formerly were Muslim subjects of the Sultan of Brunei who conquered the area around 1500.

83 Schurz, 21.

84 From the port of Tondo to Ermita, the latter being the site of *Pascoal's* Portuguese shrine called "Our Guide Lady," was a mere 3 miles. A trip from Spain to the Philippines took a year in the 17th century, meaning that *Pasco's* nautical travel from the Philippines to England (where he obviously rested) and then to Virginia must have begun around 1622-23 for him to have appeared in Elizabeth Cittie, Virginia's 1624/25 muster. Source: https://worldhistoryconnected.press.uillinois.edu, accessed August 3, 2019.

85 Schurz, 29.

86 According to Schurz, the Japanese attached special importance to their acquisition of Chinese raw silk since the Chinese were forbidden by their own authorities to trade with Japan "under a singularly vigorous penalty, which is that if any Chinese trades with the Japanese, not only he but his father, mother, and relations shall be put to death." See Schurz, 115.

87 The Manila suburb of Malate was established by the once-ranking Muslim members of pre-Hispanic Manila. Shortly after they were forced to move by their Spanish conquerors, these *maharlika* families became successful, prosperous settlers in Malate. The ancestors of *Pasco's* mother are believed to have ties to these settlers.

88 Indians.

89 As *cabezas*, chiefs no longer had to share blood lines with their village constituents.

90 Warrior.

91 In 16th century Southeast Asia, *Mestizos* were usually children of concubines. Citation above in Pinto, 179-80, and in John Leddy Phelan, *The Hispanization of the Philippines* (Madison: University of Wisconsin Press, 1959), 106.

92 Schurz, 51.

93 Ubaldo Iaccarino, "The 'Galleon System' and Chinese Trade in Manila at the Turn of the 16th Century," *Ming Qing Yanjiu*, (2011), 113.

94 Miyata, 4.

95 Most of these slaves were men, women and children from the Indian subcontinent, Southeast Asia, China, and Japan. The trade involved not just Asian slaves but also the lucrative trade involving New World silver and Chinese silk, i.e., the *Galleon* Trade between private Portuguese traders in Macao to Manila. After 1592, Portuguese Macao was replaced by Manila (see Miyata, 4 and 23).

96 Tatiana Seijas, *Asian Slaves in Colonial Mexico* (Cambridge: Cambridge University Press, 2014), 19, 20, and 21. The Hapsburgs clearly allowed Portuguese traders to control the transport and supply networks that made this slave trade possible, and the powerful family was willing to sacrifice the material interests of Manila settlers – the small number of white, blue-eyed, blond Spanish colonists – as long as Portuguese traders kept the colony supplied with valuable trade including slaves and spices. And so to 1600s Manila, Portuguese ships came from Makassar, Macao, and India with the monsoon winds – carrying clove spice, cinnamon, pepper, Black slaves and what were called Kafir slaves along with a long list of other goods. But most of the slaves they brought to Manila were from all over Asia because the Spanish authorities in Manila were afraid of the black slaves.

97 Reed, 63. It was not until July 10, 2020 that I realized the importance of this relationship.

98 Miyata, 8 and 21. Also, see Paul Kekai Manansia, "The Philippines and the Sandalwood trade in the late pre-colonial and colonial periods" in https://www.academia.edu/10401069/T My understanding of the prosperous China trade practiced by private traders like *Pasco's* father flowed more or less in the following manner: (1) from the Moluccas private Portuguese traders such as *Pascoal* initiated the trade in cloves, shipping this spice to Makassar; (2) from Makassar the bulk of these cloves were sent to China in exchange for valuable silk (or silver); (3) the Chinese sold the cloves to Spanish merchants in Manila to be shipped by them out of Tondo on the *Galleons* to New Spain (Mexico) then trans-shipped to European markets; (4) from New Spain the Chinese were paid in silver ingots. Also, the fact that *Pasco's* father traded with the Chinese and certain Asians from the coastal area of Ermita/Malate

located on Manila Bay offered him additional lucrative trade opportunities within markets located in Southeast Asia and the Philippine Islands.

99 Dennis O. Flynn and Arturo Giráldez, "Born with a "Silver Spoon": The Origin of World Trade in 1571," *Journal of World History*, Vol. 6, No. 2 (1995): 205.

100 Schurz, 26.

101 Quote from Schurz, 138. There were two important publications which I relied on in order to lead me to the conclusion *Pasco's* "rich" merchant father earned his fortune primarily through the spice trade: Boyajian's "Portuguese Trade in Asia under the Habsburgs" and Miyata's "Portuguese Intervention in the Manila *Galleon* Trade." The latter author, like several others, emphasized that Portuguese merchants participated in the *Galleon* Trade by shipping Chinese silk and ceramics from Macao to Manila/Tondo then on to Mexico (68, 69). I conclude that *Pasco's* father was not among these Macao Portuguese traders for reasons I cited elsewhere. Boyajian (237) begins his analysis in the Maluku Islands (where the Moluccas are located) to explain that Portuguese clove traders there participating in the *Galleon Trade* had the bulk of the cloves spice market located in China, in Coromandel, and in Bengal. Importantly, this second group of private Portuguese traders and distributors were *casados* who, such as *Pascoal*, participated in the *galleons* through Makassar (close neighbor to the Moluccas) and Manila where they also "facilitated the exchange of American silver for South Asian cloth and spices from [the Moluccas] Ambon and Banda [Islands]." *Pascoal* belonged to this second group. "American silver" was turned into the silver dollar coin used as currency around the world, and it was among the currencies used in colonial Virginia during the lifetime of William Crawshaw and his descendants whom Crawshaw told that his father was rich. These descendants recognized silver as being the commodity and currency held by the affluent, which they also concluded would never include people like them or those others with whom they were intimate.

102 Reed, 63.

103 In 1580, Portugal and Spain were forcibly brought together under one crown: Philp II, titular head of the extraordinarily rich Habsburg family Empire. Philip II wanted to create even more wealth for his Spanish Empire by tapping into Portugal's hold on the spice trade and the Chinese silk and porcelain trade goods, connecting the two with the rich silver mines of Mexico, Peru, and Potosí located in

present-day Bolivia. Before 1580, the Spaniards and Portuguese were bitter enemies and competitors as each sought to dominate the lucrative spice trade largely orchestrated from Maluku. Though the two empires served the same Crown after 1580, each remained suspicious of each other's trade motives.

104 To gain some idea of the lifestyle of these *casados*, read the description of a Dutch onlooker witnessing Portuguese merchants (*casados*) from Macao arriving at Nagasaki, Japan for a trading mission in 1610: "The ship coming from Macao usually has about 200 or more merchants on board who go ashore at once, each of them taking a house wherein to lodge with his servants and slaves. They take no heed of what they spend and nothing is too costly for them. Sometimes they disburse in the seven or eight months that they stay in Nagasaki more than 200,000 or 300,000 [silver] taels, through which the populace profit greatly; and this is one of the reasons why the local Japanese are very friendly to them." Charles R. Boxer, *The History of Human Society,* ed. J. H. Plumb (New York: Alfred A Knopf, 1969), 64. *"Casado"* was a bourgeoise social category unique to Portugal's old Asian Empire.

105 Boyajian, 237.

106 "Arbitraging" silver in this case means acquiring a product in one market and selling it in silver at a profit in China. Throughout the world at the time, silver had its highest value in China. For an explanation of how such arbitrage opportunities worked in 15th to 17th century Manila, see Dennis O. Flynn and Arturo Giráldez, "Cycles of Silver: Global Economic Unity through the Mid-Eighteenth Century," *Journal of World History*, 2002, 13, No. 2, 392-405.

107 E. Veen, 94.

108 Ibid. Also, André Murteira, "Dutch attacks against Portuguese shipping in Asia (1600-1625)," *TIJDSCHRIFT VOOR Zeegeschiedenis* 38, no.2 (2019), 15-18.

109 Veen., 94.

110 Ibid., and Murteira, 14-15.

111 Literally cited as: Parthesius, R. (2007). Dutch Ships in tropical waters: the development of the Dutch East India Company (VOC) shipping network in Asia 1595-1660. Amsterdam: in eigen beheer,

p. 136. "Privateers" were pirates who were authorized by marauding European powers to join them in raids and plundering of Asian and African victims.

112 Schurz, 348. Schurz suggests the blockade lasted just short of a year and a half. He cites as his source a diary written by Arnold Browne, "an Englishman who participated in these movements against the Spaniards . . . . "Paul Van Dyke suggests it was about 1 ½ years. See Paul Van Dyke, "The Anglo-Dutch Fleet of Defense (1620-1622: Prelude to the Dutch Occupation of Taiwan" in L. Blussé (ed.), *Around and About Formosa, Essays in honor of Professor Ts'ao Yung-ho* (Taipei 2003): 61-81.

113 Reed, 33.

114 Spain's colonial system and the *Galleon Trade* were intricately wound together such that neither *Pasco* nor his father could hope to escape it. The Spanish Empire consigned father and son to different castes, the father occupying a rung higher than the one his mixed-race son was born into. As a *Mestizo*, *Pasco* for all intents and purposes was a serf – one obligated to fulfill punishing work requirements to the *cabeza*. His father's wealth largely depended on the level of prosperity enjoyed by the Spanish Empire, the wealth of which was tied to Galleon Trade activity and to the tributes that free-born wards like *Pasco* were obligated by the Empire to honor. *Pascoal's* status everywhere in the Spanish Empire was precarious. He was a *new Christian* – a *converso* descended from Jews and despised by everyone. One wrong move or a baseless, arbitrary accusation made by enemies known and unknown that the wealthy tradesman secretly harbored anti-Christian, pro-Jewish sympathies was enough to send him to the Inquisition in Mexico. There, he could expect long, sleep-deprived interrogations, torture, loss of all his assets, and even death. *Pascoal* whether he wanted to or not was in no position to help his son.

115 See Tremlett, 9. Full citation provided below.

116 According to *encomienda*, certain of the king's favorites (usually conquistadores who participated in the initial settlement of the Philippines and were allotted by the king groups of Natives to perform mostly free labor for him in exchange for his supposedly making them ready to be baptized) were owed tribute payable in specie or in kind from overworked Indians who usually resided in provinces located far from Manila. Under the *vandala,* however, villages in the Manila area were obligated (given the blockades) to produce and sell food products to the government, and such products were produced and sold by dependent wards to their *cabezas*. The allotment to each ward grew higher with extension of

the blockades, but the wards were to be paid for their labor. However, because of the blockades, the government ran out of money, forcing the wards to work for IOUs that were never honored. Effectively, the wards "paid" a tax without ever receiving income. *Pasco* was among these increasingly impoverished wards – probably part of IOU-holders who included his maternal family. For further information about these *vandalas*, see Phelan, 99-102.

117 Although competitors in their efforts to control the spice trade in the Spanish Indies, the Protestant Netherlands and anti-Catholic English Courts sometimes were allies in joint military campaigns against a common enemy: the Catholic Spanish Empire. In fact, the first Africans brought to the first English Colony on August 25th, 1619 at Point Comfort, Virginia was the result of an illicit (because it was not then legal) cooperative venture between Dutch and English privateers in a raid against Portuguese-Spanish ships carrying African slaves to New Spain (Spanish America). And in the early 17th century, a young not-yet Virginia Governor George Yeardley (an Englishman) fought alongside rebellious soldiers of the Netherlands to help win Dutch independence from a Catholic Spanish Empire that both parties hated.

118 These events were what my grandfather relayed to me in the 1950/60s. When I visited Manila in March 2020 (just at the start of the Coronavirus) I visited the site on Manila Bay where all of this happened. Despite the water's profound depth, Edgar Hisoler of the Filipino Tour Center who accompanied me, said that it was not uncommon either presently or in the old days for boys to swim up to ships in the mouth of Manila Bay seeking gifts, coins, and trinkets. During certain times of the year, however, the waters of the Bay could be even more dangerous than they appeared to me on the day of my excursion due to the undertow.

119 Francis C. Assisi,"Indian Slaves in Colonial America," *India Currents: Home of the Global Indian* (May 16, 2007): 3.

120 Martha W. McCartney, *Virginia Immigrants And Adventurers 1607-1635: A Biographical Dictionary*, (Baltimore: Genealogical Publishing Company, Inc., 2007), 489-90. This is also cited in Francis C. Assisi – see endnote below.

121 Courtesy of *African Ancestry's* April 2nd, 2014 *Patriclan* DNA analysis of my saliva sample which I gave them earlier in the same year.

122 This DNA analysis was completed by *African Ancestry* using their *Matriclan* test on the saliva sample submitted by the granddaughter of my father's sister, Renee Eley, on October 7, 2014. Based on results of this test, the Howard family's maternal genetic ancestry is traced to the Yoruba and Hausa Peoples living in today's Nigeria.

123 These were the test results of various saliva samples submitted to various genetic testing services but mainly to *23andme* and to *ancestry.com*.

124 "Our guide lady."

125 These colonial mission towns (*cabeceras*) became patterned after their post-1519 colonial predecessors established in New Spain, known today as Mexico. Spanish colonial Ermita was known as a town where Portuguese traders settled alongside *Indió* traders and fishermen. In their ongoing attempt to establish Catholicism among *Los Indiós* who lived in and around the Ermita Shrine, in 1610 Augustin missionaries turned what was until then the Ermita Shrine and then Chapel into a parish church where local *Indiós* went to perform Mass, rituals, and nuptials.

126 *Pasco's* mother's family was among the "chief Tagáls" who were deprived of their homes in pre-Hispanic Manila when the Spanish conquistador and first governor of the Philippines Miguel López de Legazpi forced their ancestors to flee, whereupon they settled in Malate. There, according to Reed (63): "Rather than languish following Spanish conquest, these ranking Filipinos began to involve themselves in domestic commerce and grew fairly prosperous." *Pasco's* biological family was small (likely not more than 4 individuals – see Reed, 14 and 82). Note that the English translation of the Portuguese *Nossa Senhora da Guía* is "Our Guide Lady." The Chinese who visited the Malate-Ermita coast came from the mainland, and the other traders who frequented the area came from South Asia. After 1580 and until 1640, Portuguese traders controlled most of the Moluccan cloves distributed in China, on India's Coromandel Coast, and in Bengal (Boyajian, 237). Ermita Chapel was built in 1606 after the 1574 cessation of Chinese pirate raids on Manila Bay led by the infamous pirate Limahong. In 1610, Ermita Chapel was elevated into a parish church. [Much of the foregoing information can be found in Reed, 59-63.] For more about the origin of Ermita Village, Wikipedia mentions that it was first the site of a fishing village called Lagyo (merged with Malate) before arrival of the Spanish. People started calling the site Ermita rather than Lagyo when a Mexican hermit arrived in the place and lived in the chapel built there for "Nuestra Senora de Guía." Wikipedia goes on to say that "When the Spaniards moved

out of Intramuros, they integrated with the Indios in Ermita, which became a fashionable residential area." That was in the 19th century. Ermita is a mere 2 to 3 miles from the Port of Tondo, having made the area very convenient to *Pascoal's* trading activities at the Port of Tondo. However, it may not have been solely the commercial activities of *Pasco's* father that William Crawshaw was talking about when he said his father was rich. His mother's *Indió* family who lived in Malate was, according to Reed, "fairly prosperous," too.

127 Bagumbayan

128 According to Reed: "Ermita [and] Malate originated as . . . undifferentiated communities of Filipinos [*Los Indiós*]. Ermita was founded in 1591 by a Spanish secular priest [but by the turn of the 17th century, King Philip II had assigned the area to Augustinian missionaries] . . . becoming a small religious hermitage . . . Malate, a settlement established by *maharlika* families who had been displaced from Sulayman's palisaded port by Legazpi and his troops, was situated about a kilometer [0.621 mile] to the south of Ermita.

129 Scott, 220.

130 Reynaldo C. Ileto, *Filipinos and Their Revolution: Event, Discourse, and Historiography,* (Manila: Ateneo De Manila University Press, 2003), 42.

131 Ermita Chapel began as a shrine made of bamboo, nipa and mulawen (a plant material), and it was built in 1606 to house the image "Our Guide Lady," a Marian statue said to have been found by Spanish soldiers who accompanied explorer Miguel López de Legazpi in 1571. "Ermita" comes from the Portuguese word "eremita," defined as "hermit, a person who lives alone, away from people and society," according to Wikipedia. Google (http://www.livinginthephilippines.com/www.livi) states: "This area was a fishing village known as Lagyo prior to the arrival of the Spaniards. People started calling it "La Ermita" " distinguishing it from contiguous Malate " when a Mexican hermit arrived in the place and lived in the chapel built there for Nuestra Senora de Guía." "Lagyo" is defined in the dictionary of the language spoken in Mindanao (Southern Philippines) as a place that is "separate;" "remote;" and "apart." The place referred to as being separate, remote, and apart seems to be 17th century Ternate, located in the North Moluccas and described elsewhere in the text of this narrative. A search on the internet further reveals that the Portuguese built several other "eremitas" in various parts of the

old Portuguese Empire, including, to mention a few instances, the 17ᵗʰ century *Ermita de San Antonio de Padua* in Ceuta, Morocco, as well as other such shrines and chapels in Europe, America, and Asia. Most if not all of them are believed to have had earlier Portuguese associations going back to the period before the Spanish came to the Philippines in the 16ᵗʰ century. As described in the text of this narrative, it was Portuguese soldiers and traders who were the first Europeans in control of the clove spice trade on Ternate from the early 1500s to approximately 1605, when several hundred Portuguese left the area for the Philippines, settling around the present Manila Bay location of Ermita, and speaking a creole – "Ermiteno" – that is now extinct [Anthony P. Grant, "Substrate influences in Mindanao Chabacano," *Creoles, their Substrates, and Language Typology*, ed. Claire Lefebure (Amsterdam/Philadelphia: John Benjamins Publishing Company, 2011), 303-304.]. Academic researchers have documented Portuguese trade activity in Manila going back to the period before 1571, suggesting – contrary to popular belief – further evidence that Portuguese traders brought *Nossa Senhora da Guía* to Manila Bay before the Spanish arrived. As author Gregory C. Gunn has published through the Hong Kong University Press (regarding Spanish explorer Miguel López de Legazpi's June 3, 1571 establishment of the city of Manila): "Manila already hosted a community of some 150 Chinese; prior Portuguese trade contact was also established." See Gregory C. Gunn, *History without Borders: The Making of an Asian World Region, 1000-1800* (Hong Kong: Hong Kong University Press, 2011), 180.

132 Ibid., "Organographia Philipiniana."

133 Nossa Senhora da Guía's origins are in the history of the Orthodox Christian Church. Centuries later, a supply ship arriving from Nueva Espana and reaching anxious Filipino officials in the latter part of June 1570 delivered a letter from Philip II which "formally dismissed earlier Portuguese claims to the Philippines" even though the Portuguese were in the Islands before the Spanish arrived and had been entitled to the territory under a papal bull and the 1494 Treaty of Tordesillas signed by Spain and Portugal. See Reed, 22, 88 (n).

134 Parthesius, 156.

135 Ibid.

136 Schurz, 350-1

137 The Spanish Empire's *polo and vandala* policy required dependents like *Pasco* to help Spain in its war against the Dutch by providing forced labor and rice from Filipino fields to Spanish officials no matter the costs to the dependents themselves. As the war continued, the system became unbearable to *Pasco*. Records from the period indicate over 35,000 Filipino dependents fled the Islands to escape the onerous obligations. Most fled the Spanish-controlled Islands to the forested mountains where the Spanish could not find them.

138 Others like the author Van Dyke suggest the blockade was a few months longer but still in the same time frame. See Paul Van Dyke, 61-81.

139 Schurz, 348-9.

140 Published 16th and 17th century descriptions of Manila Bay *Indiós* often use adjectives like "indolent" and "lazy." It was thought by the Church and *encomenderos* of *Pasco's* day that Manila Bay *Indiós* needed the discipline of hard work, paying tribute, and food insufficiency to make them productive and fulfill the requirements of the Empire. And although his father's lifestyle was tolerated by the Spanish Empire such that he was allowed the perks of a "rich merchant" (enjoying the life of a *homen de negócio* – "businessman" – and affluent *converso*), his dependent Indian wife and half-dependent son had no such freedoms and remained wards of the Spanish Empire and of its Church. Such men included the Portuguese "*casado*" – a term used almost exclusively in Portugal's *Estado da Índia*, including the Indian province of Goa; Macao in China; parts of Timor; and, for a time, parts of the Moluccas. See Teodoro A. Agoncillo, *History of the Filipino People*, (Quezon City, Philippines: Garotech Publishing, 1990), 35-9; Paul-Francois Tremlett, "Power, invulnerability, beauty: producing and transforming male bodies in the lowland Christianised Philippines," *Occasional Papers in Gender Theory and the Study of Religions*, no. 1 (2006): 9, 10, accessed February 13, 2020, oro.open.ac.uk; George Bryan Souza, "Merchants and Commerce in Asia and the Portuguese Empire over the Long 18th Century," *Revista de Cultura 34*, 2010, 8, 9. Also, see Jurre Knoest, "Company Privateers in Asian Waters: The VOC-Trading Post at Hirado and the Logistics of Privateering, ca. 1614-1624," *Leidschrift, jaargang* 26, no. 3 (December 2011), no page; P. Van Dyke, 61-81.

141 *Remonstrado* (Spanish): A Christian native of the Philippine Islands who escapes the Spanish Empire by running away from his village and lives in the mountains. *Pasco* chose a different course.

142 It was to the financial advantage of the Portuguese traders by this time to operate as smugglers of the clove spice. The value of silver had fallen from the lofty heights it enjoyed during earlier years in the 1600s. Yet at least in Spain's case, the Iberians kept adding taxes on to the revenues stemming from its clove sales to try to sustain something close to previous profit levels. I assume that the same scenario occurred once the Dutch monopolized the clove market. Portuguese smugglers therefore could sell the spice at prices below that charged by at first the Spaniards and later the Dutch who followed and still earned what they – the Portuguese traders –considered to be satisfactory returns.

143 1572-1626.

144 Andrew Fitzmaurice, *Sovereignty, Property and Empire, 1500-2000* (New York: Cambridge University Press, 2014), 64.

145 Ibid., 63.

146 This physical description is not unlike that of the descendant family member I met in Africa during the early 17th century. More about him and about our meeting below.

147 He was a "servant" as opposed to "slave." According to Paul Heinegg's *Native Heritage Project* and Francis C. Assisi's *Indian Slaves in Colonial America (a 2007 publication),* baptized East Indians in Virginia during the 17th century were commonly indentured servants and not slaves like most unbaptized Native Peoples. Assisi cites evidence for these baptized East Indian servants in Jamestown as early as 1622. See: http://nativeheritageproject.com/2012/07/03/east-india-indians-in-early-colonial-records/ and https://indiacyrrebts,cin/ubduab-slaves-in-colonial-america/ respectively.

148 Some argue that the English East India Company, chartered in 1600 to trade in Asia, was like Britain's Royal African Company, chartered in 1660 to trade along Africa's west coast, in that both were mere conduits for the propagation of an international slave trade. Between 1622 and 1772, the East India Company traded between 2,773 and 3,304 African slaves. Considering the total volume of slaves trafficked by the British in the Indian Ocean from 1500-1850, England transported some 5,698 to 5,716 slaves while maintaining a primary fort in Southeast Asia's Bencoolen, Sumatra. It is purely speculation that in 1624, *Pasco* was intended to be among such cargo – especially if he were among the highly valued, but rare, human cargo who could speak understandable English. However, possible

problems of logistics aside, English East India Company-affiliated merchants could possibly have decided that the pro-Christian Indian would be put to better use if he were transferred to the Virginia Company of London's Reverend William Crawshaw – this being right after the 1622 Powhatan uprising against Anglican English colonists in Virginia. The English East India Company and the Virginia Company of London were in frequent contact and shared investor-members. Officially, slavery did not yet exist in 1624-Virginia, except, that is, for certain enslaved Natives. So, after baptism into the Church of England, *Pasco* sailed from London to Colonial Virginia (having been acquired from Dutch adventurers) as a "free-person" indentured servant. See the research completed by Ela Hefler, Class of 2017, *The British East Indian Company's African Slave Trade* (Nashville: Vanderbilt Historical Review, Vanderbilt University, 2018).

149 See Fitzmaurice, page 69.

150 According to some sources, early Manila Bay Native Christians thought that the purpose of a baptism, for instance, was to cure ills. In Peterson's 2014 dissertation, he writes: "Recent research on early Christianity in the Philippines has revealed that many (most?) conversions were superficial and misguided and that the notion of a truly 'Christian' *Indio* subject community in the sixteenth and seventeenth centuries should be regarded as an ongoing project, not a reality." *Pasco* may not yet have been baptized Catholic. For one thing, if his Manila Bay parish priest followed the book, *Pasco* was probably too young to fulfill all the Catholic sacraments – like confirmation and communion. For those, he should have been at a minimum 15 years old before leaving the Philippines. That was unlikely the case. Complicating all this was the fact that *Pasco's* father and ancestors were Catholic.

151 Pronounced <pay-puhst>, the first syllable sounding like "pay" as in paper.

152 Reverend Crashaw followed the Salamanca School of development theory which insisted on respecting the rights of Indians encountered during the economic development carried on by European countries in pagan lands.

153 Starch extracted from the pith of the palm tree stem.

154 London's Bridewell House served this population. See Tim Hitchcock, Robert Shoemaker, Sharon

Howard and Jamie McLaughlin, et al, *London Lives, 1690-1800* (www.londonlives.org, version 1.1, 24 April 2012).

155 Chet Snow,"Raleigh Croshaw (c. 1584-1667) – Genealogy," accessed April 27, 2017, https://www.geni.com/people/Capt-Raleigh-Croshaw-Ancient-Planter/6000000003815165796

156 Fitzmaurice, 61-69 (especially pages 61-64).

157 Indians.

158 See Chet Snow.

159 "How Colonists Acquired Title to Land in Virginia," accessed September 20, 2017, http://www.virginiaplaces.org/settleland/headright.html ; "Headrights (VA-NOTES)," Library of Virginia, accessed September 20, 2017, http://www.lva.virginia.gov/public/guides/va4_headrights.htm

160 Lorri Glover and Daniel Blake Smith, *The Shipwreck That Saved Jamestown*, 2008 (New York, N.Y.: Henry Holt and Company, LLC, 2008), pp. 54, 64-66.

161 James Douglas Rice, "The Second Anglo-Powhatan War (1622-1632)," last modified November 30, 2015, accessed August 10, 2016, http://www.EncyclopediaVirginia.or/Anglo-Powhatan_War_Second_1622-1632

162 "Peter Arundell, His letter to Mr. John Farrar, April 15, 1623," cited in Susan Myra Kingsbury, editor, *The Records of the Virginia Company of London,* vol. iv United States Government Printing Office, Washington, D.C., 230.

163 Ibid., Kingsbury, "Richard Frethorne, Letter to his Mother and Father, 1623 (modern translation)", no page number.

164 Edmund S. Morgan, *American Slavery, American Freedom* (London: W. W. Norton & Company, 1975), 103.

165 Ibid., 104.

166 Nevertheless, in the 1624/25 Elizabeth Cittie muster, all white servants were listed with their ages, the ship on which each reached the Colony, and importantly, the date of their arrival. Not so for William Crawshaw and the two African servants Antonio and Isabella. Without this information that was publicly listed for the white servants, there seemed to be no publicly official way to document the termination date of Crawshaw's indenture (if his work and board agreement took the form of a formal indenture), suggesting that the term of his agreement was not publicly acknowledged. Why? Were he and the African servants brought to Virginia aboard illegal and otherwise surreptitious privateer ships just like the two ships that mysteriously showed up with stolen African slaves at 1619 Cape Comfort? Was there any intention to deprive him of a previously-agreed-upon fixed term of labor? Why was information pertinent to his agreement not listed in the public record, in comparison to such agreements for white servants? Answers to these questions are addressed below.

167 Ibid., 119-124. Reports indicate Tucker treated his servants well, probably honoring Crawshaw's severance pkg. Tucker served on an August 1619 committee in Virginia's House of Burgesses who voted affirmatively that "workmen be sent to erect a university and college" to teach "savages" Christianity and civilized living. This suggests he was interested in having among his servants an already-baptized Indian such as Crawshaw was. See: Norma Tucker, *Colonial Virginia and Their Maryland Relatives: A Genealogy of the Tucker Family and also the families of . . . .* (Baltimore: Clearfield Company, 2002), 9. The same source suggests the pork-loving-Crawshaw fulfilled one more wish: among Tucker's 1625 provisions for his family and servants to enjoy were "3 swine."

168 Tucker, 8 and 9.

169 "A Study of Virginia Indians and Jamestown: The First Century," accessed May 4, 2017, https://www.nps.gov/parkhistory/online_books/jame1/moretti-langholtz/chap4.htm

170 Ibid.

171 Fitzmaurice, 63.

172 These circumstances help explain a question posed earlier in this narrative: Why was not information important to *Pasco's* indenture contract – if it was indeed written down at all – not available in the public recording of the 1624/24 muster, which normally listed such information next to the name of all (white)

servants? *Pasco* was captured by Dutch-English privateers who were cruising waters of the Spanish Philippines as part of a blockade against Manila Bay commerce. After capture, he was ultimately consigned to the English. The last thing that the Virginia Company would want to do at a time when English-Spanish Empire relations were sensitive was to give the Spaniards and Spain's supporters at the Virginia Company (including spies for the Spanish Court) any information confirming Virginia's continued participation in raids on Spanish and Portuguese ships.

173 Taken from *The Virginia Magazine of History and Biography.* Anglicans – strictly speaking – were not Protestants. They were viewed by some as a more worthy extension of the Catholic Church.

174 See Fitzmaurice.

175 Ibid.

176 Ibid.

177 Alfred A. Cave, "Canaanites in a Promised Land: The American Indian and the Providential Theory of Empire," *The American Indian Quarterly* 12, no. 4 (Autumn 1988): 277-297. Consistent with the Salamanca School of economic development philosophy applicable to European relations with Natives, it was important, according to Reverend Crashaw, that the rights of Aboriginal people in Virginia be respected and that they willingly accept Christian baptism. See Andrew Fitzmaurice, 40-79. Also consistent with Salamanca reasoning was Spain's presence in the Philippines. Accordingly, on February 8, 1597, Philip II issued a decree ordering the governor-general of the Philippines to determine ways and means to obtain, without coercion, ratification of the Natives' submission to the Spanish sovereign and that such submission needed to be *voluntarily given by the Natives.* On July 12, 1599, the King of Spain was notified that Filipino Natives approved the King's sovereignty, whereupon missionary territory of the whole district of Manila was assigned to the Augustinian Fathers. See: J. Gayo Aragon, "The Controversy over Justification of Spanish Rule in the Philippines," *Studies in Philippine Church History*, ed. Gerald H. Anderson, [book on-line] (Ithaca, NY: Cornell University Press, 1969).

178 Crashaw, "On the Baptized Ethiopian."

179 Granddad said "William" lived with the Indians although he did not seem to know of William's

Asian Indian roots. For details on what such a lifestyle entailed when Crawshaw lived in Virginia, see Edward Lawrence Bond, *"Religion in Seventeenth-Century Anglican Virginia: Myth, Persuasion, and the Creation of an American Identity."* (1995). *LSU Historical Dissertations and Theses.* 5943. This dissertation can also be found online at: https://digitalcommons.lsu.edu/gradschool_disstheses/5943 Also, see Heinegg and Assisi.

180 Morgan, 130. The paragraph is quoted from this source. Also, see Bond (dissertation cited above).

181 T. H. Breen and Stephen Innes, *Myne Owne Ground: Race & Freedom on Virginia's Eastern Shore, 1640-1676* (New York and Oxford: Oxford University Press, 1980).

182 Ibid., Bond.

183 Morgan, 223-243.

184 Ibid.

185 Ibid.

186 See Bond. Legal slavery was not yet widely spread in Colonial Virginia at the time that Crawshaw came to Elizabeth Cittie. For all intents and purposes, in Virginia his life at this point was but a step above slavery – though not for life. Still, William Crawshaw let it be known to his descendants that back home, he had a very prosperous father and that **He** was never a slave.

187 James Oliver Horton (Editor); Lois E. Horton (Editor); Ira Berlin (Contributor), *A History of the African American People* (Detroit: Wayne State University Press, 1997), no page number. According to Alexander Brown in *The Genesis of the United States . . . .*, there were 20 "negroes" (excluding William Crawshaw) living in Virginia as of February 1625. See endnote below. The 20 probably consisted of the 1619 arrivals and any children they may have had.

188 "Beaver Wars – Ohio History Central," accessed August 11, 2016, http://www.ohiohistorycentral.org/w/Beaver_Wars?rec=483.; "Ohio River Map/Map of Ohio River," accessed August 11, 2016, http://www.mapsofworld.com/usa/states/ohio-river-map.html

189 For documentation that the Manahoac Indians are apparently still referred to as the Mahock Tribe by homeowners on Virginia's Mahockney Plantation (said to have been home to the Manahoac Indians), the reader should see LEWISSHEPHERD, "Mahock Tribe fights in the Battle of Bloody Run," *Blog at WordPress.com*, accessed March 5, 2018, http://mahockney.org/1656/01/01/mahock-tribe-fights-in-the-battle-of-bloody-run/ According to the author, the *Battle of Bloody Run* (described later in the text) occurred in the first quarter of 1656.

190 Edward D. Neill, *Virginia Carolorum: The Colony Under the Rule of Charles the First and Second, A.D. 1625*-A, (CHIZINE PUBN, 2018), 245-246.

191 Sources such as "Four Directions Institute," accessed March 17, 2017, http://www.fourdir.com/manahoac.htm and John R. Swanton, "The Indian Tribes of North America," accessed March 17, 2017, http://www.saponitown.com/Swanton.htm all seem to indicate a 1654 arrival date for the Shackaconia on the James River site near Richmond, and according to Scott Prescott Collins, " . . . they [Richahecrians] came and settled back in an area the Colony had already cleared of Indians and that they found the Mahocks and Nahyssan among their town." See Scott Prescott Collins, "Saponi History," Saponi Descendants Association, accessed August 11, 2016, http://sites.google.com/site/saponidescendantsassociation/home/the-daily-grind p. 5.

To this day, the name "Manahoac" is variously used to describe a particular "confederation" of Siouan Indians living along Virginia's Rapidan and (above the Falls at least) Rappahannock Rivers, while also used to describe a "tribe" of such Aboriginals including a subtribe and/or town called "Shackaconia." When I visited the Museum of Culpeper History in Culpepper, Virginia in October 2016, for instance, an exhibit there referred to the "Manahoac Indian *Tribe"* [italics added] and to one of this tribe's "towns" called Shackaconia. Most sources that I consulted refer to the latter as a tribe (albeit a small one by the late 17th century) of the Manahoac (or Mannahoac) Confederation.

The Manahoac were neighbors of – and kin to – the Monacan Confederation (which included the Nahyssan). In fact, after 1656, many sources indicate that the significantly diminished Manahoac Confederation had merged with the Monacan Indians, who exist to this day around Amherst, Virginia. The Manahoac (including the Shackaconia) Confederation/Tribe no longer exists.

As to the best pronunciation of the word Manahoac, historical sources starting with 17th century John Smith tell us it is *mana-hock* (as in ham-hocks), but others today say it sounds like *mana-HO-ack* .

192 "The Manahoac Confederacy," Access Genealogy, accessed August 11, 2016, https://www. accessgenealogy.com/native/the-manahoac-confederacy.htm

193 What the 1641 *Act* and the 1659 Virginia *Order* both craftily ignored was that the property conveyed to Hamond belonged to Indigenous Peoples – including the Shackaconia – according to early policy established by the Virginia Company. And, according to author Edmund Morgan (pp 57, 58): "What looked like unused empty forest to the English did not necessarily look that way to the Indians . . . Although a given tribe might have only a small acreage under cultivation at a given time, a substantial acreage had to be left in long-fallow [up to 40 years] to renew fertility." Colonial officials in Jamestown and in London knew this, for as one member of the Virginia Company of London wrote as early as 1609 (quoted in Andrew Fitzmaurice on page 69): " . . . the country, they say, is possessed by owners, that rule and governe it in their owne right; then with what conscience, and equitie can we offer to thrust them, by violence out of their inheritances?" And another Virginia Company Council member, Reverend William Crashaw, added: "A Christian may take nothing from a heathen against his will . . . We will take nothing from the Savages by power nor pillage, by craft nor violence, neither goods, lands nor libertie, much less life." But despite these sentiments, the laws of Virginia decades later turned a blind eye to the plight of Chief Shackaconia (see below) when between 1654 and 1656, the Chief lost his life and property when he was chased off his land, only to have the "unused" property awarded to Francis Hamond no doubt acting in concert with his more powerful brother Major General Manwaring Hammond.

So what changed between the early- and mid-17th-century in Virginia? In the earlier period, English activity in Virginia was largely influenced by the Salamanca School of development theory whose primary arbiter was Francisco Vitoria. Reverend William Crashaw had the largest collection of this School's writings in his large library, and his own thinking about Virginia development for England was influenced by this School. The Salamanca School was replaced by harsher analysts like John Donne, who observed that "In the law of Nature and Nations, a land never inhabited, by any, or utterly derelicted and immemorially abandoned by the former Inhabitants becomes theirs that will possesse it." Alberico Gentili and José de Acosta were of similar persuasion.

Briefly then, Virginia's Natives were not thought to be members of civilized society. Instead, after the early 1600s, English colonial policy in Virginia relegated the Natives there to the level they called a "third class of barbarians . . . savages similar to wild animals, who hardly have human feelings – without law, without agreements, without government, without nationhood, who move from place to place, or if they live in one place they are more like wild animals' caves or animal cages." They have no religion but idolize the devil. The land they did not occupy or plant crops, they could not call theirs, and such land, the colonists said, was therefore available to white settlers. (See Fitzmaurice, 73-77.)

194 David I. Bushnell, Jr., *The Manahoac Tribes in Virginia, 1608* (Washington, D. C.: The Smithsonian Institution, October 9, 1935), 4-15; Scott Preston Collins, "Saponi History," Saponi Descendants *Association*, accessed August 11, 2016, https://sites.google.com/site/saponidescendantsassociation/home/the-daily-grind

195 Neill, 245-247; Eric E. Bowne, *The Westo Indians: Slave Traders of the Early Colonial South* (Tuscaloosa: University of Alabama Press, 2005), 37-88. There was actually a third Aboriginal tribe at the *Battle of Bloody Run* – a Siouan ally of the Manahoac known as the Nahyssan Indians. The Manahoac and the Nahyssan are said to have intermarried; it is possible that both groups comprise the Aboriginal ancestry of the Howards. The Nahyssan, too, had been displaced by the Beaver Wars from their sedentary life in towns and farms located near the Manahoac. Apparently the two Siouan groups along with the Westo Indians defeated the Colonial soldiers and their Algonquian allies who had been sent to the area to remove – not kill – them. See "Nahyssan Indians," last modified May 7, 2012, accessed January 5, 2017, http://www.accessgenealogy.com/native/nahyssan-indians.htm

Much has been written about the *Battle of Bloody Run*. But when mention is made of the non-Iroquois and non-Algonquin Peoples involved in the battle, such references usually apply to the Shackaconia and to their larger Siouan Nation.

196 Gatford, like Reverend William Crashaw, was a Puritan. Gatford despised white Virginians, (who were unreformed Anglicans) saying "The people that are sent to inhabit in that Colonie, are the most of them the very scum and off scouring of our Nation, vagrants or condemned persons, or such others, as by the looseness and viciousness of their lives have disabled themselves to subsist any longer in this Nation . . . ." The leaders of the Colony of Virginia, he said, " . . . corrupt and taint others of the same Colonie, but cause the very Heathen to loath both them and the very profession of Christianity

for their sakes." He later talks about "servants" like William Crawshaw, lamenting that (they are) "the very many children and servants sent into that Plantation (i.e., Virginia), that were violently taken away or cheatingly duckoyed without the consent or knowledge of their Parents or Masters by some prœstigious (sp) Plagiaries (commonly called Spirits) into some private places, or ships, and there sold to be transported; and then resold there to be servants or slaves to those that will give most for them."

197 It appears that the recently-arrived-Westos (Richahecrians) sent five of their "Kings" (chiefs) down to the Colonists to offer beaver skins in trade, whereupon the Colonial soldiers executed them, thus starting the *Battle of Bloody Run.* This also set the context for the Manahoac "King's" loss of his own life shortly thereafter.

According to John Burks, author of *The History of Virginia – From Its First Settlement to the Present Day, Vol. 2* (Petersburg, Virginia, 1805) – reprinted by Forgotten Books, copyright 2012, page 107 – the Virginia Assembly in 1656 ordered Colonel Edward Hill to remove the Richahaecrians preferably without violence. The Colonel, along with his troupes and Pamunkey allies, were soundly defeated by the Richahaecrians (and apparently by the Manahoac Aboriginals and their Nahyssan allies), but at the end of the battle, the undefeated Richahaecrians remained entrenched near the falls. (The smaller-numbered Manahoac and Nahyssan – also victorious – retreated up the James River, according to Bushnell's account.) After Hill's defeat, the Assembly ordered that: " . . . the governor and council . . . make a peace with this people (i.e., Richahaecrians), and they farther (sp) directed that the monies which were expended for this purpose, should be levied on the proper estate of Hill." Thus, it would seem, was the beginning of the infamous alliance involving these Richahaecrian-Westo Natives and their wealthy white Virginia benefactors/planters, i.e., the alliance calling itself the Rickahockans (and various other spellings of the word). Officers of the latter included Major General Mainwaring Hammond and Attorney-Major Joseph Crowshaw.

198 Who was Gatford referring to when he used the term "enemies?" Although it was not yet apparent to the "Indian King," in the end the Manahoac, Nahyssan, and the Iroquois Richahecrians all fought for their lives against their common enemy, i.e., the Colonial troops and their allied Algonquin Pamunkey recruits (see James Mooney, *The Siouan Tribes of the East* [Washington: Smithsonian, 1894], 28, 30). It was Col. Edward Hill's contingents who killed Shackaconia; given the Virginia Assembly's land grant Act of 1641 and Col. Hill's association with one or more of the Hammonds, Shackaconia may have been purposely lured to his violent end. Exactly who was supposed to be fighting against whom during parts

of the *Battle of Bloody Run* may have been just as confusing to the spectators as it is today to many modern-day writers attempting to describe what happened. All agree today, however, that before it had even concluded, the Colonial troops led by Colonel Edward Hill left the battle prematurely, leaving it to the Siouan and Iroquois to fight against the Algonquians by themselves. One of the major consequences was that many of the soldiers and virtually all of the Pamunkey were massacred. Colonel Edward Hill, leader of the Colonial soldiers and their Pamunkey allies, was censured, fined, and disgraced for his early withdrawal and for the violence his forces initiated. But it was merely a short while after his reprimand that Hill was restored to his former social and military prominence in the Colony. Hill's restoration was correlated with the restoration of Sir William Berkeley as Virginia Governor.

199 Neill, *Virginia Carolorum,* 246-247. It should be noted here that by 1654, the Natives who traditionally occupied the land had been chased away. Therefore, the Virginia court at the time could say there was no evidence that the land had been taken away from "Indians." At the time, Virginia law officially frowned upon what it called "land speculation" committed by Colonists at the expense of Aboriginal Peoples whom it could be said occupied the land. Interestingly, LEWISSHEPHERD (cited in an earlier endnote) referred to pre-Revolutionary "buckles" found on the grounds of Virginia's present-day Mahockney Plantation (former home and hunting territory of the Manahoac). In a blog, he writes: "The date range given for buckles of this type: 1500-1650." Note: Mahockney's original colonial English settlers arrived mid-seventeenth century and were actively trading goods back & forth to England throughout the remainder of that century, "when buckles of this type would have been common in Virginia," adding additional credibility to Chief Shackaconia's claim that English (speculators) were active in his Manahoac home territory before he was chased away. See LESISSHEPHERD IN BANNER IN BANNERMAN, McDuff, People, Roane, Seayres, Tomlin, "Buckles and History at Mahockney," accessed March 5, 2018, https://mahockney.wordpress.com/2015/01/04/buckles-and-history-at-mahockney/?preview_id=1238&preview_nonce=a1740ed32a&post_format=sta...

200 For nonwhites including Natives, the status of the mother determined the status of the child. On page 1480 of Ablavsky (full citation provided below), for instance, it is written that: "In prerevolutionary Virginia . . . Indians could be slave or free . . . merely proving descent from an Indian carried no presumption of freedom . . . it was necessary to establish the mother's free status . . . the treatment of Indian laborers often amounted to slavery, whatever their formal legal status." Put another way, regardless of whether Shackaconia's family accepted the advice of bystanders, Ben's mother became

enslaved. As such, Virginia custom (as opposed to not-yet-written law) rendered the child, too, enslaved which status eventually for these Natives became lifetime slavery.

201 Sources indicate that liaisons between non-Christian Native females on the one hand and their European and Black paramours were part of the customary hospitality extended by Virginia Natives (including the Sioux) to visiting white and Black traders. The visiting party would be invited to eat, drink, and share that night's bed with one of the tribe's young females. For as long as the visitor remained, she would provide him with provisions like food and the like to ensure his comfortable stay. Such unions could be for one night only, or they may go on for much longer. Any children resulting from these circumstances were full members of the tribe, and they were raised by uncles who lived in the mother's family town. Such customary "hospitality" predates first contact, and it seems to have been common among nonwhite indigenes all over the world – including among "Indians" in the Philippines. See Roberta Estes, "Where Have All the Indians Gone? Native American Eastern Seaboard Dispersal, Genealogy and DNA in Relation to Sir Walter Raleigh's Lost Colony of Roanoke," *Journal of Genetic Genealogy* (Fall 2009): 30, 31; Hazel Petrie, *Outcast of the Gods* (Auckland: Auckland University Press, 2015), 161-168. But there is another possible explanation of how Crawshaw and the Manahoac met. As part of their contract, indentured servants like William Crawshaw were generally granted land at the end of their Indenture. Such land was often "inland and near Native American territory," often causing tension between settlers and Natives. It is possible that Crawshaw's land was close to the Manahoac camp; it is possible that Crawshaw lived with the tribe or was otherwise close to Chief Shackaconia. It is likely that Crawshaw was among those " . . . other Indians" who at the end of the Battle "retired up the James" (as put by Bushnell) after the battle: "Headright," *Wikipedia*, last modified September 9, 2017, accessed September 20, 2017, https://en.wikipedia.org/wiki/Headright

202 Edmund S. Morgan, 331.

203 "Full text of 'Kecoughtan old and new . . . .,'" p. 12, accessed August 17, 2016, https://archive.org/stream/kecoughtanoldne00heff/kecoughtanoldne00heff_djvu.txt Of all the male names given to children in my paternal Howard family since 1624, the most common was *William*, followed by *Ben* and *Benjamin* (the latter two usually taking the form of a middle name). A brother of Charles William Henry Howard, who is my late grandfather, was named William, as were my father and numerous ancestral cousins and nephews over many past generations.

204 For this entire paragraph, see: Martha W. McCartney, A Study of Virginia Indians and Jamestown: The First Century, Chapter 4, accessed August 11, 2016, https://www.nps.gov/parkhistory/online_books/jame1/moretti-langholtz/chap4.htm

205 Morgan, ibid.

206 Some sources for information in this paragraph: "Hughes and Phillips; Smith and Lapham," RootsWeb's WorldConnect Project: Hughes and Phillips; Smith and Lapham, last modified October 23, 2013, accessed August 11, 2016, http://wc/rootsweb.ancestry.com/cgi-bin/igm.cgi?op=GET&db=vapsmith&id=13194; Col. Henry Norwood, "A Voyage To Virginia," *Synoptic copy from the "Force's Collection of Historical Tracts,"* Volume 111, No. 10; "New Kent County History," accessed August 11, 2016, http://newkentvahist.blogspot.com/2013/06/new-kents-members-of-house-of-burgesses_24.html; and Benjamin B. Weisiger III, "York County, Virginia Records 1665-1672" (Richmond, Va.), 7."Manwaring" is sometimes spelled "Mainwaring."

207 Information in this paragraph about the affair between Col. West and Queen Cockacoeske is drawn from Virginia Johnson, "The Queene of Pomonky," contained in LIBRARY POINT, Central Rappahannock Regional Library, *accessed* August 12, 2016, http://www.librarypoint.org/queene_of_pomonky Additional information is in: *John West (colonel),* Wikipedia, last modified August 11, 2016, accessed August 12, 2016, http://en.wikipedia.org/wiki/John_West_(colonel); and *"COL John West, II,"* Find A Grave Memorial, accessed August 12, 2016, http://www.findagrave.com/cgi-bin/fg.cgi?page=gr&GRid=145906688

208 Ibid.

209 "The Fairfax Grant," accessed July 4, 2016, http://www.virginiaplaces.org/settledand/fairfaxgrant.html; "Northern Neck Proprietary," *Wikipedia*, accessed July 4, 2016, http://en.wikipedia.org/wiki/Northern_Neck_Proprietary.

210 Lyon Gardiner Tyler, *Encyclopedia of Virginia Biography, Under Editorial Supervision of Lyon Gardiner Tyler, Volume 1 (*Virginia: Lewis historical publishing Company, 1915), 219.

211 "Hughes and Phillips; Smith and Lapham," p. 5; Norwood, 4-5; "New Kent County History," pp.

1, 2. That the two were brothers is documented in "Encyclopedia of Virginia Biography," 126, accessed February 11, 2017, http://vagenweb.org/tylers_bios/vol1-12.htm

212 Ibid., "Hughes and Phillips, etc." RootsWeb's WorldConnect Project. That the office of "Major General" was only second in rank to the Virginia Governorship is cited in Alvord and Bidgood, 41.

213 Ibid. Viz., "Bee it known to all whom this may concern that I, Manwairing [sp] Ham'ond, of Riccohocke, Esq., out of the confidence and trust I repose in my trusty and well-beloved friends - . . . Major Joseph Croshaw, . . . doe appoint and constitute the same persons, my true and lawful attornies, ov'rsee all the estate, reall and personall [sp], I leave behind in Virginia . . . this 2nd day of June 1662 – Signed M. Hammond. Wit: George Morris, Sam Huckstepp, LANCELOTT WOODWARD [sp], Rees Hughes. Rec. 7 die ffebr. Seq. [Charles City County, Court Orders, 1661-1664, p. 359 – Copy of Original Document] & [Fleet III, op. cit., p. 269]." Hammond died in England soon after this document was filed. Also, see the next endnote.

214 Ibid. Continuing with the preceding endnote, on page 22, Eric E. Bowne (*The Westo Indians*) presents an "Early colonial (sp) America" map on which he shows an "Indian Settlement" named "Rickahockan Town." This "Rickahockan Town" and the "Riccohocke" mentioned in the immediately preceding endnote were the same. It was part of Hammond's "reall . . . estate" – perhaps one of the locations where Hammond resided or conducted business. The site was very near to the famous Fort Henry, Virginia (since its 1748 incorporation called Petersburg, Virginia), and would have been the location (or near it) where the "invaders" stationed themselves when they were attacked in 1656. Fort Henry is said to have been the most important trading post on the frontier, a transportation hub, and a military base (the "Chicago" of its day). Ft. Henry's location on the map was close to the highlighted Rickahockan Town, and both were near the Virginia Fall Line (i.e., location of present-day Richmond). The wealth of the Rickahockan organization, of which Hammond and Crowshaw were officers, I believe, was tied to the activities of these two trading posts. Fort Henry was largely responsible for helping to foster economic development in the western and southern parts of Colonial Virginia. The major trade item brought to all these southeast trading posts by Natives was furs, which is what the 1656 Rickahocken tried to offer the Virginia settlers before the former were attacked.

215 As part of exiled King Charles II's 5.2 million-acre Northern Neck land grant to his wealthy Colonial and European supporters, Shackaconia's homeland and hunting territory were by decree

transferred to Sir John Colepeper, first baron Culpeper of Thoresway, and to six others – all staunch royalists. In addition to this 1649 European-based decree (Charles II was exiled when he issued the decree), the Virginia Assembly by 1659 gave exclusive patent rights over Shackaconia territory to Francis Hamond. The two actions sealed the fate of the area's Natives. Sir John Colepeper was father of Thomas Culpeper, second baron Culpeper of Thoresway, governor of Virginia (1677-1683) and proprietor of Northern Neck. Members of the Culpeper family and the royalist Hammonds had fled England quickly after the 1649 beheading of English King Charles I. Their flight was facilitated by the wealthy and politically powerful royalist friend and then-Virginia Governor William Berkeley. Once in Virginia, they remained under the protection of Berkeley from the English Parliament. Even after his polite dismissal by the English Parliament from Virginia's Governorship, Berkeley continued to protect the Virginia political and economic interests of Hammond and Culpeper. Colonel Hammond – through his brother Francis – was involved with having chased Shackaconia and the tribe off their Rapidan- and Rappahannock-River, Northern Neck lands (perhaps employing enemy Indians to assist). Such would not have been inconsistent with Culpeper's, Berkeley's, and Hammond's own ties to the Rickahockan network of wealthy white planters and illicit Iroquois/Westos who all wanted to profit from ridding Virginia of non-cooperating Natives whom the network viewed as standing in the way of the fur trade, land development and other money-making ventures to be enjoyed by the English. From the standpoint of the Colonists, the Shackaconia property was favorably situated near the Rivers Rapidan and Rappahannock – enabling excellent transportation for tobacco and other goods destined for Virginia markets. That the Westos may have been involved in such a scheme is supported by: "The Rickohockans," 2, last modified September 27, 2016, accessed November 4, 2016, https://www.accessgenealogy.com/native/rickohockens.htm)) In any case, some of Shackaconia's lands eventually became part of Virginia's Culpeper County, where portions of his homeland and hunting territory remain today.

After 1660, Charles II won the crown of his beheaded father, and William Berkeley was made Governor of Virginia again. Immediately after the restoration, Berkeley promoted his friend and colleague Colonel Mainwaring (also Manwaring) Hammond to the rank of Major General.

I visited the Shackaconia area in October 2016.

See Eugene M. Schell, *CULPEPER: A Virginia County's History Through 1920* (Orange, Virginia: Green Publishers, Inc. *and* Culpeper, Virginia: The Culpeper Historical Society, 1982), 1-23; "James

River Plantations," accessed November 3, 2016, https://www.nps.gov/nr/travel/jamesriver/gentry.htm; and "Northern Neck," *Wikipedia*, accessed November 3, 2016, http://en.wikipedia.org/wiki/Northern Neck Additional evidence of the link between Berkeley and rich property owners and cavaliers living in Colonial Virginia can be found in Burk, 114, 115, and 119.

216 For source of information in this paragraph, see Bowne, 37-88 and the balance of the same book.

217 Yorktown, Virginia records (see text) show that in 1656, the "Indian boy called Benn" was enslaved, and from all the available evidence, his father William and his "Indian" mother were in no position at the time to prevent his sale or to otherwise save the child from being merchandised by a military colonel in that same year as the *Battle of Bloody Run*.

218 The Howard-family legend that was passed on to me makes no mention of William Crawshaw's death, only that in Virginia he lived with the Colony's Indians. As cited in the text, the Manahoac were among the Battle's victors, and at its end, they retreated up the James River – presumably to live with their Nahyssan and Monacan kin whose homes lay in that area of Virginia's Piedmont.

219 Weisiger III.

220 The surname "Howard" comes from the Medieval English name "Hayward," (also "Heyward" and "Haward") meaning the ward or guardian of the hedge or fence that protected an enclosed area from vandals, poachers, animals and the like.

221 Information in this paragraph found in: Walter L. Howard, Ph.D., *Ten Generations of Virginia Howards (*Davis, Ca: Published by Author, 1949), 74-77.

222 Ibid. Also, over time, Virginia formal law codes (as opposed to so-called customary law) would sanction the long-term enslavement of both *Christianized* Africans and Indigenous Peoples, too. But as stated above, the fact that "Ben" was not listed with a surname indicates that he was not viewed by the white Colonists as a legitimately baptized Christian. So unbaptized Ben was captured/immediately enslaved by the enemy in the bloody run war.

223 Facts in this paragraph found in "Decoding the Documents: 'Indians' in Selected Seventeenth

Century Documents & Secondary Sources," – McIlwaine 197B:425 Court Order/Complaint, compiled by Katherine Harbury, accessed August 12, 2016, https://www.nps.gov/parkhistory/online_books/jame1/moretti-langholtz/chap10a.htm

224 The following facts about the Bacon Rebellion were found in: Alfred A. Cave, *Lethal Encounters: Englishmen and Indians in Colonial Virginia* (Santa Barbara: Praeger, 2011), 147-165; and in "Mises Daily: Bacon's Rebellion:" accessed August 12, 2016, https://mises.org/library/bacons-rebellion

225 Bacon did not create the popular phrase.

226 Here, it is worth quoting in long form from Gregory Ablavsky, *Making Indians 'White': The Judicial Abolition of Native Slavery in Revolutionary Virginia and It's Racial Legacy,"* (Philadelphia: University of Pennsylvania, 2011), 1473. Gregory Ablasvsky at the time was a J.D. Candidate for the Ph.D. degree in American Legal History at the University of Pennsylvania:

"The concept of race as a fixed biological identity did not exist when Europeans settled in Virginia in the early seventeenth century." (Here, Ablasvsky explains in a footnote that "Before the mid-eighteenth century, most English speakers used 'races,' 'nations,' and 'peoples' interchangeably to describe groupings of individuals who shared a common language and geographic origins . . . . "). "The English of that era perceived the difference primarily as a matter of culture, society, and especially religion." (In another footnote, Ablasvsky explains: " . . . early English colonists defined Natives in cultural and social, rather than racial, terms."). "This tendency led them to regard Indians and Africans similarly as alien peoples with an odd and unfamiliar culture and, most fundamentally, as heathens . . . This principle of the era's Eurocentric law of nations undergirded the transatlantic slave trade and the enslavement of Natives captured in Virginia Indian wars." My statement that Bacon served as a basis for eventual Virginia and American racism applies to policies employed to justify Virginia's oncoming (and continuation of the) importation of Africans as slaves and to the race-related policies of post 1776 Revolutionary America and its Jim Crow era and beyond. For eighteenth-century effects of the bias, see Ablavsky p. 1508. For his discussion of Virginia's Department of Vital Statistics Chief, Dr. Walter Ashby Plecker ("believed there were no real native-born Indians in Virginia and anybody claiming to be Indian had a mix of black blood"), and the State's series of 1920s Racial Integrity Laws "that, among other provisions, excluded anyone with more than one-sixteenth Indian blood from being 'white,' and Indian identity was finally erased from Virginian records" – see Ablavsky, 1520-21. Also see Huff,

Jennifer Marie, "A Question of Indian Identity in the Plecker Era: The Monacan Indian Nation in the twentieth century" (2012) – especially pages 26 and 27 to 31. *Masters Theses.* 240; and Walter A. Plecker, *Eugenics in relation to The New Family and the law on Racial Integrity*, issued by the Bureau of Vital Statistics State Board of Health, (Richmond: Davis Bottom, Supt. Public Printing, 1924).

227 Paul Heinegg, *Free African Americans of North Carolina, Virginia, and South Carolina, From the Colonial Period to About 1820, Volume I* (Baltimore: Clearfield Company, 2005), 650-651.

228 Jack D. Forbes – also in "The Journal of Ethnic Studies," 12.2 (summer 1984): 17; "The Classification of Native Americans as Mulattos in Anglo-North America," accessed August 14, 2016, http://www.forbes 2-africans_and_native_americans.pdf; Stacey Ricketts, "Mulatto Classification of Indian Families & Related Laws,", September 10, 2006, accessed August 14, 2016, http://nativeamericansofdelawarestate. com/Mulatto%20Classification%20of%20Indian%20Families%20&%20Laws.htm; and *Mulatto*, Wikipedia, last modified August 2, 2016, accessed August 14, 2016, https://en.wikipedia.org/wiki/ Mulatto Also, see Ablasvsky, 1510, and Heinegg, 18-21.

229 Walter L. Howard, Ph.D., p 79.

230 As cited in an endnote below, the terms "Negro" and "Indian" were often used interchangeably in the Colony of Virginia after Bacon. Later, I learned that these terms included the Southeast Asian "Indians" who came to Virginia in the 17th century. These Southeast Asians eventually disappeared as a distinct ethnic group because they married Africans and African Americans, blending in with this non-white group.

231 Ibid.

232 More on the status of East Indians in Virginia will be elaborated below.

233 Ibid., Howard, Ph.D., 78-83. W. L. Howard is this narrative's source of facts contained in this paragraph.

234 Ann Howard is more fully described later in the text.

235 Paul Heinegg, 650.

236 Ibid. As part of the indenture agreement, it was illegal for servants to marry, but records suggest that some tried.

237 "England Births and Christenings, 1538-1975," Database, FamilySearch, (https://familysearch.org/ark:/61903/1:1:J7MP-HHC : accessed 24 June 2015), Frances Haward, Christened 09 Apr 1665; Library citation I found for: DUNSTABLE,BEDFORD,ENGLAND, reference ; FHL microfilm 845,461.

238 "Raising Children in the Early 17th century: Celebrations," Plymouth Ancestors, accessed August 12, 2016, www.PlymouthAncestors.org

239 Ibid. According to the church literature that I read during my 2015 visit to Dunstable, the same chancery screen under which Frances Haward was christened in 1665 remains intact to this day in the front part of the church; Dunstable Priory, Wikipedia, page last modified April 17, 2015, accessed July 11, 2015, https://en.wikipedia.org/wiki/Dunstable_Priory; "Parishes: Dunstable," in A History of the County of Bedford: Volume 3, ed. William Page (London, 1912), pp. 349-368, http://www.british-history.ac.uk/vch/beds/vol3/pp349-368 [accessed 23 June 2015]; "A Brief History of Dunstable," accessed June 24, 2015, http://www.localhistories.org/dunstable.html; "History of St. Peters/Dunstable Parish," accessed July 12, 2015, http://www.dunstableparish.org.uk/history-of-st-peters/; "An Illustrated Guide to the Church – the Priory Church of St. Peter, Dunstable, Bedfordshire," Dunstable Church pamphlet available at the Church and which I collected while there.

240 "England Birth and Christenings, 1538-1975, Database . . . ."

241 Ibid. Was he a commoner? The spelling is traced to the Howard Ducal family whose origin is Scandinavian.

242 See blogs written and titled by Wanda Thacker: "My Medieval Genealogy; John Howard/ Heyward and Margaret Clarke;" "Sir Francis Howard and Jane Monson;" William Howard and Francis Couldwell; John Howard and Catherine Moleyns; Margaret De Mowbray and Robert Howard. Also see "FamilySearch Community Trees," Pedigree Chart for Sir Robert Howard, Lord Howard:

Community Tree Project, accessed January 28, 2015, https://histfam.familysearch.org//pedigree. php?personID=19785&tree=EuropeRoyalNobleHous

243 "England Marriages, 1538-1973," Database, FamilySearch (https://familysearch.org/ ark:61903/1:1N2SP-CN1: accessed 24 June 2015), William Haward and Anne Tommes, 22 Oct 1642; Library citation for: Eaton Bray, Bedford, England, reference; FHL microfilm 826,462. The rest of this citation has been lost.

244 He was the half-brother of Sir Thomas Howard, 3rd Duke of Norfolk.

245 Information in this paragraph was drawn from a number of sources, including (but not limited to): Robert Hutchinson, *The Rise and Fall of a Tudor Dynasty: House of Treason* (London: Weidenfeld & Nicolson, 2009); "Edward Seymour (2nd E. Hertford)," accessed February 25, 2016, http://www/ tudorplace.com.ar/Bios/EdwardSeymour(2EHertford).htm; "Thomas Howard, 1st Viscount Howard of Bindon," *Wikipedia, accessed February 25, 2016, https://en.wikipedia.org/wiki/Thomas_Howard,_ 1st_Viscount_Howard_of_Bindon; "Frances Howard, Duchess of Richmond," Wikipedia, accessed February 25, 2016, https://en.wikipedia.org/wiki/Frances_Howard,_Duchess_of_Richmond; "William Howard, 1st Baron of Effingham," Wikipedia, accessed February 25, 2016, https://en.wikipedia.org/wiki/ William_Howard,_1st_Baron_Howard_of_Effingham;* "Howard of Nottingham," accessed February 25, 2016, http://www.tudorplace.com.ar/HOWARD2.htm#Frances Howard (C.Hertford); "Toddington, Bedfordshire," Wikipedia, accessed February 25, 2016, https://en.wikipedia.org/wiki/Toddington_ Bedfordshire; TD Barnes Genealogy, "HOWARD GENEALOGY," accessed February 24, 2016, http:// td-barnes.com/howard_genealogy.htm; "Thomas Howard, 3rd Duke of Norfolk," accessed February 22, 2016, http://www.geni.com/people/Thomas-Howard/6000000000159444061

246 Facts about Dunstable in this narrative: Tim Lambert, "A Brief History of Dunstable," accessed June 24, 2015, http://www.localhistories.org/dunstable.html; "Parishes: Dunstable," in A History of the County of Bedford: Volume 3, ed. William Page (London, 1912), 349-368, accessed June 24, 2015, http:// www.british-history.ac.uk/vch/beds/vol3/pp349-368; Katie Carmichael, David McOmish and David Grech, "The Hat Industry of Luton and its Buildings," *(*Swinton, England: English Heritage, 2013).

247 Lambert.

248 Ibid., and "William Taylor, Abt 1645-1710," accessed May 24, 2015, http://www.frostandgilchrist. com/getperson.php?personID=129772&tree=frostinaz01; "The Colonial Virginia Register," accessed October 21, 2014, http://www.newrivernotes.com/topical_books_1902_virginia_colonialvirginiaregister. htm; Heinegg.

249 "selectsurnames.website," accessed February 29, 2016, http://www.selectsurnames.com/hayward. html; "The Genealogy Tree – Howard and Allied Families," last updated May 5, 2014, accessed March 1, 2016, http://www.thegenealogytree.com/articles/howard-family-facts.htm

250 Ibid.

251 See earlier end note labelled: "Facts about Dunstable in this essay."

252 See Charles J. Reid Jr., *The Seventeenth-Century Revolution in the English Land Law,* 43 Cleveland State Review 221 (1995). This source is available at http://engagedscholarship.csuohio.edu/clevstirev/ vol43/iss2/4

253 "William Taylor," accessed May 24, 2015, http://www.frostandgilchrist.com/getperson. php?personID=129772&tree=frostinaz01

254 Neill, 239-240.

255 Heinegg microfilm version received from: Library of Virginia, Richmond County Microfilm, Reel 29, Order Book, 1, 1692 1694, 202 p. Film of Original [40], viewed at Harold Washington Library, Chicago, between November 4 and November 22, 2015. In his "Native History Project," Heinegg states: "[white] Women convicted of having children by native Indians were prosecuted for the lesser offense of fornication and had to pay a fine or suffer corporal punishment." Heinegg does not distinguish between the terms "native Indians" and the "East Indian servants" whom he discusses in his following paragraph, but from the 1692 court records, Frances Haward was similarly charged and sentenced. Court records indicate that she escaped the further punishment of being lashed because the holder of her indenture paid her fine of £10. Another author states: "The legal and popular lumping of Natives and Blacks into a common racial underclass blurred the racial lines between Blacks and Indians." – See Ablasvsky, 1509. It should also be noted that mixed-race marriages in Virginia at the time were illegal. According to

Assisi, 17th century reference to "East Indians," "East India Indians," or "Asiatic Indians" as Southeast Asians living in Virginia were called, were "identified variously as 'Mulatto,' 'Negro,' and 'colored' . . ." And Warren Eugene Milteer Jr. (cited in full below), on page 24, explains: "the British categorized people with ties to the East Indies as blacks." He goes on to say about colonial officials that: "'Indian' of course was a term used to categorize indigenous Americans as well as Asians."

256 ACT XVI, *Laws of Virginia,* April 1691 (*Hening's Statutes at Large, 3:87*).

257 See Morgan, 386.

258 Heinegg, 650. And according to Ablavsky, 1520, "Virginian Indians appeared physically indistinguishable from their African-American neighbors in the eyes of whites."

259 Forbes, 202, and see Morgan, 329.

260 See Morgan, 335.

261 Ibid.

262 Ibid.

263 Ibid.

264 Ibid., Howard, Ph.D., 78-81.

265 Ibid., 79.

266 In 1707, Frances was 42 years old. Today, according to one obstetrician at Northwestern University's School of Medicine, most fertile women experience difficulties conceiving and giving birth to a healthy baby beyond this age. Heinegg on page 650 estimates 1720, but this is certainly too late. Heinegg probably did not see the Hayward 1711/12 will.

267 "England Births and Christenings, 1538-1975," Database, *Family Search* (http://familysearch.org/ark:61903/1:1:J7MP-HHC accessed 23 June 2015), Frances Haward, 09 Apr 1665; citing DUNSTABLE,BEDFORD,ENGLAND, reference; FHL microfilm 845,461.

268 William D Howard, 26, 27.

269 Heinegg, 9.

270 Ibid., 17.

271 Ibid., 16.

272 Heinegg, 650.

273 Howard, Ph.D., 78-81.

274 Heinegg, 650-51; Keith Egloff & Deborah Woodward, *First People: The Early Indians of Virginia* (Richmond: University Press of Virginia, 1997), 2-50 (especially page 48). Middlesex County was home to the Algonquian. The Tutelo were also called Totero, Nahyssan, Monahassanough, Oniasont, and Yesan.

275 "Manahoac," *Wikipedia*, last modified August 12, 2015, accessed April 15, 2016, https://en.wikipedia.org/wikiManahoac

276 Heinegg and U.S. Census records.

277 Forbes.

278 Heinegg, online summary of the book's introductory chapter, page 15, accessed August 14, 2016, http://www.genealogy.com/articles/research/12_heing.html According to this source, "North Carolina and Virginia enacted apprenticeship laws similar to those in England. In 1646 Virginia passed a law giving justices of the peace at their own discretion the right to bind out children of the poor 'to avoid sloath and idleness wherewith such children are easily corrupted, as also for the relief of such parents whose poverty extends not to give them breeding' [Hening, Statutes at Large, XXVII:336]." But in the

printed book on page 14, Heinegg writes: "We also find cases where children were willingly bound by their parents to neighbors, friends, and relatives. . . (on p. 12) as apprentices . . . trained as coopers, blacksmiths, cordwainers, or other useful occupations." Indeed, John Hope Franklin lists brick masons, bricklayers, and brick makers as among North Carolina's most sought after and highest paying skilled trades during the 1860-1880 period (see pp. 124 and 134-5 of *The Free Negro in North Carolina 1790-1860).* In addition, barbering and blacksmithing were among three of the occupations held by the male descendants of Miles Howard.

279 Victoria E. Bynum, "Free People of Color" in Old Virginia: The Morris Family of Gloucester County, a Case Study," *Renegade South: Histories of Unconventional Southerners,* November 10, 2011, 7-9, accessed April 16, 2016, https://renegadesouth.wordpress.com/2011/11/10/free-people-of-color-in-old-virginia-the-morris-family-of-gloucester-county-a-case-study/

280 Ibid.

281 Information collected from the records of the Historic Halifax State Historic Site, Monica Moody, Manager, 23 David Street, Halifax, NC 27839. Miles Howard was the father of several children, including 2 boys named "John." The first was named after Miles's own father, but he died about 1836. The second son John inherited a large part of the late Miles Howard's estate, and he became the second wealthiest "Free Negro" property owner in Halifax County, NC according to an 1860 unpublished census prepared by the "North Carolina Historical Commission and the Bureau of the Census." – See: John Hope Franklin, *The Free Negro in North Carolina: 1790-1860* (Chapel Hill: University of North Carolina Press, 1971), 228.

Miles' father John Howard and his sister Rachel lived in Botetourt County, Virginia among the white Catholic Howard family. Additionally, in 1810, Botetourt County was in the heart of Monacan territory (the Monacan was an "Indian" confederacy closely allied with the Manahoac). Like Halifax, Botetourt County is on the Roanoke River but south-easterly and close to the Indian mission called Ft. Christiana. According to the 1810 census, Rachel lived in Botetourt County along with "7 other free." It is likely that Miles Howard was born in Botetourt County among the Monacan Indians and the previously mentioned white Catholic Howard family.

282 Ibid.

283 William Waller Hening, Statutes at Large; Being a Collection of all the Laws of Virginia (Richmond, Va., 1809-23, Vol. 11), pp. 170, 260, 266, 270.

284 A Robert Howard biography appears in William D Howard, 54-58.

285 "Halifax County, NC – Free Persons of Colour, 1847-1865," listed as part of "the Halifax County Minutes, County Court, 1847-1865, Microfilm C.047.30003, North Carolina State Archives." The description of Robert Howard was included in his application for a construction job to clear parts of the Great Dismal Swamp. Following Robert's application was that of his 20-year-old brother Miles B. Howard.

286 Isaiah Howard, "Certificate of Death," State Board of Health – Division of Vital Statistics, Franklin, NC. December 19, 1911; Robert Howard, "Halifax County, NC – Free Persons of Colour, 1847 -1865," accessed November 19, 2013, http://www.files.usgwarchives.net/nc/halifax/court/free01.txt

287 Isaiah Howard, United States Census, 1880, Franklinton, Franklin, North Carolina. It is curious to see that the young Isaiah was not made a North Carolina *field* slave as were many Black slave boys in those days. The fact that he was instead apprenticed as a skilled blacksmith is in keeping with typical skilled tasks of mulatto Howard males and may be attributable to the intervention of his elders who already had a long relationship with the white Smith family, including with the white Miles Smith. Isaiah's mother was Margaret Peggie, enslaved to a member of the white Smith family. During Reconstruction (1865-1877) and its aftermath, Isaiah seems to have done well economically. In addition to blacksmith (and later a "restaurant cook") back then, I found records proving that he owned his home and other real estate in Franklinton, North Carolina. Although apparently financially able to provide a home for his son (my grandfather) Charles William Henry Howard, my young grandfather seems to have lived elsewhere during some (if not most) of his young years. Why? Whenever I asked my grandfather where his boyhood home was located, he always responded "Franklinton, North Carolina" – his biological father's home. My grandfather told me more than once that he was raised by some "mean people," namely "Paris (*Pasco*) Howard" and (if I recall correctly) that he ultimately ran away from them to New York City.

288 I visited the properties while completing research for this narrative.

289 According to the 1880 U.S. Census covering Franklinton, Franklin County, North Carolina, my grandfather's "Mulatto" mother "Bettie" and her "Black" husband Isaiah had two children older than he, identified as mulattos Emily (8) and Robert (5). Emily's biological mother was Isaiah's deceased wife Mary, wedded 12/27/1871. My grandfather was born to Isaiah and his then legal wife Bettie (Betsie) about 1885; Robert, Junior was my grandfather's full brother. When my grandfather told me that his relative "Mary" used to visit him until she got caught up in a Holiness Church, he was talking about Mary: the mulatto daughter of his grandmother Margaret Peggie, who, after the Civil War, adopted the surname "Smith.".

290 On about 6 occasions, Miles found it necessary to save family members from the slave trade by purchasing them, making himself – temporarily – their slave master. Living on the Underground Railroad, Miles's interventions in the pernicious trade may have totaled more than the number I was able to find.

291 On May 15, 1834, Miles was paid $25 "for the hire of Soloman," ("Account of Sales, Halifax County, 1830s" – Monica Moody's notes filed in Historical Halifax Office). Soloman, a person of color, could have been the enslaved male held by white Solomon Smith of Halifax/Northampton in the 1800 and 1810 U.S. Census. In 1840, the U.S. Census continued to list him in this household, but he was free.

292 Cited earlier in Mcilwaine.

293 Heinegg (2005), 650.

294 See below.

295 David Bindman and Henry Louis Gates, Jr., Editors, *The Image of the Black in Western Art* (Cambridge: Harvard University Press, 2014), 16.

296 Monica Moody.

297 Hypergamy is defined here as continually marrying a person or people of superior social and economic caste or class thereby upgrading the individual's or family's social standing.

298 As the population of Afro-, Euro-, Native- and Southeast Asian-Americans continued to increase, the Colony and State of Virginia took the lead in declaring that the South's Indigenous Peoples population had stopped growing after the Bacon's Rebellion of 1676. By the 1920s, the state's department of vital statistics went so far as to erase all recorded information that documented any ethnic mixing of its white, black, and "Indian" Peoples. But as steadfastly as America's Southland stood by its declaration of racial purity and the "dead Indian," Miles – remembering that his ancestors were "Indian" before ever reaching the shores of Virginia – declared it all a falsehood. If Virginia and some of the other territories of the South maintained that their only real Indians were the few who lived on state-sanctioned reservations and beyond the western frontier, Miles and his mixed-race ancestors stubbornly adhered to their self-defined roots and married this same mixed-race people recorded as *Mulatto; [Free] Negro;* and *[Free] Colored* in the census and elsewhere. After the Civil War, the Miles Howard family was called "Old Free Issue" (*'Ol Isshy'*) by their community – see Milteer, 223. As such, the family was said to have earned their freedom *before* 'The War' as opposed to having been post-War freedmen. Miles knew also that a pre-Virginia-Indian ancestor named William did indeed take up with a Siouan woman. Traditionally, there were a few Sioux of Virginia who included the children of mixed "Indian," Black, and (to a lesser extent) white parentage. In today's Halifax County, North Carolina, the Miles Howard family probably would be classified as members of the Saponi Indian community – a tri-racial group whose pre-20th century origins include the "Portuguese" (see Heinegg, 21). Heinegg goes on to write that at least from the eighteenth century, records in Virginia and North Carolina did not identify any "nuclear Indian families" because virtually all of the Indians in this period were children of Indian and African-American parents (Heinegg, 19). In addition to Heinegg, see Warren Eugene Milteer Jr., *North Carolina's Free People of Color: 1715-1885*, (Baton Rouge: Louisiana State University Press, 2020); David Dodge, "The Free Negroes of North Carolina," *The Atlantic,* January 1886; and the associated blog: *Native American Roots: Genealogy and history of Native Americans of Granville County and Northeastern North Carolina*, June 28, 2015, Tag Archives: David Dodge.

299 The year 1900 U.S. Census shows a Charles Howard, born about 1885 and with similar middle initials, living in both Edgecombe, NC and in Sampson, NC. See below.

300 If this is not confusing enough, my grandfather was also listed in the 1900 U.S. Federal Census household of Mathew (and Sarah J.) Howard. They lived in Dismal, Sampson, North Carolina. Mathew Howard and Paris Howard appeared to have been related. My grandfather was enumerated there as "Charley H Howard," born Aug 1885, his U.S Census documented birth month and year. Paris and

Rebecca's biological son Charlie's death certificate filed May 1943 indicated he was born in 1900. He was not listed in that year's U.S. Census because the enumerator probably visited the household sometime before this son was born.

301 One of *"Pasco's"* (biological) sons, according to a May 19, 1943 "Charlie Howard" death certificate, was "Charlie Howard," born in Edgecombe County, N.C., like his father ("Paris") and his mother Beckie. This Charlie was not the same person as my grandfather Charles W. H. Howard. The name *Pasco* ultimately is of Hebrew origin and derives from the Latin "paschalis" or "pashalis," which according to Google means "relating to Easter and from the Aramaic 'pasha (Hebrew pesach) Passover' (since the Hebrew holiday," Google explains, "coincides with the Christian holiday Easter)." The Spanish/Filipino name is of this origin and is thought to be given to a child born around Easter (Paris Howard was born in July according to the U. S. Census). See endnote number 5 above (https://forebears.io/surnames/pasco) for more information about the Filipino origins of the name *Pasco*. According to Wikipedia (https://en.wikpedia.org/wiki/Poruguese_name) the Portuguese version of the surname (i.e., in Portuguese, the Spanish *Pasco* is *Pascoal*) has religious meanings often indicating it may have originated from an ancestor who converted to Catholicism or was abandoned in the churches and raised in Catholic orphanages by priests and nuns. Wikipedia goes on to say that these children were usually baptized with a name related to the date near when they were found or baptized. Such names were often adopted as family names. *23andme; ancestry.com;* and written historical sources consulted for this narrative all indicate that my male Howard ancestors who were born after our Angola origin were of Portuguese and mixed-Portuguese ancestry. Therefore, the Spanish connection cited a few sentences earlier is irrelevant to my story. Separately, another *"Pasco,"* a white one named *"Pasco* Champion" was a 1625 servant to Capt. Wm Tucker, suggesting the word's English association (see below). Finally, Paris/*Pasco* named one of his children "Benjamin," no doubt after ancestor William Crawshaw's son ("Ben") born to a Manahoac mother about 1655. I suspect that my grandfather (Charles William Henry Howard), and his father (Isaiah Howard), and Paris/*Pasco* Howard, and Mathew Howard were all related – all seemingly descended from William Crawshaw (aka *Pasco*) and Ben Howard.

302 This is an important fact explained in court records cited below. What is important to note here is that Miles and Matilda's union was not a State-accepted Christian union.

303 The reason these four children remained slaves was due to a Virginia law at the time that made it difficult to manumit slaves other than for "meritorious" service. Nevertheless, in a March 26, 1832

letter sent to famous North Carolina Senator and 1836 Presidential candidate Willie Person Mangum, Attorney Thomas Burgess described "a free man of color" who is "a barber and musician" who had purchased children from a former master. The free man was unable to free them due to the North Carolina law. Could the legislator help? Part of the plan to free these children included details worked out by Thomas Burgess and Miles Howard to move the family to one of the slave-free states where the family would establish a new life. The states under consideration were probably Illinois, Indiana, Ohio, and Michigan. Miles did not follow through on this plan (Thomas Burgess's death may explain one of the reasons why). In August 1839, after the 1836 emancipation of children Henry, Fanny, and John, Miles sold young Mary to Willie Eppes of Virginia for $550 "to permit Martha Marshall to receive Mary and use her." This may have been part of a plan to apprentice Mary into domestic work. The information was compiled by Monica Moody of the Historic Halifax State Historic Site office on January 23, 1996. Mary Howard went on to marry John Wilkins on April 10, 1849. She and her husband joined Frances Howard as plaintiffs in the *Howard v Howard* North Carolina Supreme Court case.

304 "An Act to emancipate Henry, Fanny and John, the slaves and children of Miles Howard," NC Archives, Public and Private Laws of North Carolina, 1836-37, Chapter LXIV, 327.

305 M. Moody files; U.S. Department of the Interior, National Park Service, National Register of Historic Places, Church of the Immaculate Conception – Michael Ferrall Family Cemetery. See p. 8 for the number of Catholics living in 1820s North Carolina (cited later in the paragraph) when the State's total population was 628,829.

306 See my "Howards of San Juan Hill," 50-51.

307 Morgan, 329.

308 "John England," Encyclopedia Britannica, accessed 5/30/14, Facts about England gathered from this source.

309 Joseph Kelly, *America's Longest Siege: Charleston, Slavery and the Slow March Toward Civil War* (New York: Overlook Press, Peter Mayer Publishers, 2013), no page number.

310 "William J. Gaston (1778-1844)," North Carolina History Project, accessed May 30, 2014, http://

www.northcarolinahistory.org/commentary/45/entry Facts about Gaston cited here were gathered from this source.

311 See Margaret and Doug Phillips citation below.

312 See references to Gaston in my previous endnotes, above.

313 Catholic missionaries began as staunch defenders of subject Filipinos against secular Spanish authorities who often were unscrupulous, corrupt caretakers of the Islands. As the demands of a Dutch war increased and the available resources declined sharply, over time the missionaries – realizing the difficulty of their tasks and the potential wealth that lay before them – grew corrupt and an enemy of the people. For *Pasco*, these unfortunate seeds had yet to take root.

314 At the Haliwa-called Pow-Wows that I attended in 2014 and 2015, I learned that the surname Valentine was included among the surnames of those Indigenous Tribal Peoples who were Siouan.

315 Franklin, 228. Also, see the 1860 U.S. Census, Halifax County, North Carolina, Eastern Division.

316 William D Howard, 53.

317 For a discussion of 19th century apprenticeship and guardianship law in North Carolina, see Franklin, 123-30.

318 *Howard v. Howard*, 6 Jones Law (N.C.) 235. (1858).

319 Ibid.

320 *Small Town North Carolina: Life in the rural South* (Halifax, N.C.: Historic Halifax, 2013).

321 Margaret and Doug Phillips, *History of the Halifax Baptist Church: A Continuation (*Halifax, North Carolina, 131 West Prussia Street, P. O. Box 465, 2001), no page number.

322 Ibid.

323 Monica Moody papers at Historic Halifax State Historic site, Halifax, NC.

324 Howard, 53.

325 Ibid., 42.

326 On November 30, 1858, when the Supreme Court of North Carolina released its decision to the public, the case was titled *Doe on demise of FRANCES HOWARD v. SARAH HOWARD, et al.* See: Supreme Court of North Carolina, Nov 30, 1858, 51 N.C. 235 (N.C. 1858).

327 I visited the street before completing research for this paper.

328 Halifax, North Carolina County Will Book, 4, Page 132 May Session, A.D. 1836.

329 Monica Moody papers.

330 Robin Law, *The Oyo Empire c. 1600 – c.1836, A West African Imperialism in the Era of the Atlantic Slave Trade* (Oxford: Oxford University Press, 1977).

331 Discussion of Mbata, the Mbundu, and Kongo found in this, and the next two paragraphs is summarized in Roland Oliver and Anthony Atmore, 166-168.

332 See Joseph C. Miller, 38-42, 55, 60.

333 Oliver and Atmore, 166.

334 Ibid.

335 Discussion in this paragraph about Kongo, Portugal, and the Mbundu is detailed in a recent publication by John K. Thornton: *Afonso I*, citation given below.

336 John K. Thornton, *Afonso I, Mvemba A Nzinga, King of Kongo: His Life & Correspondence* (Indianapolis: Hackett Publishing Company, 2023), 212-213.

337 Pronounced JHAHVAHT, interestingly the name is of male Filipino (and French) origin – not Portuguese. When I met Jovette in 2023, I was told his name was Josette – a Portuguese first name. I did not learn about the Filipino connection until I returned to Chicago after my 2024 visit. Regarding the name's Filipino association, see Subrahmanyam, 185 (referred to earlier): "Mulaka-Macau-Nagasaki-Makassar-Manila network . . . sustained a good part of the Portuguese trade in the 1610s, 1620s, and 1630s . . ."

338 See Heywood and Thornton, below.

339 Linda M. Heywood and John K. Thornton, *Central Africans, Atlantic Creoles, and the Foundation of the Americas, 1585-1660* (Cambridge: Cambridge University Press, 2007), 76.

340 Miller, 61.

341 See: "American Plantations and Colonies, Settlers living at 'Elizabeth Cittie' in Virginia, February 7, 1624/5." Sources: "Hotten's Lists" and "Adventurers of Purse and Persons," http://www.genealogy.com/ftm/s/e/e/Sylvia-See-AB/FILE/0052page.html

342 Nafafé (see below), pp. 55, 169-174.

343 Given Jovette's Filipino name, were any of his ancestors connected to *Pasco*? See Subrahmanyam, 185.

344 Jose Lingna Nafafé, *Lourenco da Silva Mendonca and the Black Atlantic Abolitionist Movement in the Seventeenth Century* (Cambridge: Cambridge University Press, 2022), 191.

345 Ibid., 190.

346 Ibid., 282.

347 Ibid., 190.

348 Ibid., 14-23.

349 Miller, 85.

350 Nafafé, 19-23.

351 Nafafé, 386.

352 Nafafé, 19-23.

353 Ibid., 300-306.

354 Ibid., 20.

355 Ibid., 382.

356 Ibid., 317.

357 Ibid., 380.

358 Miller, 85.

359 Nafafé, 148.

360 Ibid., 148-152, Heywood and Thornton, 74-77.

361 Heywood and Thornton, 74-79.; Nafafé, 170.

362 Jovette Raimundo Eduardo, August 2024.

363 Ibid.

364 Nafafé, 163-169.

365 Linda M. Heywood, *Njinga of Angola: Africa's Warrior Queen* (Cambridge: Harvard University Press, 2017), 65; Heywood and Thornton, 130.

366 John K. Thornton, " Legitimacy and Political Power: Queen Njinga, 1624-1663," *The Journal of African History,* Volume 32, Number 1 (1991): 25-40.

367 Ibid.

368 Ibid.

369 Ibid.

Author at home

Printed in the United States
by Baker & Taylor Publisher Services